The Catholic Side of Henry James is the first work to reveal the profound Catholic imagery in the work of Henry James. Edwin Fussell questions conventional critical assumptions about James' secularity and shows that James' career began with narratives of Catholic conversion and ended with his masterpiece of Catholic eccentricity and alienation, *The Golden Bowl*. The interplay of men and women, of America and Europe – those acknowledged Jamesian themes – comes to be overlaid with the interplay between Protestant and Catholic.

In the first part of the book, Fussell discusses the influence of James' Catholic friends like John La Farge; and the ambivalent attitudes toward Catholic sensibilities in writers like Cooper and Emerson and Hawthorne, James' more or less immediate predecessors on the literary scene, as well as in his contemporaries like Mark Twain and Howells. Fussell then examines the beginnings of Catholic fiction in America and the rapidly growing number of Catholics in the population and in the reading audience for fiction. He claims that the religious mix in the literary scene provided James with a commercial opportunity to explore his penchant for the Protestant–Catholic theme. The rest of the book explores the presentation of Catholics and of Catholicism in James' fiction, using criticism, letters, and notebooks to illuminate the fiction. Fussell's examination ranges from James' early reviews of religious books for the *Nation* and early tales like "De Grey: A Romance" through much of the canon, along the way reexamining James' overlooked play *Guy Domville* and climaxing with a magnificent reading of *The Golden Bowl,* convincingly demonstrating James' involvement with Catholic themes.

CAMBRIDGE STUDIES IN AMERICAN LITERATURE AND CULTURE

The Catholic Side of Henry James

Cambridge Studies in American Literature and Culture

Continued on page following the Index

THE CATHOLIC SIDE
OF HENRY JAMES

EDWIN SILL FUSSELL

Published by the Press Syndicate of the University of Cambridge
The Pitt Building, Trumpington Street, Cambridge CB2 1RP
40 West 20th Street, New York, NY 10011-4211, USA
10 Stamford Road, Oakleigh, Victoria 3166, Australia

First published 1993

Printed in the United States of America

Library of Congress Cataloging-in-Publication Data
Fussell, Edwin S.
The Catholic side of Henry James / Edwin Sill Fussell.
p.   cm. – (Cambridge studies in American literature and
culture)
Includes bibliographical references and index.
ISBN 0-521-43202-2 (hardback)
1. James, Henry, 1843–1916 – Religion.   2. Fiction – Religious
aspects – Christianity.   3. Catholic Church in literature.
4. Catholic Church – Doctrine.   5. Theology in literature.
I. Title. II. Series.
PS2127.R4F8   1993
813′.4 – dc20   92-20140
                                                            CIP

A catalog record for this book is available from the British Library.

ISBN 0-521-43202-2 hardback

For my brother Paul and my sister Florence

By the same author

Edwin Arlington Robinson: The Literary Background of a Traditional Poet (1954, 1970)

Frontier: American Literature and the American West (1965, 1970)

The Purgatory Poems (1967)

Cesare Pavese, *American Literature,* translated with an introduction (1970)

Lucifer in Harness: American Meter, Metaphor, and Diction (1973)

Your Name Is You (poems; 1975)

The French Side of Henry James (1990)

Contents

Preface

The Catholic side of Henry James is of course only one of many sides. At a venture, it affects perhaps one-quarter of his literary production, quantitatively considered. It is an unusually important quarter, however, because this "side" looms large at significant points in James' career (for example, its fictional beginnings in the "conversion narrative"), because it touches major documents (for example, *The Golden Bowl*), and because it sheds light on works difficult or virtually impossible to fathom (perhaps most notably *The Turn of the Screw* and *The Wings of the Dove*). I once called this book *The Literary Catholicizing of Henry James* but gave the title up for its want of euphony. Certain implications of that lost title are well worth preserving and keeping in mind, however. Literary Catholicizing means the representation in narrative, dramatic, or poetic form, of identifiably Roman Catholic rites, sacraments, beliefs, practices, and fictive personages, for aesthetic reasons additional to or instead of religious reasons. Clearly it will make some difference whether the writer in question is or is not Catholic. It is one thing when people in a novel by Graham Greene or Evelyn Waugh dubiously receive communion or cross themselves while dying, Greene and Waugh being such notorious Catholics, but it is quite another thing when a writer ostensibly not Catholic, such as Willa Cather, devotes so much of her late fictional *œuvre* to Catholic matters. Now biographical questions, however unanswerable, join the literary question: "Why *isn't* she, if that's the way she feels?" or, conversely, "If she doesn't really feel that way, why does she *do* it?" She does it, of course, for literary as much as or more than for personal reasons, and it is such literary reasons as these to which my lost title points: It points specifically to Henry James, who clearly belongs to the Cather rather than to the Greene–Waugh category.

I am not trying to make Henry James into some kind of secret Catholic – how loudly and clearly need that be said? and more than once? – neither to portray him as more Catholic, more Christian, or more religious than he actually was. My intention has been to illuminate an important side of James' writings to which almost no critical attention has been paid, it has been so much a matter of course among Jamesians that their man was altogether and blessedly secular. The actual evidence of the writings leads to somewhat different conclusions, but that still does not make James a Catholic. For myself, I have no regrets that James was other than he was, I feel no personal need for him to have been different, and indeed I confess no great interest in his nonliterary life. I have tried quite scrupulously to let him go his own way while I continue to go mine, which happens to be Roman Catholic, a fact I have neither concealed nor obtruded (but it has often been a help knowing what to look for).

Now I invite the well-disposed, open-minded reader to take a fresh look at a number of works by Henry James, with a special eye to "a lively and cultivated sense of what one may call the aesthetics of religion" (as he writes in an 1875 book review). I further suggest and recommend emulation of Fleda Vetch as she responds to Mrs. Gereth in *The Spoils of Poynton* (1897), who says: "You seemed to speak just now as if really nothing of any consequence had passed between you," and Fleda replies, "Something always passes when one has a little imagination." Henry James also lures us on. In the preface to the *Lady Barbarina* volume in the New York Edition, vis-à-vis "the interest of *contrasted* things," he points out how he might seem "struck with no possibility of contrast in the human lot so great as that encountered as we turn back and forth between the distinctively American and the distinctively European outlook. He [James] might even perhaps on such a showing be represented as scarce aware, before the human scene, of any other sharp antithesis at all." It is as if James were daring us to look for other sharp antitheses. One of them is certainly the topic of religious difference, no matter if it be phrased as Protestants and Others (Mainly Catholics) or Catholics and Others (Mainly Protestants) – James seldom goes further afield than that. The Protestant–Catholic antithesis appears sporadically throughout the works; it is in James' book reviews and essays, in his letters and notebooks, in his tales and novels, and it is clearly implied by his most ambitious and most original, if also his most disastrous, play.

The organization of this book is analytic, thematic, formal, critical, all four, and only as subject to those exigencies is it chronological. After supplying in Part One some essential historical and literary background, I felt it necessary to examine various conspicuous aspects of James' literary Catholicizing, such examination doing double duty in covering a broad range of published and (by James) unpublished materials, reviews, essays, tales, letters, notebooks. This second part was all along intended to close with reflections about James' attitudes toward death, according to my suspicion that no other topic is so revelatory of a person's religious state. Death led to Minny Temple, as foreseen, but Minny Temple led, as not at all foreseen, and by however tremulous a bridge, to what I call in the third part the narratives of Catholic conversion. That vein I then attempted to follow from its origins circa 1870 until it appears to run out circa 1898 (some will perhaps think earlier – they may, if they like, shift my two "supersubtleties" to Part Six and make them at home there with other examples of noninterpretability). In Part Four I survey a quartet of more fairly typical works variously illustrative of James' literary handling of religious issues, centrally Catholic still, but not exclusively, nothing being more useful at any point than sidelights. Part Five extends from 1868 to 1904 – thirty-seven years, roughly – bracketing some curious resemblances between a quite early and very curious Catholic tale and a very late and very curious Catholic novel. Both tale and novel concern Catholic and family, that is to say the relations between those two terms. So does *Guy Domville,* which is therefore placed with and between them – three examples of Catholic *"ménage,"* James' view of a religious group inordinately folded in upon itself and consequently, inevitably, and inordinately folded away from "the world." In Part Six I survey a septet of famous James novels having in one way or another to do with Catholicity and ranging from the most lucid to the most impenetrable. Thus we trail off and are lost in that relative uncertainty that must continue – forever, I fear – to shroud our understanding of Henry James on his religious side.

In retrospect, I do not conceive of any very apt alternative to this arrangement of the materials, but I confess a half-hearted regret that it fails to throw a blinding light on chronology – a half-hearted regret, because the chronological light is itself only partially illuminating. As the "Calendar: Chief Items of Catholic Interest in Henry James" shows, there are two chief clusters of apparent Catholic intensity in Henry James' literary career (but there are also many "Catholic" works outside these two periods, before, between, and after). The first cluster is circa 1870–5 and follows the death of Minny Temple (8 March 1870). The second cluster is circa 1895–8 and follows the death of Constance Fenimore Woolson (24 January 1894). There is no reason to believe that either of these deaths pressed James toward any personal involvement with the Catholic faith. But each of these deaths closely preceded, and maybe precipitated, a flurry of literary Catholicizing, not necessarily or altogether pro-Catholic, the second cluster being, however, distinctly more favorable than the first.

Aside from the biographies and the many edited texts that are owing to Leon Edel, I have found little of any direct use in the criticism of Henry James; most of it is based on assumptions completely different from, and even opposite from, mine. (To such remarks there are always exceptions, e.g., a useful if limited chapter, "Blest Images and Sanctified Relics," in Robert L. Gale's *The Caught Image,* 1964.) On the other hand, I have been singularly blest in the works of recent church historians, of which I would particularly mention Thomas Bokenkotter's *A Concise History of the Catholic Church* (rev. ed., 1979), James Hennesey, S.J., *American Catholics: A History of the Roman Catholic Community in the United States* (1981), Martin E. Marty's *An Invitation to American Catholic History* (1986), and Edward Norman's *Roman Catholicism in England from the Elizabethan Settlement to the Second Vatican Council* (1986) and *The English Catholic Church in the Nineteenth Century* (1984). David S. Reynolds' *Faith in Fiction: The Emergence of Religious Literature in America* (1981) is often suggestive for the period *before* James (up to the Civil War). The Bible of American anti-Catholic misbehavior in roughly the same period is of course Ray Allen Billington's *The Protestant Crusade, 1800–1860* (1938).

On the more personal side, I am pleased to thank Leon Edel, Adeleine R. Tintner, and Daniel Mark Fogel, for encouraging and helpful correspondence; Albert Gelpi and Julie Greenblatt, for gentle and generous pre-acceptance handling; Eric Newman, for the same in the period of production; the two outside readers for Cambridge University Press, whose identities I do not know, for acute and provocative prodding; The Johns Hopkins University Press for permission to reprint the chapter on *The Golden Bowl* from *The Henry James Review,* where it appeared in different form and under a different title; Barbara Horner, for continuous patience in the perpetual retyping and word processing; Barbara Tomlinson for a painstaking anatomy of textual difficulties, with suggestions for their removal; and Mary Burton Fussell for just about everything, from Introibo to Missa est.

Calendar: Chief Items of Catholic Interest in Henry James

1871   *Watch and Ward*
        Atlantic, August–December

1872–4 *Transatlantic Sketches*
        Nation, Atlantic, Galaxy, Independent, July 1872–
        September 1874

1873   "The Madonna of the Future"
        Atlantic, March

1874   "The Last of the Valerii"
        Atlantic, January

1874   "Adina"
        Scribner's, May–June

1874   Review of Parkman, *Old Régime in Canada*
        Nation, 15 October

1875   *Roderick Hudson*
        (*Atlantic*, January–December

1875   Review of Haven, *Our Next-Door Neighbor*
        Nation, 8 July

1875   Review of Wallon, *Jeanne d'Arc*
        Galaxy, August

1875   "Honoré de Balzac"
        Galaxy, December

1876–7 *The American*
        Atlantic, June 1876–May 1877

1878   *The Europeans*
        Atlantic, July–October

1880–1 *The Portrait of a Lady*
        Macmillan's, October 1880–November 1881
        Atlantic, November 1880–December 1881

1883   "Alphonse Daudet"
        Century, August

1885–6 *The Princess Casamassima*
        Atlantic, September 1885–October 1886

1888   *The Reverberator*
        Macmillan's, February–July

1895   *Guy Domville*
        5 January (opening night)

1895   "The Altar of the Dead"
        In *Terminations*

1896   *The Spoils of Poynton* (as *The Old Things*)
        Atlantic, April–October

Documentation

All letters are identified in the text by date and by name of correspondent. Unless otherwise stated, they are cited from Leon Edel, ed., *Henry James Letters.* 4 vols. (Cambridge, Mass.: Harvard University Press, 1974–84). The provenance of letters from other collections is given in the Notes.

Unless otherwise specified, all citations of literary criticism by Henry James are from Leon Edel and Mark Wilson, eds., *Essays on Literature, American Writers, English Writers* (New York: Library of America, 1984) and *French Writers, Other European Writers, The Prefaces to the New York Edition* (New York: Library of America, 1984).

Henry James novels *through 1890* are likewise cited from the three Library of America collections thus far available, viz., William T. Stafford, ed., *Henry James Novels 1871–1880* (New York, 1983) and *Henry James Novels 1881–1886* (New York: 1985); and Daniel Mark Fogel, ed., *Henry James Novels 1886–1890* (New York, 1989).

Novels *after 1890* are cited from the New York Edition (New York: Scribner's, 1907–9), unless otherwise indicated.

Citations of the shorter fiction, including *The Turn of the Screw,* are from Leon Edel's twelve-volume edition *The Complete Tales of Henry James* (Philadelphia: Lippincott, 1961–4).

Details of publication (place, date, periodical, as appropriate) are from Leon Edel and Dan H. Laurence, *A Bibliography of Henry James,* third edition, revised with the assistance of James Rambeau (Oxford: Clarendon, 1982).

"I'm not a real Catholic, but I want to buy it."
The American, 1907 version

He might in these sessions, with his eyes on the grey-green sea, have been counting again and still recounting the beads, almost all worn smooth, of his rosary of pain – which had for the fingers of memory and the recurrences of wonder the same felt break of the smaller ones by the larger that would have aided a pious mumble in some dusky altar-chapel.

"The Bench of Desolation," 1909–10

PART ONE

Bibliographical Leads,
Historical Considerations

> In this world we have seen the Roman Catholic power dying . . . for
> many centuries. Many a time we have gotten all ready for the funeral
> and found it postponed again, on account of the weather or something.
> Mark Twain, *Following the Equator,* 1897

Because an early topic of this book is novels of Roman Catholic
conversion, the reader may wish to learn about them as soon as possible;
alas, the only bibliography I know of is "Novels of [Catholic] Conversion," in Albert J. Menendez' *The Road to Rome: An Annotated Bibliography* (New York: Garland, 1986). Of the 112 titles given, 28 were published in 1871 or earlier, that is, before *Watch and Ward.* (See also, by the
same author, *The Catholic Novel: An Annotated Bibliography* [New York:
Garland, 1988].) Lyle H. Wright's *American Fiction 1851–1875, A Contri-
bution Toward a Bibliography* (San Marino, Calif.: Huntington Library,
1957) lists no titles directly referring to Catholic conversion, a few that
refer to convents, and a more generous selection of Catholic items, pro
and con, mostly the latter, laconically labeled "Anti-Catholic." The more
popular topics were home, love, the War, the "West," and, by far, al-
cohol. Mrs. Julia (McNair) Wright is credited with 4 anti-Catholic novels and at least 7 against drink. A few of Menendez' titles also appear in
Wright, but there is much want of correspondence. Indeed, no two lists
of "Catholic literature" correspond, for want of agreement with respect
to what is Catholic. James wrote no book reviews about conversion novels, except *Lothair* by Disraeli, a title not mentioned by Menendez because of the author's not being a Catholic convert, and not mentioned
by Wright because of his not being an American. No conversion novels
are mentioned in James' published correspondence or in his *Notebooks.*
There are no allusions to specific titles in his tales, novels, plays, or non-
fictional prose. David S. Reynolds' *Faith in Fiction* has an extensive

1

"Chronology of Fiction" by types, "Roman Catholic Fiction," and "Anti-Catholic Fiction through 1850," plus "Sampling of Religious Fiction After 1850," the latter running to 1980. Even a survey of titles in the "Anti-Catholic Fiction" listing reveals that Catholic conversion and Catholic convent are the two leading topics. The convent is regularly figured as a prison. Cuba, Canada, and France are the favored settings.

The items given by both Wright and Menendez are of course relatively recent, and they are all Anglo–American, but reflection soon reminds us that conversion narratives, presumably oral before they were written, date back to the first appearance of human life on this planet. In the Hebraic–Christian religious tradition that is also the literary tradition of Western civilization, examples of conversion are easily found in the Biblical texts, frequently among prophets (Elijah, Elisha, Isaiah, Jeremiah, Ezekiel, Amos), perhaps even more frequently among founders or apostles, these latter conversions sometimes involving a significant change of name, Abram (to Abraham), Jacob, Moses, Simon (to Peter), Paul (from Saul). Indeed, one might well consider all prophets and apostles as converts inasmuch as they come to the light from comparative darkness and in so coming acquire new obligations and rewards. The blinding-light conversion of St. Paul, with subtle change of name (Acts 9.1–30, 13.9), is surely the most spectacular conversion in world history, at least among those we know about, although the "conversion" of the Blessèd Virgin, if we may call it that, her unavoidable alteration after the Annunciation, was surely the more far-reaching (St. Joseph also).

Everyone will recall other famous conversions, such as those of Constantine (James cites his famous slogan in his preface to *The Awkward Age*); the pagan priest in England who held that the purely secular life was like a bird flying through the mead-hall; St. Augustine in his *Confessions,* the most deservedly famous of all conversion narratives (and much more than that); Dante Alighieri, *Vita Nuova,* and arguably the *Commedia* as well. Most of these famous Christian conversions involved change from outside to inside the faith, but there are also conversions within the faith, from less intense to more intense, as in the well-known case of St. Francis of Assisi. Like everyone else, Henry James was acquainted with these general types of conversion and with their most luminous exemplars. After the Reformation the conversion narratives that appear to hold the highest interest for the reading public in Great Britain and in the United States, and consequently for Henry James, are those that deal with conversions from Protestant to Catholic. (Catholics who go over to Protestant do not *convert* but are said to *lapse,* and no one wants to hear about them.) In the eighteenth century "the birth of the novel" concomitantly brings to birth historical novels about medieval Catholicity, romantic, lurid, and admonitory (plus the parodies thereof). These so-called Gothic novels illustrate the rather obvious fact that if you (the writer) insist on placing your personages and their actions amidst a populace that is preponderantly or entirely Catholic you will have a Catholic novel on your hands. Aside from historical novels, such as the anti-Catholic, pro-Protestant apologia of Sir Walter Scott (*The Monastery* and *The Abbott,* both 1820), the pertinent nineteenth- and twentieth-century texts are allegedly realistic representations of Catholics, cradle or convert; and if the novels are English or American they are representations of Roman Catholics as what are nowadays called "minorities," persecuted or maligned, yet often envied, living their anachronistic and alienated lives among schismatics and heretics. Protestants and other non-Catholics simply adore reading about these matters.

How does any of this background connect with the life and times and literary production of Henry James? There were Mrs. Clarence Strong and other Catholic convert women who sometimes amused him and sometimes got on his nerves; perhaps there were more amiable forerunners who suggested Mrs. Keith in *Watch and Ward,* James' first novel of Catholic conversion (or its avoidance). But *the* Roman Catholic who clearly most affected Henry James *in propria persona* was John La Farge. Their friendship goes back to James' adolescent years in Newport and was still being celebrated as late as *The American Scene* (1907) and *Notes of a Son and Brother* (1914). La Farge was a painter and a writer; he encouraged his younger friend to pursue the arts; he was European in manner and ambience; he had a French name and had lived in Paris; he was sophisticated, cosmopolitan, and rich; he introduced James to Mérimée, Musset, and, most important, Balzac. It may be imagined how rapidly and how deeply his immediate example called into question (if it did not entirely obliterate) any American anti-Catholic prejudices James might otherwise have grown up with.[1] Yet it was increasingly, in the United States and even, to a degree, in Great Britain, an era of tolerance and indifference. Had it not been La Farge it might well have been another.

More *literary* Catholics may be divided into those James knew personally and those he did not know but knew about; into cradle Catholics and converts, the latter, as always, more evident and more vocal; into English, French, and American Catholics, the English being the most numerous but not necessarily the most influential; and into writers who were Catholic themselves and those who were not but who wrote about Catholic matters, whether in an antagonistic or in a friendly way. English Catholic *littérateurs* were mostly poets, mostly converts, not friends of Henry James, but he would have known about them. They descend, if one may so put it, from John Henry (later Cardinal) Newman, whose *Apologia Pro Vita Sua* (1864) is the archetypical Catholic conversion narrative of modern times; who also wrote a conversion novel (*Loss and*

Gain; or, The Story of a Convert, 1848)[2]; who received into the church none other than Gerard Manley Hopkins, S.J. ("I have been up at Oxford just long enough to have heard fr. my father and mother," Hopkins wrote Newman at the time, "in return for my letter announcing my conversion. Their answers are terrible: I cannot read them twice"); Newman who figures, surreptitiously enough, some readers will be shocked to discover, in dubious connection with Henry James' protagonist of the same last name in *The American* (1876–7). Then there were in James' day many lesser lights, many of them notably eccentric, many of them swirling around the pole of Catholic aestheticism, Aubrey De Vere, Coventry Patmore, Francis Thompson ("The Hound of Heaven"), Lionel Johnson, Ernest Dowson, with other Ezra Pound heroes of the nineties, none of these, apparently, except De Vere, known to James. Known to him, not always to his complete satisfaction, were G. K. Chesterton and Aubrey Beardsley (via *The Yellow Book,* quite Catholic, quite aesthetic); Oscar Wilde (whose lover, Lord Alfred Douglas, was later a Catholic convert); Ford Madox Ford, who wrote the first critical book about James, in which he identifies himself as "a black Papist"; Compton Mackenzie, another convert, the son of Edward Compton, who had produced *The American* as a play in 1891. Overarching the lot in novelistic talent and literary relevance was Joseph Conrad, but it is not likely that he and James had any Catholic conversation: Conrad's religion was well concealed, and it was only when you scratched the surface of his fictive text that you discovered the basic principles and an occasional scintilla of the true faith fetched over the years and all the way from Poland through the French and British merchant marines onto the dry soil of Protestant England at last.

Among American writers, James knew slightly and only late in his life "poor dear old Mark Twain," with whom his brother William exchanged tips about health cures. Henry James was not an unqualified admirer of the humorist, as the condescension of his phrasing shows, but he could hardly have avoided acquaintance with such anti-Catholic (anti-Anglican?) occasions as *A Connecticut Yankee in King Arthur's Court* (1889) or the mixed performance in *Personal Recollections of Joan of Arc* (1895) – honor and glory to the Catholic Maid, anathema to the Catholic court – even if both these volumes came well after James' own religious attitudes were formed. The same goes for the major works of Henry Adams, also a friend of John La Farge, whose literary Catholicizing somewhat more nearly resembles James', but there is no question of "influence," only of "period tone." Adams' "Catholicity" is of course almost exclusively Marian, as James' is not, and plainly appears in his major works, *Mont-Saint-Michel and Chartres* (1904), *The Education of Henry Adams* (1907), and "The Prayer to the Virgin of Chartres" (c. 1900–1, 1920). James' most interesting Catholic contacts with an American non-Catholic writer are with William Dean Howells. His novel *A Foregone Conclusion* (1875) was reviewed by James – *twice*, in the same month of the same year. Howells' novel is, as James oddly says, "a singularly perfect production." It is the tale of a Venetian priest who has lost his faith but is still in orders and who falls in love with an American tourist girl and is rejected, "greeted," James says, "with the inevitable horror provoked by such a proposition from such a source." If James was in this remark as typically American as I suspect him of being, his horror was twofold: (1) that a celibate priest should be tempted to abjure his vows and (2) that he should have been celibate in the first place (it wasn't "normal," i.e., not like "us," a common message of literary Catholicizing by non- or anti-Catholics, e.g., in Charles Reade's *The Cloister and the Hearth*, 1861). James wonders if Howells' novel mightn't have been better had the priest's Catholicity been more secure, so that he should have been assailed by love only rather than by love and doubt together, but then he concludes not. The priest, as things stand, is blessedly unprovided with "prayers stupidly mumbled and of the *odeur de sacristie*." Presumably James read Howells' other novels, but probably we shall never know what he thought of such remarks as "the priest [making his rounds at a hospital] of the religion to which most of the poor and lowly still belong" in *The Minister's Charge* (1887) or the discussion in *An Imperative Duty* (1891) whether all black Americans would eventually be Catholic. Of other American writers who treated Catholicity and whom James knew, the one with the closest personal tie was Henry Harland, an expatriated Roman Catholic convert and editor of *The Yellow Book*. It was Harland who magnanimously allowed James to write out his tales to any length he liked. In 1898 James wrote a pleasant account of *Comedies and Errors*. Harland's novel *The Cardinal's Snuff-Box* (1900) appeared just in time to furnish a detail or two about multilingual conversation in a rustic outdoor dining area indispensable for the riverside revelation scene of *The Ambassadors* (1903).

American and English Catholics generally announce themselves, especially if they are converts. French Catholics you tend to take for granted – France is after all the eldest daughter of the church, and she has been at times a loyal and dutiful child – but you seldom know what kind of French Catholics they are, whether Jansenist, Jesuit, Masonic, socialist, anti-clerical, Erastian, Gallican, Ultramontane, or nominal. Even so, Henry James' relations with French literary Catholicizing are readily summed up: (1) except in his early reviews of French Catholic books, he was not as affected as by American or English Catholics; (2) of all things French, French religious life is what he felt least at home with; and (3) even more than with American or English Catholics, James liked them better on paper than in person (John La Farge being the notable exception). He could forgive Balzac everything because Balzac was dead; he could even admire the spectacle of Balzac's writing his novels dressed in Benedictine garb. Paul Bourget was alive and in his anti-Dreyfusard or reactionary moods a considerable trial. On other subjects, James liked his conversation a good deal better than his novels.

Balzac was of course the chief influence on James from French or any other literature, and one or two Jamesian responses to Balzac's commerce with Catholic representation will duly appear in the following pages, albeit briefly. There is sadly no record of what James thought about superman-criminal Vautrin disguised as a Spanish abbé or about the sensational-sentimental Catholic conversion of Venus-for-hire Esther Gobseck, who felt that God would "like" her (*Splendeurs et misères des courtisanes*, 1839–47). James was too busy enjoying the Maison Vauquer and the spotty career of Valérie de Marneffe. The first French *littérateur* James knew personally was Flaubert, to whom he was introduced by Turgenev; through Flaubert he met Edmond Goncourt, Alphonse Daudet, Emile Zola, and Guy de Maupassant. James' critical essays on them display no great interest in their religious convictions, and of course it is entirely possible that James knew nothing about them. On the whole, he tends to deplore their morals while applauding their formal-stylistic zeal. Aside from ignorance, there is plenty of room for critical disagreement about the Catholicity of (for example) Flaubert. Catholicity and romanticism seem like interchangeable terms in *Madame Bovary* (1857), according to the Chateaubriand-Stendhal connection (Emma Bovary hears Génie du Christianisme read aloud on a Sunday in her convent); the disdain for paganism displayed in *Salammbô* (1862) suggests a strong if unstated Christian point of view; so do the *Trois Contes* (1877), not to mention the end of *La Tentation de Saint Antoine* (1874): "Tout au milieu et dans le disque même du soleil, rayonne la face de Jésus-Christ. Antoine fait le signe de la croix et se remet en prières." Of the French writers James knew, he admired Flaubert most, for his aesthetic passion and integrity, while disliking virtually everything he wrote. Of the French writers James knew, Daudet was the one he liked the most and the longest (but also Bourget). The possible connection of *L'Evangéliste* (1883) and *The Bostonians* (1886) will be noted in passing. It is not, in my view, rewarding. It may further be doubted if James was even aware that the Daudet children in their home theater had been allowed to play at celebrating mass, in costume, which is more than can be said for the James children, however liberated.

For American Literature earlier than James, I have already mentioned David S. Reynolds' *Faith in Fiction,* a useful survey within its limits. Reynolds unfortunately seems to believe that to be "Catholic" a novel must be "about" Catholic topics and written "by" a Catholic, whereas the literary representation of Catholics in nineteenth-century America – the tradition that provides a certain context and background for Henry James – is almost entirely owing to Protestants. It is that tradition of mixed romantic adulation and skeptical or hostile distaste that defines the *feel* of American attitudes toward Catholicism, and it is this *feel* that James inherits and attacks and approves and even develops. There are ancillary contributions from such British Catholicizings as Dickens' *Barnaby Rudge* (1841), Thackeray's *History of Henry Esmond* (1852), George Eliot's *Romola* (1863) – one way or another, James had met all three authors – but such novels are less close to him than their American counterparts, the British examples lacking that special American blend of political toleration, paranoia, secret admiration, and contemptuous superiority.

In the first American novel, the infamous *Power of Sympathy* (1789) by William Hill Brown, the protagonist Harrington plots to remove his seductee Harriot to a private apartment, for living with a family as she does she "might as well be immured in a nunnery." In Hannah Foster's *The Coquette* (1797), the giddy girl writes a friend, "You are not so morose as to wish me to become a nun, would our country and religion allow it." In these early novels we find not only prejudice but assumption and misinformation: Did Foster really think "our country" had constitutional provisions against nuns, or was it only "our religion"? Another common convention was imposture. In Charles Brockden Brown's *Wieland; or, The Transformation. An American Tale* (1798), the narrator muses on the villain Carwin: "It was not easy to reconcile his conversion to the Romish faith, with those proofs of knowledge and capacity that were exhibited by him on different occasions. A suspicion was, sometimes, admitted, that his belief was counterfeited for some political purpose." The suspicion is justified. After all, the alternative is unbelievable: "Carwin was an adherent to the Romish faith, yet was an Englishman by birth, and, perhaps, a protestant by education." Why should he "abjure his religion and his country?" (in Spain). In *Edgar Huntly; or, Memoirs of a Sleep-Walker* (1799), Catholic luridity is associated with Portugal. It is always a romantic Latin European land where these things happen, never the United States or other English-speaking places. In the novels of Brown, even Ireland gives the impression of being non-Catholic.

"James's critical genius comes out most tellingly in his mastery over, his baffling escape from Ideas," according to T. S. Eliot, "a mastery and an escape which are perhaps the last test of a superior intellect. He had a mind so fine that no idea could violate it." It might be better said that James lifelong displayed an uncanny resistance to clichés and cheap ideology. He is almost the only writer of the American nineteenth century who declines to remark (as often as possible) on the superiority of Roman Catholic churches in not having pews (pews are undemocratic). He is not, however (T. S. Eliot still) "a continuator of the New England genius" but a reaction against it, whether as a native New Yorker or as an adoptive European. James has virtually none of that New England belief in "progress" so dear to the lady novelists (Lydia Maria Child, Catherine Maria Sedgwick, et al.) which holds, in the religious sphere, that the Church of England (Protestant Episcopal in this country) is an advance on the Church of Rome; that the Puritans (*our* ancestresses) did well to depart from the Church of England; that we, post-Puritan and post-Protestant, post–everything but American (i.e., New England), are in our liberation superior to all: We are arrived at such a final height that we may well look down on everything. This sort of fiction enables the liberal writer and reader of the 1820s to indulge in lofty views of history all the way from the present back to the seventeenth century. The novels are set in the seventeenth century, to which their authors condescend. But the seventeenth century is also useful in mounting attacks on nineteenth-century Catholics; for these attacks the nineteenth-century author is not responsible. So in the first chapter of Child's *Hobomok* (1824) a classic passage for those in search of the supercilious anti-Catholic in its sources and assumptions and tones:

> That light, which had arisen amid the darkness of Europe, stretched its long, luminous track across the Atlantic, till the summits of the western world became tinged with its brightness. . . . In this enlightened and liberal age, it is perhaps too fashionable to look back upon those early sufferers in the cause of the Reformation, as a band of dark, discontented bigots. . . . The peculiarities of their situation occasioned most of their faults, and atoned for them. . . . [Of course,] we cannot forbear a smile that vigorous and cultivated minds should have looked upon the signing of the cross with so much horror and detestation. But the heart pays involuntary tribute to conscientious, persevering fortitude, in what cause soever it may be displayed. At this impartial period we view the sound policy and unwearied zeal with which the Jesuits endeavored to rebuild their decaying church, with almost as much admiration as we do the noble spirit of reaction which it produced. Whatever merit may be attached to the cause of our forefathers . . . they certainly possessed excellencies, which peculiarly fitted them for a van-guard in the proud and rapid march of freedom.[3]

Anti-Catholic remarks in *Hobomok* will consequently be heard issuing from the mouths of the comparatively benighted and are not to be taken for the author's opinions (yet there they are, on the page). Queen Henrietta, wife to Charles I, is "their [the Anglicans'] papistical step-mother," "his Romish queen." (Romish is standard nineteenth-century Anglo-American anti-Catholic abuse. Even Henry James stoops to it.) Anglican bishops, deans, and deacons "are all whelps from the Roman litter." It goes on and on: "the hell-born Loyola," "the scarlet woman of Babylon," "the mummeries of Rome," "the popish sign of the cross," "the whorish woman of Babylon." Best of all, "the Jesuits are stretching their arms north, south, east and west, to hold up the reins of the falling church." Not only *then,* but *now.* The near cause of inflammation would appear to be French Canada.

Imposture and Rome-abuse continue in Catherine Maria Sedgwick's *Hope Leslie* (1827). The villain Sir Philip Gardiner comes to Massachusetts Colony bent on various mischiefs, among them seduction. He has seduced one young lady (probably under age) in Europe, and now he is after Hope Leslie. He affects an advanced grade of Puritan hypocrisy but is really a Roman Catholic in disguise! (Hope Leslie spots him abstaining from meat on Friday.) Like other Catholics in this novel, he is an inveterate crucifix-kisser. A French Canadian connection (implicit) is made through Hope's sister Faith (Mary). Faith is early in life abducted by Indians and she marries one. In effect, she *is* an Indian. She will not come home. She appears to have forgotten her English. As her Indian sister-in-law explains to Hope: " 'She hath been signed with the cross by a holy father from France; she bows to the crucifix.' 'Thank God!' exclaimed Hope fervently, for she thought that any christian faith was better than none.' " The girl may well have another think coming. In earlier anti-Catholic American Literature, the Menace was east in Europe, and the American Message was: Dear God, don't let them come *over.* Now the Menace is north, and the American Message is: Don't let them come *down.* On a real map, the French-speaking Roman Catholic province of Quebec lies north of New England, but it also lies both west and east of New England. If its inhabitants, speaking whatever language, and of whatever color-coded skin, ever "came down," New England would be driven into the west with the Indians or back east into the Atlantic. There is also in *Hope Leslie* a ridiculous Italian sailor (Catholic, of course) who mistakes Hope Leslie for the Blessèd Virgin (much jeering at Catholic superstition). There is plentiful talk of convents and monasteries and religious orders. The good Indian girl Magawisca is urged by Sir Philip to take Rosa, his first victim, "to your western forests, and give her to a Romish priest, who will guide her to the Hotel Dieu, which our good Lady Bouillon has established in Canada." Maria Monk of the *Awful Disclosures* (1836) is less than a decade away.[4]

James Fenimore Cooper Catholics seldom kiss the crucifix but are perpetually crossing themselves (thus you may know them). They do so throughout *The Bravo* (1831) and sporadically in Cooper's other Roman Catholic novel, *Mercedes of Castile* (1840). In these novels, everybody is Catholic. On the whole, Cooper seems to prefer European situations in which Catholics and Protestants commingle (*The Heidenmauer*, 1832, set in Bavaria; *The Headsman*, 1833, set in Switzerland). In *Wing-and-Wing* (1842) he splits a romantic couple, she Italian Catholic, he French atheist. In the United States, Cooper prefers single isolated Catholics, high or low, embedded in Protestant milieux, as Inez in *The Prairie* (1827); as the Scotch Protestant in *Wyandotté* who refers to an Irish Catholic as one "who belangs to a kirk that has so little seempathy with protestantism"; as Biddy in *Jack Tier* (1848), who informs us that "If Jack will go to a praste and just confess, when he can find a father, it will do his sowl good." Unlike most American and English writers of the nineteenth century, Cooper was very dubious about the Protestant doctrine that Catholics lacked proper capitalistic zeal. He makes a great point of his border crossings into Catholic countries: They are not crossings from splendor to squalor. Entering a Catholic canton in Switzerland, he writes (in his travel book of the same name), "[T]he hill-sides began to teem with churches; *crosses reappeared, and the views suddenly became more picturesque*" (emphasis added). This is pure Henry James. Entering Italy, Cooper wrote: "Tall, gaunt-looking church towers rose out of this grateful forest, in such numbers as to bespeak at once the affluence of Romish worship, and the density of the population." *Affluence* to Cooper meant churches and crosses and people, not money.

In *The Bravo*, all Cooper's Catholics are Italians. As in *The Golden Bowl*, by Henry James, they gladly swear to and by pagan and Christian deities alike: Corpo di Bacco, Body of Diana, Madre di Dio, St. Gennaro (whose blood liquefies), Blessed St. Anthony of the Miraculous Draught (who preached to the fishes). The Carmelite monk (Cooper as imposter) is the central character. The factitious Venetian government personifies itself as St. Mark. ("St. Mark will not tolerate such free opinions of his wisdom.") There are allusions to missals, convents, confessions and the confessional, penance, absolution, the sacrament of matrimony, candles, altar, mass, sins of omission, the Pope, the Cardinal Secretary, money for masses, the States of the Church, a private oratory (Gothic). Catholicity is by Cooper misconstrued (thus deducting slightly, for Catholic readers, from local color) in reference to purgatory, the immortality of the soul, confession, and angels. Blessings are always and everywhere bestowed and received. The intercession of the Blessèd Virgin and other saints is invoked. Prayers and masses for the dead make up a large item. "Praised be the blessed Mother and the incarnate Son."

Cooper's tolerance and sociological accuracy are a great step toward James. In *The Oak Openings* (1848) he describes the religious situation in the United States circa 1812 and continues: "All this is rapidly changing. Romanists abound, and spots that, half a century since, appeared to be the most improbable places in the world to admit of the rites of the priests of Rome, now hear the chants and prayers of the mass-books. All this shows a tendency towards that great commingling of believers, which is doubtless to precede the final fusion of sects, and the predicted end." Cooper's observation is not far from today's best eschatological ecumenicism, and some time he will receive his due. Two months before he died, Cooper was received into the Protestant Episcopal church, which he had advocated almost all his literary life and at times had tried to pretend was the same as the Catholic. It was as far as he found himself able to go.

If it is true, as is frequently alleged, that post-Protestant modernity increasingly divides between the Catholic and the atheist, Ralph Waldo Emerson is the veritable harbinger of division. Commencing as a conventional Protestant, he increasingly bifurcates into the proto-Romanist and the virtual unbeliever. These extremist views are for the most part prohibited from his public utterances but are easily discovered in his journals and letters. In 1822 Emerson sounds like just such another New Englander as Child and Sedgwick. We hear all about "the worldly and impious policy of the Roman Church who take advantage of man's terror before his Maker, to win away his earthly riches to the service of their sinister institutions," and that the "curse which is landed on the Roman Church records that she substituted *authority* for *reason*, that she took the Bible from the hands of men and commanded them to believe. This bondage was so crafty and so strong that it was long ere the mind was hardy enough to break it. But it was finally broken, and thenceforward the true Age of Reason commenced." As for Progress, no people ever had it better: "The true epochs of history should be those successive triumphs which age after age the communities of men have achieved[,] such as the Reformation, the Revival of letters, the progressive Abolition of the Slave-trade" (this in 1823).

As with other American un-Catholic types, Europe brought out the worst and best in Emerson. It splintered his conformities into prejudices more exact. In Rome, he went to the Trinità di Monte "to see some nuns take the veil" and rhetorically inquired if "any ceremony be more pathetic." At Malta, he imagined how wonderful it would be to have a basically Catholic service in a Roman Catholic church but without a priest, he attended mass and made the obligatory American remark about the absence of pews, and he urged the Father of the Church to "speak out of his own heart" to each and all, including, presumably, himself. Two years later, home again, he complained that "The arts languish now because all their scope is exhibition. . . . [On the other hand, the] Catholic Religion has turned them to continual account in its service." The prose version of his poem "The Problem" is found in a journal passage of 1838. In it Emerson claims to share the general (American) antipathy to the

Roman (or Anglican) priesthood while at the same time admiring their churches (especially if they are large, when they are called cathedrals). But in an 1841 entry he admits: "If I judge from my own experience I should unsay all my fine things, I fear. . . . I think then the writer ought not to be married, ought not to have a family. I think the Roman Church with its celibate clergy & its monastic cells was right."

"I regret to learn that Miss Howard is a Catholic" (letter to his wife of 4 January 1872). Very much like Henry James, Emerson liked certain external aspects of Catholicity, and even the Catholic "idea," a whole lot better than he liked particular Catholic people. The Catholic people he liked least were American converts. (They should have known better.) Roman Catholic conversions among his friends tried Emerson's patience sorely: "Least of all will I call sacraments those legendary quips of yours which break the sacraments which are most my own, my duty to my wife, husband, son, friend, country, nor can I suffer a nasty monk to whisper to *me, to whom God has* given such a person as S.G.W. & such children, for my confessors and absolvers." As his son and editor Edward Emerson notes, "RWE's Reflections on a valued friend lately turned Romanist." (The friend was Anna Barker Ward, an old-time magnolia-South associate of Margaret Fuller's.) In 1847 Emerson noted "The superstitions of our age are," and then first on a list "the fear of Catholicism," and in 1849 "New England Catholics disgusting. And the spread of Popery futile. As to fearing the Pope, we in America should as soon think of fearing a muskmelon." Twenty years later, he was still on the same tack: "Charles Newcomb said, he liked Catholics born to it, but American Catholics were disgusting. And I have never seen any such converts who did not seem to me insane."

Yet Emerson also has an anti-Protestant side so strong that it drives him far in the Catholic direction. Back in 1847 when he was listing fear of Catholicism as a superstition, he was also writing, at some length, also in his journal (pews again):

> The Catholic religion respects masses of men & ages. If it elects, it is yet by millions, as when it divides the heathen & christian. The Protestant, on the contrary, with its hateful "private judgment," brings parishes, families, & at last individual doctrinaires & schismatics, & verily, at last, private gentlemen into play & notice, which to the gentle musing poet is to the last degree disagreeable. This of course their respective arts & artists must build & paint. The Catholic church is ethnical, & every way superior. It is in harmony with Nature, which loves the race & ruins the individual. The Protestant has his pew, which of course is only the first step to a church for every individual citizen – a church apiece.

And in 1843, in letters to Margaret Fuller and to his wife, from Baltimore, we find three passages that bear on the Emersonian churchgoing lapses when out of town. First, attending High Mass in the cathedral: "It is so dignified to come where the priest is nothing, & the people nothing, and an idea for once excludes these impertinences. . . . It is a dear old church, the Roman I mean, & today I detest the Unitarians and Martin Luther and all the parliament of Barebones. . . . 'Ah that one word of it were true!' " Then, second: "It is well for my Protestantism that we have no Cathedral in Concord . . . I should be confirmed in a fortnight. The Unitarian church forgets that men are poets." Third and last: "Tomorrow, to the Catholic Church once more." In "The Divinity School Address" (1838) Emerson claimed that the "Puritans in England and America, found in the Christ of the Catholic Church, and in the dogmas inherited from Rome, scope for their austere piety, and their longings for civil freedom." Such a view would seem to suppose that "America" was in its origins "Catholic," a view that we can hardly imagine shared by such regional patriots as Lydia Maria Child and Catherine Maria Sedgwick.

We can hardly imagine it shared by Hawthorne either, whose mind, although far better in some respects than Emerson's (in the writing of fiction, for example), was in comparison simple and unsubtle. Hawthorne's notebooks, especially *The French and Italian Notebooks,* show him looking at this side and that of various religious positions, especially the Roman Catholic, but they show no particular tendency toward conversion. He was born into Protestantism, and he would stay there: It was loyal, it was obvious, and it was easy. In *The Scarlet Letter* (1850) he dallies with the false resemblance between Hester Prynne and "that sacred image of sinless motherhood" the Blessèd Virgin ("Had there been a Papist among the crowd of Puritans, he might have seen in this beautiful woman . . . an object to remind him of the Divine Maternity," etc., etc., etc.). It is almost never said – perhaps now is the time for it to be said – that one of the major unstated significations of this novel, issuing at a time and in a place where, as I have been trying to show, the Protestant–Catholic division was a major topic of concern, at least among the literate and the literary, is that no such tragedy as befalls Arthur Dimmesdale and to an extent Hester would so likely have occurred in a Catholic milieu, where it would not have been long before *that* priest would have been on his knees to another priest, confessed, absolved, and, it is devoutly to be hoped, headed in a better direction than the seduction of beautiful young women parishioners with God knows what sorts of delusionism to follow. That is not the novel Hawthorne wrote, of course, nor even the novel he ought to have written. It is one of many imaginable novels hovering in the wings behind the textual facade.

In *The Marble Faun* (1860) – which James says he reread, with the rest of Hawthorne, at the outset of his own career – Hawthorne presses the issue of Catholic conversion and nonconversion about as far as any major American novelist would do, prior to James. Hilda lives in Rome at "The Virgin's Shrine," where she tends the lamp and, like St. Francis, converses with birds. Like everyone else, she is a frequenter of Catholic churches. Many good things are said (by the narrator) in favor of the Catholic faith, but of course in the end it is impossible – not for any reason, it just is. Then, burdened with her knowledge of another's guilt, Hilda finds herself in San Pietro. She dips her fingers in holy water and "almost signed the cross upon her breast, but forbore, and trembled, while shaking the water from her finger-tips." Yet San Pietro is, in the chapter heading and beyond, "The World's Cathedral" – not the Catholics' alone, not even when Protestants and tourists and other unbelievers are drifting around, but everyone's cathedral. The confessional, Hilda thinks, or feels, must "belong to Christianity itself." She enters a Pro Anglica Lingua confessional. Her confessor happens to be a New England priest (Hawthorne's wonderful stroke!) who has not been home for fifty years. He observes that this is her first confession. Is she reconciled to the church? Certainly not! What then is she doing in a Catholic confessional? She has no answer. He attempts to convert her. She declines. And then the miracle:

> "I am a daughter of the Puritans. But, in spite of my heresy," she added, with a sweet, tearful smile, "you may one day see the poor girl, to whom you have done this great Christian kindness, coming to remind you of it, and thank you for it, in the better land!"
>
> The old priest shook his head. But, as he stretched out his hands, at the same moment, in the act of benediction, Hilda knelt down and received the blessing with as devout a simplicity as any Catholic of them all.

It is almost as neat a fictional trick as Lord Marchmain's silently crossing himself while the last breath expires.

One consequence of that scene in real life is that Hawthorne's youngest child, Rose, became in later life a Roman Catholic convert and a nun. She founded an order for the care of terminally ill cancer patients, which is now called the Dominican Sisters of Hawthorne and is based in Hawthorne, New York. The sequence of events, with several assorted references to Hawthorne's works, plus their implications for his daughter and for her special work, are spelled out in Flannery O'Connor's "Introduction" to *A Memoir of Mary Ann* (1961), almost half a century after the death of Henry James. So do things ramify yet so we must leave them. It is time to turn to James himself as a young man and see if we can fit him into the stream of historical Christianity during the late nineteenth and early twentieth centuries, where in Western Europe and North America it continued to play itself along in glories and disasters, for what but a mixed performance would you expect of the Holy Spirit blowing through instruments so unsanctified as literary people, however expressive and revealing?

PART TWO

Representing Catholicity

1. The Protestant Base

The religious base from which Henry James set out to be a writer was unquestionably a liberalized nondenonimational American Protestantism rather than that happy-go-lucky irreligious indifference so blithely imputed to him in virtually all Henry James criticism. That he was uninterested in religious matters, for what they might yield him as a writer of fiction, if for nothing more, is copiously refuted by the textual evidence of his tales and novels, and at least one play, as well as by an early (31 March 1873) letter from Rome to Charles Eliot Norton in which, among other things, he says: "[T]he religious passion has always struck me as the strongest of man's heart. . . . I don't know how common the feeling is, but I am conscious of making a great allowance to the questions agitated by religion, in feeling that conclusions and decisions about them are tolerably idle." The perfectly balanced paradox of religious centrality and vague liberalistic tolerance is pure James. In the same paragraph, he admits that "civilization, good and bad alike, seems to be leaving it" – "Christianity in its old applications" – "pretty well out of account." And yet, even "when one thinks of the scanty fare, judged by our usual standards, in which it has always fed," we must all the more recognize and remark on "the powerful current continually setting towards all religious hypotheses," with the result that "it is hard not to believe that *some* application of the supernatural idea, should not be an essential part of our life." The marginality of belief – it is at least a receptivity to belief – is indicated in the grammar of assent by the double negative, and by the casual phrasing, "the supernatural idea," which adequately signifies James' comparative innocence of certain issues and emotions centrally involved with the "religious" or "spiritual" life, both generally and

in detail, as well as his distance from the specificities of Christian doctrine, no matter of what persuasion.

James' Protestant proclamations are mostly, but not entirely, found in
his early book reviews: in book reviews rather than in any other literary
genre because a book review lends itself to statements of personal opinion; early rather than late because it was in the early years that James
reviewed religious books. In the beginning his religious opinions display
a certain broadly genial yet unmistakably Protestant majesty of tone, one
notable Protestant denomination excepted. In an 1865 notice of Elizabeth
Rundle Charles' *Hearthstone Series,* he most emphatically writes: "We are
all of us Protestants, and we are all of us glad to see the Reformation
placed in its most favorable light, but as we are not all of us Methodists,
it is hard to sympathize with a lady's *ex parte* treatment of John Wesley."[1]
In the same review James deplores a certain absolutism of Reformation
zeal – people then were "dreadfully nervous," he explains, as during the
Civil War – and welcomes the fact that as Protestantism has developed,
"we are all of us [that phrase again] more or less Unitarians in spirit
compared with the founders of our creed" – it is not clear what creed he
has in mind. Nor does he seem to mean Unitarian doctrinally but rather
as a guerdon of sophisticated civility – Emerson is cited. Oddly enough,
some may think, James makes a rather automatic opposition between
religion and morals: "When religion enters in force, moral pre-occupa-
tions withdraw." Even more oddly, still others may think, especially in
the light of subsequent developments in the Jamesian *œuvre,* if not in
Protestantism itself, James makes no allowance at all for the possibility
that some of his readers might be Jews or Catholics. No: "We are all of
us Protestants." It was a position he would soon learn to aggregate, but
we may better understand the aggregations if we first clarify what they
are aggregations of; here, James' position is quite obvious – readers of
the *Nation* are naturally all Protestant (Americans) and may be so addressed by one of themselves, on the assumption that an overwhelming
majority, *that* majority in particular, constitutes for practical purposes a
homogenized totality.

But in 1865 and 1866, James also twice reviewed, and for readers of
the same *Nation,* the Catholic *Journal* and *Lettres* of Eugénie de Guérin.[2]
In these reviews he naturally makes no statements about all of us being
Protestant – indeed, the very subject matter suggests that some of "us"
are not. The standpoint is not the less Protestant, however, and is quite
in keeping with views previously expressed by the same writer in the
same periodical. In general, Catholicity is simplistic dependence: "Religion without imagination is piety; and such is Mlle. de Guérin's religion." And yet her piety is reversibly another word for her strength:
"She was a woman of character. Thoroughly dependent on the church,

she was independent of everything else." In the second review, the limitations of (European) Catholicity are explicated along more hemispheric lines. It is not with them as it is with us, where saintliness in the older sense is passé; on the other hand, "Nowhere are exquisite moral rectitude and the spirit of devotion more frequent than in New England," only in New England the religious sentiments are more complex (a judgment James would soon reverse); here, he goes on to say, the saints travel, they "hold political opinions; they are accomplished Abolitionists," they read magazines, newspapers, and novels, they attend lyceum lectures, they subscribe to libraries (as in *The Bostonians*) – "in a word, they are enlightened. The result of this freedom of enquiry is that they become profoundly self-conscious. They obtain a notion of the relation of their virtues to a thousand objects of which Mlle. de Guérin had no conception." Mlle. de Guérin is for early James the virtually perfected Roman Catholic, admirable in her way, and for whom a certain charitable toleration is elicited, if not necessitated, by the inescapability of her provincial plight. Such catchy phrases as "spiritual submission," "intellectual self-stultification," and "fundamental repulsiveness" sustain the argument and carry the tone. The basic Catholic problem is a lack of intellectual liberty, receptive and procreant alike: "The penalty paid by Mlle. de Guérin and those persons who are educated in the same principles, for their spiritual and mental security, is that they are incapable of entertaining or producing ideas." Granted, the limitation of ideas encourages "an incalcuable host of feelings. . . . No wonder Mlle. de Guérin writes well!" Nor is she to be called a bigot: "She knows only the Catholic Church. A bigot refuses; she did nothing all her life but accept." Neither is Henry James a bigot, for that matter, but he is coming out of it slowly; he was himself educated in certain principles conducive to a certain spiritual and mental security, and likewise exacting a certain penalty.

James' increasingly sophisticated and increasingly knowledgeable anti-Catholicism (perhaps too strong a term) continues into the year 1868, rendering it difficult (but maybe not impossible) to read "De Grey: A Romance," his first fiction blatantly about Roman Catholics, as anything else, however qualified – if only he were less mysterious and paradoxical! In another review for the *Nation,* of *The Inner Life of the Very Reverend Père Lacordaire, of the Order of Preachers,* by the Rev. Père Chocarne, O.P. (most of the Catholic items noticed by James in these years happen to be French), James once again proclaims his own religious allegiance but now with some illuminating irony and considerable inexactitude as to fractional proportions: "Belonging as we do to the profane and Protestant half of society" is now his formulation. There is a welcome shift of modesty away from the locution "all of us," meaning the entire American readership worth bothering about, to the regal or papal "we," meaning the reviewer. The review surprisingly begins with the citation of Lacordaire's belief, or hope, which James neither endorses nor protests, "that the Catholic Church was destined in the course of time to reassert its sway over the stronghold of Protestantism" (England), as naturally all Catholics hope and believe and even some Protestants. Lacordaire gets high marks for a putative Americanism: His "motive feeling" was "a desire for the perfect independence of the Church under the state, and he found his conception satisfied by the situation of the Church in this country." Careful readers will notice James' conventional opposition of church and state, and which one is under which, and which one is capitalized, as well as the opposition of religion and the world as James gets around to giving Lacordaire low marks for intellect and expression: "[H]is compositions exhibit that poverty of thought which smites with its hideous barrenness all those works which come to the world through seminaries and cloisters." James' sporadic rejections of worldliness will be found later, as will his bemused, horrified fascination with convents. As in the narratives of Catholic conversion, we find a deep distaste for, and perhaps a considerable fear of, the very idea of conversion, all the more if any proselytizing be involved. What Lacordaire asks, James says, and what James sturdily withholds, is, precisely, that we "be moved, enlightened, converted. Ah! we exclaim, what a far different thing is the light of our profane desire." As for the monastic or conventual life ("seminaries and cloisters"), that secondary topic of the conversion narratives and other James performances (such as "The Great Good Place"), "They order these things much better in the Catholic Church than we do in the world," a mixed compliment that leaves no doubt where James is and where he is not. James' main objection to Roman Catholicity is the same as in previous reviews – a century later it seems an obvious response to what church historians sometimes refer to as the Catholic state-of-siege mentality – what might be alternatively phrased as a lack of relevance or a lack of fashion: "[T]here is hardly a faint echo of the sounds and movements of our age. He ignored it. He averted his head and cried that it was not worth looking at." That was just what Thoreau recommended in *Walden,* and it is ironically more or less what Henry James will be accused of doing in his "retreats" from "reality" into what one or another of his critics takes to be his "aestheticism."

A few years later, in an August 1875 review for the *Galaxy,* James vigorously and revealingly dealt with Henri Alexandre Wallon's *Jeanne d'Arc;* seldom did he show himself more sophisticated, more equally inclined both to belief and to disbelief, more coy. What we may read between the lines is James' secularizing the sacred while at the same time managing to sound like an au courant Roman Catholic himself. Wallon is taken to task because "he considers his heroine too much from the standpoint of orthodox Catholicism, and attaches undue importance to the fact that she has never been canonized" – and now watch James slide over into the camp of the knowing and the decently faithful – "though, at last, there is very good hope that she will be." (She was, in 1920.) "Few episodes in human annals," James continues, taking a broad sweep of secular and sacred history alike, "compare with this in interest; we are tempted to say that there is only one that exceeds it." Catholicistically advancing in his profane Protestant concessions, James brilliantly equivocates: "Narrating the capture of the Maid beneath the walls of Compiègne, M. Wallon risks the expression that now her Passion had begun." There follows further equivocation: "Even if the reader does not believe, with M. Wallon, that Jeanne was divinely inspired, he will not resent this association," James' curious reason being that "Certainly only in that other case [what a tone!] is there such an example of a person being lifted up from the lowest fortune to the highest," this bizarre language apparently referring to the Crucifixion and Resurrection, in which there is no strong evidence that James "believed" (and there is considerable suspicion that he did not). Either way, he seems for the moment sublimely insensitive to the physical–material components of a crucifixion, that is, he fails to control his metaphor ("lifted up" – "lowest" – "highest"), and it recoils upon him as the exasperated reader begins to supply the actual details of the execution.

Still, James continues to write, and it is still as a comparative insider (it may be only a reviewer's tone) that he half concurs in his author's "belief that his heroine was divinely commissioned, in the sense that the saints were," James now knowing all about saints, and then he immediately switches to an opposing argument, sounding like Mark Twain in his village-atheist mood, namely that if Providence "appointed her to her task" why then did Providence allow her to languish in chains and be "roasted alive"? And yet, without the aid of this belief, "Jeanne's career is insolubly strange." He will solve it, therefore. What of her visions and her voices? "We think it is by no means impossible to account for these subjectively," that is to say in purely psychological and secularistic terms (and now he sounds like a parody of William James): "They were the natural outgrowth of a mind wholly unaccustomed to deal with abstractions," that is to say unlike minds of the saints in New England and other enlightened Protestant or post-Protestant thinkers, but "beguiled into expressing its emotions to itself, as it were, in images." Once again James lines up Catholicity with the emotions and the aesthetics. *Was* she inspired? No *and* yes – "inspired, if you will, but inspired by familiar human forces. Her brief career is a monument to the possible triumphs of a powerful will," as Ligeia in the tale by Poe. Jeanne d'Arc also sounds like an attribute of extrascientific Darwinism. Religious phenomena are to be understood in the light of the survival of the fittest, these defining themselves by their extraordinary assertion of intelligible volition, that energy which was only another name for nature in the circular circulating argument of power, "familiar human forces."

In a letter of 8 September 1894 to A. C. Benson, James curiously alleged that he was neither English (technically true) nor Protestant (what did he mean?) – that was about the time of *Guy Domville* and just before "The Altar of the Dead."[3] But in 1900, "The Great Good Place" makes quite clear that he was Protestant "again," if he had ever been otherwise. I think it may be assumed that his Protestantism was more or less perdurable lifelong but that it suffered an occasional wobble, and that, as we shall soon see, it was overlaid with several different and even contradictory religious emphases, chiefly Roman Catholic. Meanwhile in the years 1883–4 there is a cluster of critical documents in which James once again proclaims himself as Protestant. His 1883 essay on his friend Daudet speaks of (and for) "us readers of Protestant race"; the essay has an additional interest in its reference to Daudet's anti-Protestant (anti-Calvinist would be a more accurate term) novel *L'Evangéliste,* often held to have influenced *The Bostonians,* and maybe so, even if *The Bostonians* can hardly be taken as a counter-celebration of New England's religious sanctity. To "us readers of Protestant race," James suggests "almost a kind of drollery in these fearsome pictures of the Protestant temperament. The fact is that M. Daudet has not (to my belief) any natural understanding of the religious passion," such as, we are to understand, is in possession of the reviewer, who furnishes expert inside characterization of "the large, free, salubrious life which the children of that [Protestant] faith have carried with them over the globe," including, presumably, what had been and in large part still was, the Catholic world.

James is not necessarily backing off from that claim in his 1884 essay on his friend Turgenev, even though there seems to be a marked shift of tone brought on by the very thought of Turgenev as freethinking Orthodox: "Our Anglo-Saxon, Protestant, moralistic, conventional standards were far away from him" is how James puts it. And in "The Art of Fiction" (also 1884), despite the compliments to the lady who wrote so nicely about "the French Protestant youth," we find Protestantism in general now turned against itself, stood on its head, made, in a sort, the villain of the piece, no longer the bastion of liberty but the prison-house of the aesthetic worker: " *'Art,' in our Protestant communities, where so many things have got so strangely twisted about,* is supposed in certain circles to have some vaguely injurious effect upon those who make it an important consideration" (emphasis added). It might also be said that it is James who has got twisted about. To put Protestantism against art, as James would again appear to do and at great length in *The Tragic Muse,* is not of course necessarily to take a pro-Catholic position, but it is decidedly to take a pro–Matthew Arnold position contra the British Philistia, who perhaps by historical accident just happened to be overwhelmingly Protestant and often, until very recent times, quite vigorously anti-Catholic. As James notes in his 1884 essay on Arnold, "He is impregnated with the associations of Protestantism, saturated with the Bible, and though he has little love for the Puritans, no Puritan of them all was ever more ready on all occasions with a text either from the Old Testament or from the New." No critic was ever more ready on all occasions with an idea or two from Matthew Arnold.

The most pertinent Arnoldian idea concerns the relations of literature and religion. In the 1884 essay James approvingly notes "the taste, the temperance, with which he [Arnold] handles religious questions," coupled with "the impression he gives of really caring for them. To his mind [and James' mind? we recall that 1873 letter to Charles Eliot Norton] the religious life of humanity is the most important thing in the spectacle humanity offers us, and he holds that a due perception of this fact is (in connection with other lights) the measure of the acuteness of a critic, the wisdom of a poet." Let that perception be ours as well as we continue to probe the variegated and fluctuating recesses of the Jamesian wisdom, bearing in mind the Jamesian caveat: "To say that this feeling, taken in combination with his love of letters, of beauty, of all liberal things, constitutes an originality is not going too far, for the religious sentiment does not always render the service of opening the mind to human life at large."

2. Liberalism

> I am not going to criticize here that vast body of men, in the mass, who at this time would profess to be liberals in religion. . . . The Liberalism which gives a colour to society now, is very different from that character of thought which bore the name thirty or forty years ago. Now it is scarcely a party; it is the educated lay world.
>
> John Henry Cardinal Newman, *Apologia Pro Vita Sua,* 1864

And the name *liberal* (or *Liberal*) went on changing, and goes on changing still, as American political campaigns attest, through a considerable range of different, even contradictory, meanings, at times secular, at times religious, at times both.[4] How confusing the word can be is easily seen in James' 1877 review of Charles de Mazade's *Life of Count Cavour:* "For M. de Mazade," James writes, "Cavour is the model of the moderate and conservative liberal." Evidently aware how confusingly misleading such language can be, James rushes in with further qualification: "[H]is liberalism was untinged by the radical leaven. . . . [I]f he was a liberator, he had nothing in common with some of the gentry who aspire to this title." Specifically, "Great innovator as he had been, he was remarkable for the moderation of his attitude toward the Church; and the last words he uttered to the good friar who attended his deathbed were a repetition of his famous formula – 'Libera chiesa in libero stato.' "[5]

Liberalism was a centralizing pejorative term in the encyclicals addressed by the Holy Fathers to the Catholic faithful and to the world at large (Pius IX, 1846–78, and Leo XIII, 1878–1903, are the pertinent Popes for Henry James). But *liberalism* with quite a different set of meanings was an honorific to James and one of his favorite words. That opposition, on top of his inherited Protestant allegiance, might seem logically to have driven him toward an even more anti-Catholic position than the one he began with; what actually happened was the reverse of that. James simply applied his own concept of *liberalism* – a charitable vague tolerance – to the Catholic church and faith and people.

The process of liberalization was in fact almost predictable. Particularly in his fictions, James' mind functioned most richly as well as most comfortably in the acceptance and manipulation of conflicted pairs, as America–Europe, male–female, Protestant–Catholic. Having supplied himself with a conflicted pair, James regularly and happily proceeded to represent one half of the opposition to the other half, as if he were the accredited diplomat of a speechless constituency. Quite often he delighted in switching sides. It is so obvious and so well known how he represented Europe to the Americans and the Americans to Europe, and equally how he represented the woman's point of view to a male audience and alternatively the male point of view to a presumptively and disproportionately larger female audience, that it should come as no surprise that he should increasingly have found himself representing Protestants and Catholics to each other and, of course, and inevitably, to themselves. As a born and bred Protestant feeling his oats, James would naturally relish most the representation of the other party. Perhaps he also felt that, like women dominated by men, Catholics surrounded by Protestant Anglo-Saxondom stood in special need of a partisan.

These considerations, plus a highly developed and increasingly powerful sense of historical relativism and fair play, largely account for James' highest praise of another critic, in avowedly Arnoldian terms, namely Edmond Schérer, whose *Nouvelles Etudes sur la Littérature Contemporaine* he reviewed (again for the *Nation*) in 1865: "M. Schérer is a solid embodiment of Mr. Matthew Arnold's ideal critic. Those who affirmed Mr.

Arnold's ideal to be impracticable may here be refuted; those who thought it undesirable may perhaps be *converted"* (emphasis added). James' evaluation is sweeping and precise:

> There are [in Schérer] plenty of theories, but no theory. We find – and this is the highest praise, it seems to us, that we can give a critic – none but a moral unity: that is, the author is a liberal. It is hard to say, in reading M. Schérer's books, which is the most pleasing phenomenon, this intellectual eclecticism or this moral consistency. The age surely presents no finer spectacle than that of a mind liberal after this fashion; not from a brutal impatience of order, but from experience, from reflection, seriously, intelligently, having known, relished, and appropriated the many virtues of conservatism; a mind inquisitive of truth and of knowledge, accessible on all sides, unprejudiced, desirous above all things to examine directly, fearless of reputed errors, but merciless to error when proved, tolerant of dissent, respectful of sincerity, content neither to reason on matters of feeling nor to sentimentalize on matters of reason, equitable, dispassionate, sympathetic.

It is quite the reticulated and eloquent credo; and as the review goes on we find that the praise is religious as well as literary (and indeed it carries us back once more to those first-quoted statements by James in his letter to Charles Eliot Norton about the essentiality of the religious idea):

> Of M. Schérer's religious character we have not explicitly spoken, because we cannot speak of it properly in these limits. We can only say that in religion, as in everything else, he is a liberal; and we can pay no higher tribute to his critical worth than by adding that he has found means to unite the keenest theological penetration and the widest theological erudition with the greatest spiritual tolerance.

Schérer, the editor of *Le Temps* (predecessor to *Le Monde*), was in fact a lapsed Protestant, his chief point the essential relativity of truth.

By now we are perhaps sufficiently oriented in James' customary literary-religious practices – basically or at least initially Protestant yet open to plentiful divagation, but only of certain kinds and only in certain directions – to derive intellectual pleasure and profit from the spectacle of his side-switching, which often is hard to distinguish from his fence-sitting. In an 1868 review of *Life and Letters of Madame Swetchine* (whom he will refer to in "The Two Ampères," 1875, as "the famous ultramontane pietist"), James continues to object to Catholic presumption: "To enlarge people's sympathies was no part of her desire nor of her mission. If one were a good Catholic, one had always sympathies enough. What Madame Swetchine would have welcomed would have been an exchange of the reader's actual [present] sympathies for those which she herself indulged"; in plain English, she would gladly have put up with at least the results of proselytization and conversion. In other respects, James is generous; some readers may think him too generous, may see in his generosity an unseemly bending in the direction of Rome (this would almost certainly be a misinterpretation, and still it is notable how accurately James appears to grasp the Roman Catholic point of view, if only politely to reject it):

> Mme. Swetchine came out from her retirement with a conviction of the validity of the claims of the Romish Church, of the force of the historical evidence of its divine establishment, and of its adherence to the sacred principles of its foundation, which she never afterwards allowed to be shaken. Not only in the present, but in the past and in the future, the Catholic Church was for Mme. Swetchine the sole reality – the omnipotent fact – in history. We may differ from her conclusions, but we are obliged to admit that they are indeed conclusions, and that they were purchased at the expense of her dearest treasure, – the essential energies of her mind and heart. Mme. Swetchine had staked her happiness upon the truth which she finally embraced. It is not uncommon for people to die for their faith: Mme. Swetchine lived emphatically for hers.

We shall soon come to the spectacle of James' secularizing sacred entities in a variety of literary genres, and vice versa, sacralizing secular entities. In his review of Mme. Swetchine we may observe an early rationale for these processes, which are mainly, with James, a matter of metaphor. In advance, as it were, of his fictional *œuvre,* most of it, he appears to delineate a goundwork for his own sacred-secular doings and at the same time to provide considerable light on how he might be read: "Her originality, and her great merit, to our mind, is, that thoroughly attached as she was to the world to come, she maintained on its behalf the dignity of our actual [present] life. . . . Her soul was the soul of an ardent devotee, – her reason was equally strong and subtile, – *her mind was that of a woman of the world. . . . She had practically reconciled the two spheres of our thought, – the natural and the supernatural, – and she made them play into each other's hands. She was a most efficient link between the Church and the world"* (emphasis added).

In the previous year (1867) he had taken to task, as ever with a fierce show of justice to all, James Anthony Froude in *Short Studies on Great Subjects.* As a vague sort of loyal Protestant, James objects to Froude's apology for Martin Luther's marriage ("an act for which no apology is needed"): " 'The marriage,' he says, 'was unquestionably no affair of passion.' If it was not, so much the worse for Luther." Seven years later, in "Adina," James would express the same case for erotic passion but from the Catholic side of the post-Reformational wall. Now his main objection to Froude has to do with historical falsification based on religious prejudice: "Bad as the monasteries may have been, moreover, it is certain that the manner in which Henry VIII. went to work to sift them out was in the last degree brutal and unmerciful. He [Froude] finds the greatest ingenuity at his service to palliate acts for which, in the annals of Catholic governments, he finds only the eloquence of condemnation." Religious bigotry held no appeal for James, early or late. He was, as is often said, a pacifist. Mostly he was, as he said himself, a liberal. Always he was a devotee of honesty and honor. In an 1868 review of two books about the Huguenots, he wrote that "The suppression of the Huguenots was inhuman, but it affords no excuse for historians being inhuman to the king."

Reviewing Disraeli's popular and peculiar novel *Lothair* for the *Atlantic Monthly* in 1870, James again tilted at anti-Catholic prejudice, and we must remind ourselves that to be anti-anti-something is not necessarily to be pro-that-something, as, for example, Dickens' vehement attacks on anti-Catholic feeling and behavior in *Barnaby Rudge* (1841) do not make him pro-Catholic, as he took pains to point out in his preface to that novel; what they make him is disgusted with certain Protestant goings-on. "The motive of the romance" (Disraeli's), James says, "is simply the attempt of the Cardinal and his accessories to convert the young noble-man" to "the cunning Romish Church." If *Lothair* "can be said to have a ruling idea," James goes on to say, completely ignoring all the political history informing the novel, "that idea is of course to reveal the secret encroachments of the Romish Church. With what accuracy and fidelity these are revealed we are not prepared to say." What James is quite pre-pared to say is that Disraeli's anti-Catholicism is a fictive fizzle, not so much because it is anti-Catholic as because it wants literary force: "Mr. Disraeli's attempt seems to us wholly to lack conviction, let alone pas-sion and fire. His anti-Romish enthusiasm is thoroughly cold and me-chanical. . . . [I]t is not on such terms as these that religion stands or falls. . . . It will make no Cardinal's ears tingle." What seems to have made James' ears tingle is Disraeli's "almost infantine joy in being one of the initiated among the dukes." And perhaps in a quite different way he tingled at the idea of a prospective Catholic priest tempted by his reli-gion's opponent (or is it her coadjutor?): "The Church of Rome . . . having marked him [Lothair] for her own, we are invited to see what part the world shall play in contesting or confirming her influence." It is the germ of *Guy Domville* a quarter of a century ahead of time.

In *A Small Boy and Others* (1913), James adopts a wistful and comic tone of regret on the subject of his religious upbringing – liberal to a fault, as he seems to have felt it – and yet the conditions of that early time were apparently to remain more or less his own down to the time of his death: "[O]ur young liberty in respect to church-going was abso-

lute and we might range at will, through the great city [New York],
from one place of worship and one form of faith to another, or might on
occasion ignore them all equally, which was what we mainly did." He
recalls being embarrassed as a boy at having no answer to his friends'
question: "What church do you go to?" It was not that the James family
lacked religious instruction – "we had plenty, and of the most charming
and familiar" – but that they lacked religious identification: "It was colder
than any criticism, I recall, to hear our father reply that we could plead
nothing less than the whole privilege of Christendom, and that there was
no communion, even that of the Catholics, even that of the Jews, even
that of the Swedenborgians, from which we need find ourselves excluded."[6] Ludicrous as all this may be – it is virtually a satire of the
secularistic American approach to religious pluralism, the conception of
religious communions as so many competing brand-names – it was not
the worst possible religious background for James as a writer. But as
James' family milieu was preponderantly Protestant, the extra-Protestant
ideal of unlimited burgeoning could only mean a moving out and away
from Protestant bounds in the direction of something else. As James'
works clearly demonstrate, he so moved.

To the end of his days he was deliciously vague about certain religious
details (e.g., he will say *absolution* when he means *dispensation*). On 17
September 1913, he wrote his old friend Thomas Sergeant Perry to ask
about a mutual teenage friend, John La Farge: "Was John La Farge's
Maryland (Catholic) college the *William and Mary??*" Any American
schoolgirl could have told him that a college counting among its gradu-
ates Presidents Jefferson and Monroe was hardly a Papist seminary. Another bright young thing might gladly have added that William and Mary
is not in Maryland but in Virginia. Few, if any, American schoolchildren
could ever be so amusing as Henry James in a July 1899 letter to his friend
Mrs. Humphrey Ward, who wanted help in clarifying, for her novel
Eleanor, the American religious background. "Why, this isn't *us*" – James
quotes an imaginary American reader as saying – "it's English 'Dissent.'
For it's well – generally – to keep in mind how very different a thing
that is (socially, aesthetically &c.) from the American free (and easy)
multitudinous churches, that, practically, in any community, are like so
many (almost) clubs or Philharmonics or amateur theatrical companies."
As for liberal American attitudes toward Catholicity, he goes on comically to clue her in: "I *don't* quite think the however obscure American
girl I gather you to conceive would have any shockability about Rome,
the Pope, St. Peter's, kneeling, or anything of that sort. . . . She would
probably be either a Unitarian or 'Orthodox' (which is, I believe, 'Congregational,' though in New England always called 'Orthodox') and in
either case as Emersonized, Hawthornized, J. A. Symondsized, and as

'frantic' to *feel* the Papacy &c, as one could well represent her. . . . This particularly were her father a college professor."[7] The senior Henry James would have relished these comical characterizations, just accurate enough to escape the charge of downright falsehood; what redeems them, what almost always redeems the remarks of Henry James, Junior, is style. Style would lead him further in the Catholic direction, which is not to say (let me repeat) that he was personally turning Catholic, only that in a number of ways the representation of Catholics was increasingly serving his turn. He was never, so far as we know, a card-carrying Catholic, but he became on occasion a fellow-traveling Catholic of a certain literary type. Ultimately we might say he was about one-quarter Protestant, where he began; one-quarter secular, post-Protestant leakage into "the world"; one-quarter Catholic, an acquired social–aesthetic patina for the expression of certain points, values, shapes, shades, colors, emphases; and one-quarter mixed ignorance, innocence, and indifference. One of his best combinations lay in a blend of Catholic and secular elements – this blend was at once fashionable, romantic, exotic, cosmopolitan, *moderne,* and safe. Books about Judaism frequently contrast the Jewish atheist with the impossibility of there being a Christian counterpart, a Christian atheist being a contradiction in terms.[8] The distinction is perhaps too neat, for surely there is such a thing as a Catholic atheist, a person who, with a minimum of Catholic belief, manages to give off a distinctly Catholic *tone.* It is the tone of one who "belongs" to a communion or regime as ancient as Christendom and as far reaching; which is hard on provincials, upstarts, and related vulgarians; which declines to palter with ugliness or boredom; which is, in those senses and in none other, aristocratic. Needless to say, this tone is designed for Anglo-American use; it would get you nowhere in France. Quite often Henry James managed to give off that tone.

3. The Picturesque

When there are three or four brown-breasted contadini sleeping in the sun before the convent doors, and a departing monk leading his shadow down over them, I think you will not find anything in Rome more *sketchable.*

"A Roman Holiday," 1873

New England life is not the most picturesque in the world, but there is something [especially] regrettable in this pale, unlighted representation of a dry and bloodless population, and a style of manners farther removed from the spectacular than a cranberry-bog from a vineyard.

Review of Helen Hunt Jackson's *Mercy Philbrick's Choice,* 1876

No literary–aesthetic term in all the manifold writings of Henry James is more frequently met than the term *picturesque,* and none is so immediately unedifying. In its most limited, literal, and specific sense, the picturesque was anything you might want to represent and preserve in your ever-ready sketchbook, predecessor of today's photographic equipment. By an obvious extension it referred to anything that might be felt to possess unusual possibilities for such representation and preservation, anything with a high degree of more or less enduring visual interest (complexity, variety, subtlety, typicality, rarity, novelty, importance, and so forth). By a further extension, widespread since the success in 1819–20 of *The Sketch-Book* by Washington Irving, the picturesque quite easily referred to anything, aside from the visual, that possessed parallel kinds of intellectual or literary merit. Whatever was "interesting" (another favorite James word) to the mind for meditation just as much as to the eye for perception was, accordingly, "picturesque."

Roman Catholics, their latter-day coreligionists may be gratified to learn, were on many an occasion, for Henry James, *picturesque,* while Protestants, almost by definition, were not. In "The Solution" (1890), a fairly late tale of a much earlier Rome – "the slumberous, pictorial Rome of the Popes, before the Italians had arrived or the local colour departed" ("splendid Catholic processions and ceremonies") – Mrs. Goldie is said to have an "old cardinalesque chariot." Far more inclusively, we are informed that "At the British [diplomatic] establishment . . . no form of dissent less fashionable than the Catholic was recognized." Catholic readers then and now may be mildly annoyed at being defined as a variety of "dissent," James once again ahistorically assuming some sort of Protestant hegemony – here, the Church of England – but surely they might be pleased at being found so comparatively fashionable; in fact, most American and English Catholics at that time were quite poor, uneducated (except, perhaps, in religious matters), unsophisticated, precisely *not* fashionable. Catholics are fashionable in James, however, because to him they are picturesque, and they are picturesque because they combine difference (from "us," that is) and style. Only certain kinds of difference are fashionable-picturesque. Mrs. Wix, in *What Maisie Knew* (1897), at least before her curious transformations, is not picturesque, despite the eccentricity of her get-up. Mr. Mudge, of "In the Cage" (1898), is decidedly not picturesque – he frequents a Wesleyan chapel. English Dissenters are never picturesque in James. Neither are American Protestants, although they are more readily tolerated. These kinds of people have altogether the wrong tone, that is to say they have no style at all, or if they do we wish they didn't.

The reader of James' Italian sketches, or of *William Wetmore Story and His Friends* (1903), will recall the genial and exuberant preference, by visitor James, for Papal Rome over national or post-Risorgimento Rome. Rome earlier, prior to the imposition of secular government, was more picturesque, not merely for the existence of ancient ruins but for the highly visible presence of the Roman Catholic church, meaning mainly its hierarchy. All this is abundantly evident in a 30 October 1869 letter from Rome to William James: "At last – for the first time – I live! . . . For the first time I know what the picturesque is." Among the details we find St. Peter's "filled with foreign ecclesiastics – great armies encamped in prayer on the marble plains of its pavement – an inexhaustible physiognomical study. To crown my day, on my way home, I met his Holiness in person – driving in prodigious purple state – sitting dim within the shadows of his coach with two uplifted benedictory fingers – like some dusky Hindoo idol in the depths of its shrine." Then on 7 November to Alice James, "that flaccid old woman waving his ridiculous fingers over the prostrate multitude" – and so on. Remarks like that were evidently for family consumption.

James' *public* dealings with Catholicity involve a powerful sense of social, external, visual, aesthetic, stylistic, formalistic, processional, ceremonious attributes, a passionate devotion to ritualistic observances for their own sake – a devotion to visual display, rather sentimental and worldly – a penchant for vestment, sacramental, image, gesture, and the like, almost completely bereft of any conceivable sense of their meaning to and within the Catholic communion. James' views of Catholicity were prevailingly outsider's views, sympathetic in part, antipathetic in part, almost always detached, better informed than we might expect yet curiously ignorant in the most important directions and in any and all instances highly aestheticized. In "The Diary of a Man of Fifty" (1879) a fictive personage writes, "Things that involve a risk are like the Christian faith; they must be seen from the inside" – but James conspicuously failed to take his own advice. Naturally he tended to represent Catholics in most of his fiction and even in *Guy Domville,* his Catholic play, from the outside, as different, unusual, odd, peculiar, alienated, eccentric, bizarre, glamorous, exotic, traditional, ancient, European, continental, Latinate, interesting, quaint, *picturesque,* even if, in fact, the typical English or American Catholic of his readership happened to be none of these. At the very least, Catholics were *not us.* Henry James would gladly, therefore, write about them, ensuring himself an easy romanticism; and the populace, from whatever point of view, would gladly read about them. Or so he quite obviously hoped and assumed. At the same time we must never forget that religion and aesthetics seem to have lain closer together in the soul of Henry James than in the souls of most people.

The strange coupling of James' aesthetic fascination with Catholic practices and mannerisms and his moral reservations about what he seems to have felt were Catholics' devious ways past, present, and future is best seen in his 1875 essay on Balzac, virtually a prescription for the curious behavior of Maggie Verver, an intensely strong-willed cradle Catholic, in *The Golden Bowl,* three decades later. James cites Balzac's "two eternal truths – the monarchy and the Catholic Church" and proceeds to embroider them with his own fervently aestheticized and psychologized transatlantic Protestant–Catholic–secular threads:

> A monarchical society is unquestionably more picturesque, more available for the novelist than any other, as the others have yet exhibited themselves; and therefore Balzac [but not James] was with glee, with gusto, with imagination, a monarchist.

As for the church:

> Of what is to be properly called religious feeling [no definition vouchsafed – Protestant moralizing?] we do not remember a suggestion in all his many pages; on the other hand, the reader constantly encounters the handsomest compliments to the Catholic Church as a social *régime.*

The distinction is perhaps more James' than Balzac's; the charge of no religious feeling is completely inaccurate; but James goes on:

> A hierarchy is as much more picturesque than a "congregational society" as a mountain is than a plain. Bishops, abbés, priests, Jesuits, are invaluable figures in fiction, and the morality of the Catholic Church allows of an infinite *chiaroscuro.*

There are not, in fact, among James' represented Catholics more than a small handful of priests or other ecclesiastical personages, and in *Guy Domville* they are cunningly kept off stage; his represented Catholics are drawn almost entirely from the laity.

In all these quotations it will be noticed how dependent are James' opinions on the overriding conception of Catholicity as picturesque – what it *means* is far away from him. But for purposes of fictional representation, anything, one sometimes senses, that is *not* Protestant will do (and yet, if it is not Protestant, it *won't* do). So James continues, now speaking quite unreligiously of

> that great worldly force of the Catholic Church, the art of using all sorts of servants and all sorts of means. Balzac [and James?] was willing to accept any morality that was curious and unexpected, and he found himself as a matter of course more in sympathy with a theory of conduct [Jesuitical?] which takes account of circumstances and recognizes the merits of duplicity [!], than with the comparatively colourless idea [Protestant, one presumes] that virtue is nothing if not uncompromising.[9]

And there, finally, is Balzac's praise of "duplicity," with James' evident connivance, a topic to look at again when we come to *The Golden Bowl*.

James' representation of Catholics was undeniably mixed and unstable. If you desire a responsible reading you had better get up your skepticism and cultivate a zeal for contexts. And anticipate many a surprise. Readers of *The American Scene* (1907) may well be surprised by James' acid observation that the "field of American life is as bare of the Church [so capitalized] as a billiard-table of a centre-piece." What conceivable "Church" had he in mind? The one, holy, catholic, apostolic Roman Catholic Church (in the United States)? Hardly. And not, just as surely, the Church of England, known in this country since the American Revolution as the Protestant Episcopal. In any case, both these churches, and a couple of dozen more, were easily to be made out. In the same work, James, having at least once located a church (building) to look at and talk about, speaks knowingly, as he doubtless felt, but others may wonder, of "the Ascension . . . that noble work of John La Farge, the representation, on the west wall, in the grand manner, of the theological event from which the church takes its title."[10] Should we smile or groan at Our Lord's Ascension conceived as a "theological event," as if it were a performance, invented by churchmen, more or less along the lines of a popular number in a variety show?

In his 1867 review of Maurice de Guérin, brother to Eugénie, James refers to "the most paternal and comfortable of creeds," meaning the Catholic, a frequent designation often accompanied by the sentiment that Catholicity, like Art, takes care of her own, but had he himself ever read that creed, Nicene, Apostles', or other, did he recite it regularly, believe it, understand what it "meant"? It may be supposed that he did not. To cite once again "The Solution," in reference to St. Peter's in Rome James speaks of the Catholic Church generally as "the faith that has no small pruderies to enforce," so that as a consequence the cathedral may serve as "a splendid international *salon*" for Protestant and other un-Catholic tourists and expatriates (Catholics too); but earlier tales – for example, "Travelling Companions" (1870) – appear to deplore the same practice of using Catholic churches for primarily sightseeing purposes.

Reviewing Francis Parkman's *The Jesuits in North America* in 1867, and now in a decidedly pro-Catholic-picturesque mood – you might even call it an Indian-summer Catholic-picturesque mood – James positively wallows in the pleasure of his perception that "Their story is far more romantic and touching than that of their Protestant neighbors; it is written in those rich and mellow colors in which the Catholic Church inscribes her records," not to mention Henry James, but then he adds his characteristic reservation: "[I]t leaves the mind profoundly unsatisfied." Once he exploded in a letter (27 December 1869) to William James from of course Rome, "I'm sick unto death of priests and churches. Their 'picturesqueness' ends by making you want to go strongly into political economy or the New England school system." How uncharacteristic, we are tempted to say, but we would be wrong. At least one secret of Henry James is that he has no fixed character but instead a multiplicity of luminous characteristics, most often ambivalent. The same Henry James who for a moment was ready to worship, if only as a joke, at the altar of the New England school system, as a welcome relief from a surfeit of Italian Catholicity, could also note, scathingly, in "A New England Winter" (1884), the prejudice of Mrs. Daintry, whose maid was "so carefully selected, as a Protestant, from the British Provinces," lest that maid, all offensively, prove to be a French or even an Irish Catholic, insupportable either way. The phrase "as a Protestant" dangles.

4. The Question of Religious Audience

There are doubtless many people all ready to regard themselves as injured by a suggestion that they should for the hour, and even in the decent privacy of the imagination, comport themselves as creatures of alien (by which we usually understand inferior) race. To them it is only to be answered that they had better never touch a foreign book on any terms, but lead a contented life in the homogeneous medium of the dear old mother-speech.

"Guy de Maupassant," 1889

Generally speaking, the question of religious audience is analogous to the question of multilinguistic or international audience; like any other sort of cultural pluralism, religious toleration invites and rewards transcendence of bigoted boundaries (including the boundary of pretending to have none). Transcendence in turn often depends on factual knowledge. Recent scholarly works considerably extend and fortify our practical sense of James' literary situation vis-à-vis publishers and readers.[11] Unfortunately, these studies neglect to inquire into the religious composition of James' presumed readership, either in the conviction that little can ever be known of these matters or in the conviction, rife among academic Jamesians, that nothing is more secure or more welcome than continuing validation of the Master's unquestioned secularity.

Of course we know, if we wish to, that James' audience was preponderantly, but not exclusively, composed of American and British Protestant adults, variously lapsed or lapsing under the influence of Charles Darwin and other the like inducements, with an acquired taste for the substantive and stylistic entertainments his tales, novels, and other writings so abundantly furnished. And we can guess at the relative proportions of non-Protestant readers, Catholics, Jews, and others, in the United States, Great Britain, or elsewhere, who might have been readers of James. But even if we had better census reports we would be little the wiser. We will never be able to determine with any degree of security who read what or how they reacted. We proceed to conjecture in the comparative dark, mostly reasoning backward from the text to the probabilities of different kinds of readers responding in different kinds of ways – and we may assume that the maker of the text would be aware of that obvious fact in advance. What Victor Terras says of Dostoevsky is *ceteris paribus* true of James: "Depending upon the reader, *The Brothers Karamazov* will have more or less of a 'subtext' of some kind – a meaning that is not explicitly stated in the text. A great deal depends on the reader's external frame of reference. . . . Of the greatest importance is the reader's attitude toward religion. A reader whose external frame of reference includes a belief in the basic dogmas of Christianity . . . will read the novel quite differently from a reader who lacks these beliefs." More closely: "The effect of such stylization will depend on how well attuned a reader is to religion. A believer will be deeply moved, for Father Zosima's wisdom is Russian Orthodox religious eloquence at its quintessential best." [12] That James is not Dostoevsky is no reason for willfully ignoring his religious subtexts or his religious style.

On the other hand lie obvious dangers of reckless interpretation and attribution. We are not to suppose that Catholics read only Catholic books, Protestants likewise, and so on down the line, as (to take some really outrageous example) a foolhardy feminism might find itself tempted to allege that women read, and ought to read, women only. Such divisiveness might then be multiplied through any number of imagined categories such as the middle-aged reader, the Republican reader, the New Mexico reader. Moreover, if there is sometimes a pleasure in reading one of your own there is also a pleasure in reading one *not* of your own. It is a typical Jamesian pleasure, as enunciated in a 10 July 1915 letter to H. G. Wells: "It is when that history and curiosity [on the part of some other novelist] have been determined in the way most different from my own that I myself want to get at them – precisely *for* the extension of life, which is the novel's best gift." In somewhat the same spirit, recent studies of American Literature emphasize pluralism and difference, heterogeneity, mixture rather than melting-pot; race, gender, and class is the usual formulaic. Religious differentiation is surely not less important and not less interesting, and it is a curious assumption of recent criticism almost automatically to rule it out of account. For many people – including, at times, Henry James – it is the most important consideration of all.

It is true, as I am warned by a reader for a literary journal, identity unknown, that "comments on James' attitude toward a Catholic audience seem purely speculative. Some kind of primary source, such as James' letters, would be needed. . . . I don't know if this kind of evidence exists." It does, but not richly; it is clear but not plentiful. I think of James' epistolary wail to brother William over the British theatergoing public's caring no whit for his Catholic play, as if, somehow, they ought to have – we will come to that, by and by, in connection with the *Guy Domville* debacle. For the moment, I think of James' 1874 review of Francis Parkman's *The Old Régime in Canada*. Among its variously laudatory remarks about Parkman's history, we may be stimulated and reassured by James' attention, however brief, to the evident fact of differentiated religious readerships. James is himself frankly speculative, as having no absolute grip on the facts of the differentiation yet at the same time being convinced of its existence and equally convinced that it should be recognized and met in the interests of justice, fair play, and expediency, combined. "We have been especially struck with his fairness. He is an incorruptible Protestant," proof against even the faintest stirrings of Catholic conversion, I think we must take James to mean, a reliable and loyal stand-pat, "dealing with an intensely Catholic theme." In such a situation the historian will be neither anti- nor pro-Catholic; he will be simply a historian, and this is how James says that Parkman does it: "[H]e appears wholly free from any disposition to serve his [Catholic] personages' narrow measure, or bear more heavily on their foibles than his facts exactly warrant." It is then that James proceeds to speculate about the (American) Catholic reader, showing at the very least an awareness that such a creature did indisputably exist, and showing, what is more, a desire never unnecessarily to alienate that or any other kind of putative reader whatsoever. James writes, in his customary liberal and balanced mode, that Parkman "can hardly expect to have fully pleased Catholic readers, but he must have displeased them singularly little." James clearly knew the religious varieties within the American reading public; he was solicitous that they be treated with a decent respect; and he was cognizant of the fact that, religious divisions being what they have been and are, no writer dealing with religious topics could possibly please in equal degree all possible constituencies; still, he should try to be fair, factual, dispassionate, and charitable. James goes on to the end of his paragraph, "Never, it must be added, was there a case in which Catholicism could so easily afford to be judged on its own strict merits as in the early history of Canada," thus demonstrating his own affiliation to the values praised in Parkman. It should be added that while there are cases and cases in historical literature, in fictitious literature – tale, novel, play – you make your own cases. Surely you might make them so as to please as much, and displease as little, as possible – if, that is, you wanted to be read and admired and remembered fondly. Uncensored and freely circulating in the market-place, literary works almost automatically tend to a liberal tolerance and an inclusiveness of appeal.

The overarching fact of the matter is that Henry James is far more Catholic in print than there is any evidence for his ever having been in his personal life. There must be reasons for this phenomenon, and they must be some combination of the following: (1) Catholicity was to James aesthetically pleasing, interesting, novel, provocative, complex, deep, mysterious, romantic, *picturesque,* both as a thing in itself and as an element in literary representation; (2) a certain representation of Catholics, not only Italian and French but American and English as well, would make for a more rounded and more realistic representation of the actual world, for there, indeed, they were, and why should you deprive yourself of the literary pleasure of showing them forth? – this consideration may be called the Balzac consideration, that is to say, as literary worker you are to deal with what you find before you, not some of it but all; (3) circumspect attention to Catholics was a courtesy to a minority of the readership such as a civilized Christian (or other) gentleman might extend to that segment of a hoped-for audience – and now we seem to slide over into reasons (4) hoping that they would reward you and (5) knowing at the same time that such attention would simultaneously serve as the spice of life to readers other than Catholic, (6) not to mention what I already said about James' conflicted pairs and his penchant for diplomacy. Just as he would make himself a part of English Literature and of French Literature and by so doing make himself virtually tantamount to American Literature in the birth pangs, so he would make himself the generous and gentle representer of all Christendom and beyond, overpassing division by co-option.

The religious proportions of the American and the English populations were rapidly changing, not so much through individual conversions as through immigration – mainly from Ireland in the case of Great Britain and largely in the case of the United States as well, though less predominantly so – but the individual conversion was always more conspicuous, and in a literary work it could be made to stand for the demographic changes. In England there were perhaps 80,000 Catholics in 1767 (13 years before the alleged date of *Guy Domville*); a quarter of a million in 1851, the year after the restoration of the English hierarchy (James about 7 years old); and by 1912, in his old age, about 1,710,000.[13] Estimated figures for Catholics in the United States by 30-year periods suggest the following redistribution of religious affiliation:

1830	500,000
1860	3,103,000
1890	8,909,000

"So large was this increase that by 1850" – James was born in 1843 – "Roman Catholicism, which at the birth of the nation was nearly invisible in terms of numbers, had now become the nation's largest religious denomination."[14] (In 1850, the total American population was 23,191,876; in 1890, it was 62,947,714.) Commencing to publish in 1864, Henry James is among other things the seismograph of the change.

There remains the question of genre as it relates to the question of religious audience. That only one of James' dozen or more plays should be blatantly Catholic calls for no particular explanation. But why is there more Catholicity in the novels than in the tales, even if so much of it is diaphanous and debatable, apparently by design? It can't be altogether because of a sense on James' part that book lovers are more sophisticated, and therefore more tolerant, than magazine consumers – many of the novels were serialized in the magazines that published the tales. Perhaps James was a trifle uneasy about letting too much religious zeal loose in a small enclosed space. If Catholics were to be admitted to the fictive page, there to romp around in their picturesque yet potentially subversive way, they had better be given plenty of room within which to disport themselves and plenty of surrounding matter to contextualize the dynamic of their fascinatingly un-Protestant convictions and behaviors.

5. Sacred Seculars in the Tales

She was being, yes, patronized; and that was really as new to her – the freeborn American girl who might, if she had wished, have got engaged and disengaged not six times but sixty – as it would have been to be crowned or crucified.

"Julia Bride," 1908

Sacred seculars or secular sacreds – the phrase goes equally well either way. Throughout his career, and in every literary form, including the comparatively personal form of letters and the indisputably private form of notebooks, Henry James habitually and with consummate stylistic felicity referred to ordinary, diurnal, worldly, secular objects, events, emotions, behaviors, and so forth, in the language of religious belief and practice. His religious language is almost always Christian and more often than not specifically Roman Catholic. Catholic language was at once more exact, more extensive, more inclusive, and more romantically *picturesque* – in James' view, apparently, as not being the language of his presumptively majoritarian Protestant readership – than just any old religious language. In the terms of linguistics, James' signifiers and his signifieds, the signs and the concepts, are Christian tending to the Catholic, whereas the referents, what the signifiers-signifieds point to or stand for, tend to the secular. It is precisely the division we might have expected.

And indeed the whole process is so obvious that it mostly goes unnoticed, but clearly it will be responded to, directly or subliminally, with different degrees of approval, disapproval, pleasure, annoyance, whatever, by different kinds of readers. Some will be quick to conclude that the signifiers-signifieds "don't matter, only the referents count," so that James is once more reduced to the totally secular and certified as safe.[15] Such a reading, however fashionable, amounts to critical irresponsibility – you can't in decency admit and revel in that half of the metaphor which happens to chime with your own views and then obliterate the half which does not; and the relation between James' sacralized language and its secular applications is precisely a case of metaphor, metaphor indeed often structuring, and not merely embellishing, the Jamesian text throughout the Jamesian *œuvre*. It appears to be his way of simultaneously dealing with this world and the life of the world to come, as the Nicene Creed has it in English translation. You can endlessly argue if this habit of mind more denigrates the Kingdom of God or romanticizes the diurnal – the latter is the more literary and the more generous as well.

The very act of writing, because it normally takes place at a desk or table, but also because of the attitudes of reverential piety (to indulge my own secularization) that James seeks to invoke in its honor, is regularly made into a metaphor with talk of altars, while almost any person, object, emotion, or event, if it is seriously or importantly "good," is regularly made into a metaphor as *sacred* or *consecrated* – and this, especially, if it involves the past, something or someone old, dead, or at least "gone." There are of course real altars in James, though not many – for example, in "The Altar of the Dead" – readily discriminated from the figurative altars of literary consecration. (But I do not recall a single instance in all James of a "real" consecration.) Jamesian altars are naturally profuse in the more literary tales. In "Sir Dominick Ferrand" (1892), the hero's writing table is "his altar of literary sacrifice," all simply "a literary altar"; and when the child of his beloved scratches his new desk it is "as if an altar had been desecrated." In "The Middle Years" (1893), Dr. Hugh is the "servant of his [poor Dencombe's] altar." In "The Death of the Lion" (1894), the narrator's devotion to Neil Paraday is his "little customary altar," complete with flowers and candles (but conspicuously lacking the Body and Blood of Our Lord Jesus Christ). In the same tale, a lost manuscript is said to be "an object of adoration." As is easily seen, the relations of letter and figure are various: In "The Coxon Fund" (1894) we are treated to a "temple of talk and its altars of cushioned chintz." In "The Next Time" (1895), admiration for aesthetic superiority is the desired "altar of sacrifice." In "The Figure in the Carpet" (1896), George Corvick "had no wish to approach the altar [i.e., communicate directly with Hugh Vereker] before he had prepared the sacrifice [i.e., comprehended Vereker's works]." A piece of literary criticism is in "John Delavoy" (1898) designated "that altar," and the literary biographer of "The Real Right Thing" (1899) is "the young priest of his altar" ("the place had suddenly become as if consecrated"). In "The Velvet Glove" (1909), at a literary party, we read of "a consecrated corner of a writing-table."

Sacred and *consecrated*, applied to obviously non-sacred unconsecrated things, sometimes seem as infinite as the eternal mysteries to which in the Jamesian text the most mundane considerations are so regularly attached. In "The Story of a Year" (1865), the absent soldier's personal possessions become his "sacred relics." In "My Friend Bingham" (1867), the titular hero's being in love is "the sacred fact" ("God has brought us together in a very strange fashion," as has Henry James). In "The Romance of Certain Old Clothes" (1868), precious garments are "to be sacredly kept for this little innocent," a mere girl. "A Passionate Pilgrim" (1871) abounds in sacralized secularities precious to tourist romanticism: Americans take a pleasure in England "more fatal and sacred" than they take in Italy or Spain, England's very dust being, most particularly, "sacred dust"; the narrator is as open to such equivalences "as to the spirit of the Lord"; Oxford is "a kind of dim and sacred ideal" (no ecclesial reference is necessarily intended, any more than a eucharistic reference is intended by "the mediaeval and mystical presence of the Empire," and still it is eucharistic language), with its "sacred and sunless courts" and a "little monkish doorway"; Clement Searle is said to speak of Oxford banquets "with a sort of religious unction." In James texts the word *unction* regularly signals Catholicity.

Readers of "At Isella" (1871) ultimately discover that "the sacred pinnacles which take their tone from heaven" are no other than the Alps and are maybe thus prepared to learn of "Italy gained," another sacralized secular, presumably by way of John Milton's title. In "The Sweetheart of M. Briseux" (1873), two art lovers with a single mind are "pilgrims in the same faith," and in "Four Meetings" filthy lucre is elevated to the status of "sacred savings." So, too, women shopping are comically conceived as engaging in "sacred rites," this in "The Pension Beaurepas" (1879). And so in "The Siege of London" (1883), Sir Arthur Demesne's self-love is satirically labeled "too sacred" (Mrs. Headway has "a religious appreciation" of his "exemption from social flaws"). In "Georgina's Reasons" (1884), the incomparable Georgina fondly fancies "that their intimacy, however brief, must have a certain consecration," a profane desecration of *The Scarlet Letter*. The Jeffrey Aspern papers in "The Aspern Papers" (1888) are of course "sacred relics" and Juliana is a "terrible relic" – "as if the miracle of resurrection had taken place for my benefit. Her presence seemed somehow to contain his." Perhaps that is why the Bordereau women are American Catholics, a phenomenon not otherwise explained. In "The Liar" (1888), old Sir David is appropriately a "sacred . . . relic," and Capidose declines to lie about the military ("that august institution was sacred from his depredations").

"A London Life" (1888) is chock-a-block with allusion to the sacredness of home, family, and departed parents ("sacred images of the dead"), upon which dubious sanctities adulterous perjury may perch and wave her hedonistic wings. In "The Pupil" (1891), the possibility that Morgan Moreen may go off with Pemberton is an "unexpected consecration." Like "A London Life," "The Marriages" (1891) is full of misplaced religiosity, mainly Adela Chart's "passionate piety" (unscrupulous selfishness, in fact) toward her dead mother, whose "hovering spirit," like a ghost or a balloon, is said to be "sanctifying" because of her "sacred place in their past" ("a kind of religion," a frequent locution in James). "She loved the place," associated with her mother, "as, had she been a good Catholic, she would have loved the smell of her parish church." Rose Tramore's social redemption for her mother (in "The Chaperon," 1891), is, simply, a "consecration" ("so mixed were her superstitions and her heresies"). Eschatology appears in "Sir Edmund Orme" (1891) when the narrator sends up "a mute prayer" – prayers in the published works of Henry James are often alluded to, but the reader is hardly ever apprised of the prayerful language – and for reward hears a sound "like a wail of one of the lost," a tone to be used again in *The Turn of the Screw* but in a radically different context, and by the incarnational subsumption (or assumption) of Miss Churm in "The Real Thing" (1892), who disappears into her painted representation "only as the dead who go to heaven are lost – in the gain of an angel the more," nineteenth-century evangelical-sentimental talk, just as loose in James as in feminized domestic fictions. In "Greville Fane" (1892), the narrator sarcastically purports to view Leolin as Mrs. Stormer's "consecrated child" (consecrated to bad fiction). In "The Wheel of Time" (1892) we have, as often, the "sacred past." In "The Death of the Lion" (1894), a promise is "sacred," especially because the promise is literary, the same with the girl of "In the Cage" (1898), whose half-hour of free time, for the reading of novels, is a "sacred pause." But in "The Special Type" (1900), the statement "my purpose is a sacred one" turns out to mean the desire for a divorce. In "The Beast in the Jungle" (1903), May Bartram's scarf is "consecrated by the years," as is all else. The old house in "The Jolly Corner" (1908) is predictably "consecrated" by time, located as it is on "so consecrated a spot" (not yet torn down). Antediluvian New York is further consecrated in "Crapy Cornelia" (1909) – the past is "old shades once sacred" to "the very altar of memory," and so forth.

Many of these sacred-secular conflations, as already cited, are at least generally Roman Catholic; others are even more explicitly so. Poor

Richard, in the tale bearing his name (1867), goes to bed "fasting as grimly as a Trappist monk." In "A Passionate Pilgrim" (1871), Searle asks his transatlantic cousin if, beneath an ancient object, he lights "a votive taper." The hero of "Eugene Pickering" (1874) strikes the narrator "like certain young monks I had seen in Italy; he had the same candid, unsophisticated cloister-face. His education had been really almost monastic." In "An International Episode" (1878), Mrs. Westgate, clearly no Catholic, comically alleges herself "always a heretic" in hats (she gets them in Paris, not London). Lady Vandeleur, of "The Path of Duty" (1884), comes clad in "nun-like robes," that is, she wears mourning. Selina, of "A London Life" (1888), looks like "a picture of Saint Cecilia," but her appearance deceives. Angela Chart in "The Marriages" (1891), "as a cloistered girl," not literally, "was poorly equipped for speculation," recalling James' remarks in early reviews about cloisters and intellectual mediocrity. Holding "her beautiful child in her arms," Mrs. Ryves of "Sir Dominick Ferrand" (1882), one of the few bastards in all James who is not a Catholic, "looked dimly like a modern Madonna." Florimond's mother, in "A New England Winter" (1884), although intensely Protestant, is said to be "perpetually swinging the censer" at her son. In "Owen Wingrave" (1892), the military coach is blessed with "the infallibility [not Petrine] of his experience." In "The Next Time" (1895), "the brotherhood of the faith," literary rather than Christian, "have become, like the Trappists, a silent order"; other people in the same tale prate "like chanting monks in a cloister" – or Carmelite nuns in *The American*. In "Paste" (1899) a "reliquary" turns out to be only a jewel case. In "The Third Person" (1900), no theological allusion intended, the old hanged pirate's ghost is felt to want Absolution, confusingly equated with Viaticum ("peace, rest, his final reprieve"). In "The Papers" (1903), the two young journalists undergo a "novitiate," that is, an apprenticeship. In "The Velvet Glove" (1909), the Princess is ecumenically presented as "some miraculously humanised idol, all sacred . . . all votively hung about . . . in the recess of its shrine," like Pio Nono. And in "Mora Montravers" (1909), the foolish, lascivious Travers is figured as "morally fingering, as it were, the mystic medal under his shirt."

There is thus, quite obviously by intent, a notably religious, Christian, and even Catholic tinge to the stylistic tissue of the tales, caused, as I have suggested, by motives of fictional representation, modified by awareness of religiously separated audiences – but the tinge should not be supposed an accurate expression of James' private religious views any more than its obviously fictitious nature should be assumed to preclude them; there is too much jumping at conclusions in James scholarship, and too little attention to evidential fact. A conspicuous exception is Adeline R. Tintner's *Book World of Henry James* (1987), which handsomely demonstrates the rich Biblical background, by way of Milton, in *The Wings of the Dove* and *The Golden Bowl*. Here are a few additional gleanings from Scripture, but the harvest is not, I think, overabundant – James probably refers to Catholic altars, shrines, images, candles, holy water, votive offerings, unction, and the like more often than he refers to the Bible. In "Osborne's Revenge" (1868), Graham's "spirit had been exquisitely willing, but his flesh had been fatally weak" (he "had never seemed so living as now that he was dead"). In "The Modern Warning" (1888), Macarthy Grice, a patriotic American zealot, has "something in his face which seemed to say that there was more in him of the spirit than of the letter," more hot air than real life. Mary Gosselin reminds Guy Firminger in "Lord Beaupré" (1892) that "Your cross" – being chased by young women – "is small compared with your crown." In "Owen Wingrave" (1892), the young pacifist "would have turned both cheeks." Anecdotes of Frank Saltram ("The Coxon Fund," 1894) are so innumerable that "Their name is legion." Stunningly, in "The Beast in the Jungle" (1903), May Bartram tells John Marcher, "I'm your dull woman, a part of the daily bread for which you pray in church." There are many more Biblical references in James, and they will turn up from time to time (many have turned up already); but they will never establish James as especially fond of or adept at Biblical allusion.

With many exceptions, the overall tone of religious reference in James' short fiction is familiar and easy, light and aesthetic; proportionally more Catholic than Protestant, even if the great majority of the tales have Protestant settings and personages, at first New England Protestants, Congregational ("Orthodox") and Unitarian mostly, and then in the later English tales communicants in the Church of England. James tends to lay Catholic reference on top of these vaguely Protestant backgrounds – or he inserts it. And there is a distinct difference in religious flavor between early and late James. In "Poor Richard" (1868), all is high seriousness. Gertrude has "despite her preponderantly prosaic and, as it were, secular tone, a certain latent suggestion of heroic possibilities" – "like the priest behind the king." When a suitor tells her that love is "sacred," she retorts that love and religion are two different things, which never prevented her creator from speaking of them in the same breath. "I give you a good deal," she says, "but I keep a little . . . which I suppose I shall give to God." We enjoy a radically different flavor in "Covering End" (1898), as Mrs. Gracedew speechifies the aestheticized Gospel: "What do politics amount to, compared with religion? . . . This [an old house] *is* the temple – don't profane it! Keep up the old altar kindly – you can't set up a new one as good. You *must* have beauty in your life, don't you see?"[16] What intervenes, from 1868 to 1898, is the Jamesian fusion of art and religion – largely by way of Balzac? – another ostensibly Catholic emphasis (in sacred-secular terms, the incarnational sacramental sub-sumption). His preferred image of the quest for literary form was the Holy Grail, which appears in "The Author of 'Beltraffio' " (1884), "Collaboration" (1892), and other places. The same image is suggested in "Sir Dominick Ferrand" (also 1892) in obscure language about "secrets of form . . . the sacrificial mysteries." However medievally romanticized, and however vaguely imagined by secular moderns, the Grail is the cup of the new and everlasting covenant, consecrated on the night he was betrayed, as the mass in English has it. James' increased religious aes-theticism is contemporary with – although not necessarily caused by – an upsurge of Catholic aestheticism especially among the poets, as suggested in Part One, allusions to the English Catholic literary scene.

6. Sacred Seculars: Novel, Letter, and Notebook

They were so provincial as to think that brilliancy came ill-recom-mended, and they were shocked at his ceasing to care for the prayer and the sermon. They might have perceived that he *was* the prayer and the sermon: not in the least a seculariser, but in his own subtle way a sanc-tifier.

"Emerson," 1887

Poor is the art, a thing positively to be ashamed of, that, generally speaking, is not far more pressing for this servant of the altar than any-thing else, anything outside the church, can possibly be.

"George Sand," 1902

Typical James statements, those; we need not subscribe to them, but we must understand them – and so I continue to look at issues broached in the preceding pages. Novels first, and very briefly; many sacred sec-ulars will be found in later chapters; most of them are of the same kind as those surveyed in connection with the tales; here, only an instance or so, too good to bypass, such as Olive Chancellor to Verena Tarrant in *The Bostonians* (1886), "Priests – when they were real priests – never married, and what you and I dream of doing demands of us a kind of priesthood" ("Olive perceived how fatally, without Verena's tender notes, her crusade would lack sweetness, what the Catholics call unction"), or such as Miriam Rooth's opinion in *The Tragic Muse* (1890) that Madame Carré was "founded [on] a rock." Nothing takes my fancy, however, religious and aesthetic alike, so much as May Server in *The Sacred Fount* (1901), the title itself being a sacred secular and perhaps her name as well. What I have in mind is May Server in "the great pictured saloon" at Newmarch, "with her eyes raised to the painted dome": "[A] kind of profane piety had dropped on her, drizzling down, in the cold light, in silver, in crystal, in faint, mixed delicacies of colour, almost as on a pilgrim at a shrine. . . . She was like an awestruck child . . . an old dead pastel under glass." As the narrator much later remarks to her and of her (in prayerful situations James is regularly fond of shifting pronouns): " 'God grant I don't see *you* again at all!' was the prayer sharply determined in my heart as I left Mrs. Server behind me. I left her behind me forever, but the prayer has not been answered. I did see her again; I see her now; I shall see her always." The conjoined passages have a way of striking the reader receptive both to satire and to religious sentiment as "something transcendent and absolute, like the sign of the cross or the flag of one's country," an oddly balanced pair of similes (technically Gilbert Osmond's) in *The Portrait of a Lady* (1881) – one sacred, indeed quite Catholic, and one secular, and each, in context, apparently intended as exchangeable with the other. "I had divided it, didn't they see?" James inquires in the *Awkward Age* preface, "into aspects . . . and by that sign we would conquer." He wrote Edith Wharton 16 January 1905, somewhat obscurely, "By that sign you shall conquer" (he will visit her?).

We have met instances of prayer in the tales, and we have perhaps even noticed how curious they are. In his personal correspondence James likewise speaks often of prayer and with such a comparable ambiguity as must have rendered his semantic intentions more often than not opaque to his original recipients – and to poor us, who do not even know the man, as the phrase is, "personally"? What we observe, from our retrospective distance, is that once again James' religious expression is frequently characterized by a fluctuating combination of Roman Catholic and secular (psychological or aesthetic) elements. A letter of 27 November 1871 to Grace Norton offers a perfect example of the characteristic blend: "I count off the days like a good Catholic a rosary, praying for your return." The statement is neither literal nor insignificant: That James is like a good Catholic clearly identifies him as not Catholic, but nothing explains his comparison, conflation, of himself as with one telling a rosary – he might as easily have referred to the calendar. About thirteen years later (24 January 1885), James writes Grace Norton again, "I am always praying for you (though I don't pray, in general, and don't understand it, I make the brilliant exception for *you*!)." On 21 January 1887 he writes Robert Louis Stevenson in the same puzzling mode, "[T]hough not addicted to prayer I petition that at the present speaking you be in some tolerable pass." The sentiment can easily be translated to fervent good wishes, but only by ignoring the language – the words *prayer* and *petition* plus the subjunctive mode of the verb (*be* rather than *are*) betoken an expression deeper than or beyond mere sociable *gemütlichkeit*. To Stevenson he writes again on 29 April 1889, "[Y]ou are for the time absolutely as if you were dead to me – I mean to my imagination of course –

not to my affection or my prayers." *"Ora pro nobis"* – to the same, 21 October 1893.

In addition to the Catholic–secular blend, James' allusions to prayer in his letters often blend the emotive and the witty. The wittiest letters of all are to William James and concern Henry's shaky dramatic prospects. Anticipating the first night of *The American,* he writes 7 November 1890: "I will tell you *when* to pray." He dispatched the same petition variously: to Edmund Gosse, 3 January 1891, "I count upon you both to spend this evening in fasting, silence and supplication"; to William again, same date, same message, "spend *you* the terrible hours in fasting, silence and supplication"; to Urbain Mengin, same date, same message, different language, "priez pour moi." Then on 8 January 1891 to Mr. and Mrs. Hugh Bell he remarks that "one clings, in the wing, to the curtain-rod, as to the *pieds des autels.*" Far and away the best letter of prayer concerning the theater is of 5 January 1895, *Guy Domville* time, to William: "I am counting on some Psychical intervention from you" – both brothers being superstitious but one of them being more comical about it than the other – "this is really the time to show your stuff." James then adds his usual Catholic note, *"Domine in manus tuas – !"* and then just as typically takes it back: "This is a time when a man wants a religion." What James wanted was a good Catholic prayer compelling an un-Catholic audience to admire his Catholic play.

Perhaps in a somewhat more serious vein, he tells Cora Crane, widow of the American novelist, on 5 June 1900, "I constantly think of him and as it were pray for him." A slightly different combination of tones appears in a 26 September 1901 letter to Mrs. William James: "Pray for me, but don't despair of me; and I will do as much, on my side, and as little, for you. Give my tender love to William and tell him to lift up his heart!" Lift up your heart(s) – *Sursum corda* in the Latin mass – was a favorite Henry James allusion. It is found in a letter of 2 May 1896 to A. C. Benson, "Pray for me . . . be of good and uplifted heart."[17] To Jessie Allen on 20 February 1910 he writes that a prospective visit from his nephew Harry "lifts up my heart."[18] Mrs. W. K. Clifford on 22 August 1914 is advised to "Lift up your heart."[19] So too Clare Sheridan 30 May 1915: "Lift up your heart and spread wide your faith" (faith not specified). James' fondness for the phrase seems to have been lifelong: In an 1866 criticism for the *Nation* James opines that "To be completely great, a work of art must lift up the reader's heart."

In August 1910 he writes Bruce Porter, recovering from the disease, to "go in peace – be measly no more."[20] James seems to possess and to relish a fond knowledge of tags from the Latin mass, but where and when he picked them up there is probably no way of knowing, nor is it known how he almost always manages to have them in English. A 21

November 1912 letter to Edith Bigelow asks her to tell an autograph hunter to snip off the end of his letter and "to sin no more" (in the same letter, "Pray for me hard . . . pray for me with every form and rite of sacrifice and burnt-offering").[21] Jocularity is also found in a 19 January 1902 announcement to his nephew Harry that "This apartment grows in grace."[22] A week later (25 January) he beseeches Howells, "[P]ray for me *you,* over this," namely, how to sell to tourist readers millions of *William Wetmore Story and His Friends,* with "poor dear W.W.S. *out,*" and plenty of Hawthornesque Rome *in* − and "Please the Family too!" On 18 June 1915 he writes Compton Mackenzie, "I hang about you at any rate with all sorts of vows and benedictions."[23]

Catholic or generally religious reference in the letters that is concerned with matters other than prayer is even more playful − for example, a letter to his father Christmas morning 1872, "The Pope's Christmas blessing on you all! − I feel the kindlier to him [Pio Nono], since seeing Rome profaned at such a rate under his apostolic nose." Noticing one of his Catholic conversion tales ("Adina") in *Scribner's* causes him to cross himself with gratitude (or so he writes his mother on 17 May 1874) that he appears there no more often. To Howells he writes on 20 July 1880: "The only important things that can happen to me are to die and to marry, and as yet I do neither. I shall in any case do the former first; then in the next world, I shall marry Helen of Troy." To Robert Louis Stevenson on 12 January 1891 he sends belated Christmas greetings, "We always go on at a great rate about you − celebrate rites as faithful as the early Christians in the catacombs." To Edmund Gosse he writes on 2 October 1891, just after the opening of *The American,* "Your picture of your existence and circumstance is like the flicker of the open door of heaven to those recumbent in the purgatory of yours not *yet* damned − ah no! − Henry James." The stylistic virtuosity tends to conceal the erroneous statement of doctrine − Catholic, of course, in its original, orthodox, pre-Jamesian form. On 23 March 1895 he comically writes Isabella Gardner, "I return to England to enter a monastery for the rest of my days," meaning that he will avoid parties and write a lot.[24] Ever the theological wag, he tells H. G. Wells on 21 September 1913 that he values Wells' writings "with thanks to the great Author of all things," including H. G. Wells (James also). But a radically different tone appears in a 28 February 1902 letter to Hendrik C. Anderson about Anderson's brother: "Beautiful and unspeakable your account of relation to Andreas. Sacred and beyond tears." That tone is again pure James, and it leads us straight to the *Notebooks.*

James' religious language in the *Notebooks* is naturally of a piece with everything we have seen in the fiction and in the letters but more ominous in tone, less witty, for there is the radical difference that now he writes to himself, a self doubled as a present and as a future reader. And surely it is tempting – it is so easy! – to say that he writes to himself as if that second self were God, in a manner of speaking. But this same shifting identification and alienation of the self, this division and doubling of the self is almost certainly an ineradicable element in all prayer, and so it would be critical ineptitude of the worst sort to attribute the linguistically prayerful practice of self-address to Jamesian vanity, arrogance, or the Napoleonic equation. What we actually find in these quasi-religious passages in the *Notebooks* is Henry James' conceiving himself, or projecting from his very inmost soul, with its eternally creational aesthetic orientation, a dual or divided consciousness, fictively imagined as a speaker or initiator, comparatively immanent, and a listener or respondent, comparatively transcendent, that listener or respondent being optionally, but again with a difference, second or third person grammatically. Thus James typically puts it to "himself": "Let me not, just Heaven – not, God knows, that I *incline* to! – slacken." Surely this is more than a self-help memo. Such language ought not to be reduced to the purely secularistic flatlands. Complexity is always and vastly preferable to spurious simplification, as readers of James ought to be aware. In that potent sentence just quoted we have in fact, in intention, and in form, a prayer. An "I," with a reflexive object "me," refers itself in the second person to "Heaven" but also, indirectly, addressing itself, refers itself in the third person to "God," that is to say, there are two clearly existent and discriminated entities to which, or to whom, the subject appeals (prays), whose (more than) approval, or blessing, the subject seeks, and whose approval or blessing the subject is sure of in advance.

How revelatory that the famous *Notebooks* passage, famous for other reasons as well, the passage dated 23 January 1895, soon after the theatrical disaster of *Guy Domville,* that curious play about a Catholic-priest-in-the-making who resisted worldly temptation and entered the church as the curtain fell – how revelatory that this passage in which Henry James took up his old novelistic pen once more in a passion of dedicational transitive return should be phrased in the self-same sacred–secular language encountered in such a variety of genres and contexts: "I take up my own old pen again – the pen of all my old unforgettable efforts and sacred struggles. To myself – today – I need say no more. . . . It is now indeed that I may do the work of my life. And I will. . . . But all that is of the ineffable – too deep and pure for any utterance. Shrouded in sacred silence let it rest." The language of ineffability points to literature and beyond literature to the divinization of art, to the sacred nature of created form (intention as incarnate), and, we shall soon see, to ideas and feelings about death as death relates to aesthetic and perhaps other modes of creation.

Such language is by no means unique to this particular passage but is James' inveterate lexical preference for the expression of his highest and deepest experiences in the life of writing. Unfortunately I have no warrant for quoting at any great length these passages, but here is a fair selection: "joys too sacred to prate about," "Glory be to the Highest," "a matter as to which the clear and sacred light can only come to me with prayer and fasting, as it were, and little by little," "the sacred fluid of fiction," "the real thing is silence and sanctity," "Ah, *miséricorde divine,* ah, exquisite art and privilege and joy!", "the sacred mystery or structure," "God knows I know what I mean," "it is the only thing that really, for *me,* at least, will *produire* L'ŒUVRE, and L'ŒUVRE is, before God, what I'm going in for," "Oh, divine old joy of the 'Scenario,' throbbing up and up, with its little sacred irrepressible emotion," "*turn and turn and turn about* is the gospel of it," "the divine diabolical law under which I labour!", "the 'process,' the intimate, the sacred, the divine," "the small fond prayer," "Heaven preserve me," "Laus Deo!", and perhaps best of all, "the old divine light, re-kindling the little old sacred possibilities, renewing the little link with the old sacred days. Oh, sacred days that are still somehow *there.*"[25] Time and death seem to lurk about and behind these apostrophic statements, and we may notice how frequent are the words *old* and *little:* Old is what James was or would be; little is what he was in the beginning.

Occasionally James will sound less Christian than ecumenically pagan, even animistic, as "I simply invoke and appeal to all the powers and forces and divinities to whom I've ever been loyal and who haven't failed me yet – after all: never, never yet!" In what seems to be a subsequently inscribed passage in the same entry he talks to himself in French (but *mon bon* is not to be translated or designated; *mon bon* is *mon bon*): "Oh, blest *Other House,* which gives me thus at every step a precedent, a support, a divine little light to walk by. *Causons, causons, mon bon* – oh celestial, soothing, sanctifying process, with all the high sane forces of the sacred time fighting, through it, on my side!"[26] It is reductive and foolish to read James as altogether secular. His texts are more serious than that, more ambivalent, more heroic, more desperate, more helpless. The objects of James' prayers may be secular, but so are the objects of most people's prayers. What makes these Jamesian passages so moving is the intense and ardent concentration of soul, the moving humility and assurance of the petitioner, the brilliance of the adorational language. Like Emerson, James sanctified whatever he touched. And like the true priest, he never apostacized. As he laconically remarked in his preface to the *Lesson of the Master* volume in the New York Edition, "Sacred altogether to memory, in short, such labours and such lights." In any case, the distinction between sacred and secular, useful in its limited way, blurs and fades so soon as we begin to notice a couple of phrases found in the Nicene Creed, endlessly proclaimed but not much thought about – in connection with God the Father, "maker of heaven and earth, of all that is seen and unseen"; in connection with the Son of God, "through whom all things were made." The Son is also the Word. *In principio erat Verbum, et Verbum erat apud Deum, et Deus erat Verbum.* All things are linguistic. *Mysterium Fidei.*

7. Death and Literary Form

His world was all material, and its outlying darkness hardly more suggestive, morally, than a velvet canopy studded with silver nails.

"Théophile Gautier," 1873

Back of everything is the great spectre of universal death, the all-encompassing blackness. . . . In short, life and its negation are beaten up inextricably together. But if the life be good, the negation of it must be bad. Yet the two are equally essential facts of existence; and all natural happiness seems infected with a contradiction. The breath of the sepulchre surrounds it.

William James, *The Varieties of Religious Experience*

It was when life was framed in death that the picture was really hung up.

The Sense of the Past

In *A Concise History of the Catholic Church* (1979), Thomas Bokenkotter concludes chapter 1 ("Jesus"): "Then the decisive event occurred: The risen Lord appeared to Peter"; and he begins chapter 2 ("The Church Spreads Across the Empire"): "The resurrection of Jesus was the starting point of Christian faith." Obviously, Henry James had heard of the Resurrection – reference to it has already turned up more than once, and in a letter of 5 March 1907 to Grace Norton he speaks of "raising" his early works for the New York Edition[27] – and just as obviously he did not believe in it, "really" (literally). Invincibly ignorant, as the phrase is, or at least constitutionally bereft of the starting point of Christian faith, bereft of any solid sense of its historical validity – for unbelievers its historical claim, its myth, its fraud, its lie – he was obliged to face the idea of death with few resources or none beyond his own courage, imagination, and wit, fending off the fear of annihilation with such reported *mots* as "At last, the real distinguished thing," and with such indisputable *mots* as "So life goes on even when death, close beside one, punches black holes in it" (1 April 1888 to Henrietta Reubell) and "But heart-breaking are ends and one's sense of the Lash" (15 February 1901 to Edith Bronson), and concocting his riotously funny farces about death and resurrection, for example, "The Papers" (1903) and "Fordham Castle" (1904). As we have seen all along, there are some fascinating problems with James' religious orientations, problems of the relation between "belief" and "language," problems of literary representation. It is one thing to find it picturesque that Catholics have an odd habit of crossing themselves. It is another thing to know the reason why. It is a third thing to assent to the truth, the relevance, the desirability, perhaps even the necessity, of the reason for the bodily gesture.

"The voluntary life seems to me the only intelligent one, and if there be such a thing as heaven, I take it to mean the state in which *involuntary* life is secure" (6 May 1872 to Charles Eliot Norton). Behind that somewhat obscure distinction one senses, as everywhere in James, a distinction between the temporal and the spatial. Life he conceives as temporal, narrative, sequenced, processual, expressive – in a word, literary. Death is thereby figured as clôture of the series of planned progressive pages leading to it. To Mrs. Gereth, Fleda Vetch in *The Spoils of Poynton* (1897) remarks, "It's a soul, a story, a life," as if the three were one – it may stand as a Jamesian translation of Trinitarian mystery. "It was, " he writes with incredible insouciance in *The Bostonians* (1886), "a lovely death," Miss Birdseye's; it is lovely because the woman is *spent;* and she is spent because James has *expended* her. Her extinction, like the conclusion of a properly constructed tale, novel, play, essay, or book, is peaceful because inevitable and appropriate, aesthetic experience perfected and rounded off, followed by silence, absence, vacuum, nonbeing, as in that wonderful phrase, found in "Georgina's Reasons" (1884), life's "closing scenes," a dead metaphor derived from theatrical production. By way of stark contrast we may think of James' frustration, perhaps even horror, at the irrational violation of formal propriety involved, as he felt, in the death of his brother William. As he wrote Thomas Sergeant Perry on 2 September 1910: "And his noble intellectual vitality was still but at its climax – he had two or three ardent purposes and plans. He had cast them away, however, at the end – I mean that, dreadfully suffering, he wanted only to die."[28] It is as if the last two books of *The Ambassadors* were found missing and, worse, with the concurrence of the author. William missing led Henry into curious speculations, even, at times, indirectly and uncharacteristically theological, perhaps partly resulting from his lifelong absorption of Catholic "tone": On 28 August 1913 he wrote William's widow about William's "ghost that hovers yearningly for us – doesn't it? – at once so partakingly near and yet so far off in darkness!" which sounds like spiritualism, but then he goes on in a more Catholic vein, "I throw myself into the imagination that he may blessedly pity *us* far more than we can ever pity *him,*"[29] and we are back to the idea of purgatory with a Jamesian difference (distortion). The idea of a wrongful death recurs in connection with Stephen Crane, to whose widow James wrote (7 June 1900) in some heat: "What a brutal, needless extinction – what an unmitigated unredeemed catastrophe! I think of him with such a sense of possibilities and powers!"

That reaction and that sort of statement is far from how James liked to express himself, so that Leon Edel is right in the main when he describes the many letters to the bereaved as "the moving tribute[s] of the sort the novelist invariably wrote, making his condolences into a muted episto- lary elegy":[30] not invariably, however, but as he could. (We will soon come to an occasion when he could not.) Thus in two personal letters of 1894, first on 10 August to Edmund Gosse, of Pater's life and death, "It presents itself to me – so far as I know it – as one of the successful, felicitous lives and the time and manner of the death a part of the suc- cess," and second on 26 December to the widow of Robert Louis Ste- venson, "There have been – I think – for men of letters few deaths more romantically right. . . . I have in my mind, in that view, only the rounded career and the consecrated work." And what a wonderful paradoxical mix of sorrow and elation we find in his letter of 24 January 1901 to William James about Queen Victoria: "We here, on our side, have been gathering close round the poor old dying and dead Queen, and are plunged in universal mourning tokens – which accounts for my black-edged pa- per. It has really been, the event, most moving, interesting and *pictur- esque*" (emphasis added).[31] James' ability to cope with death depends on his ability to dominate it in aesthetic language, perhaps never better than in "The Next Time," a tale of 1895: "He had merely waked up one morning again in the country of the blue." (The country of the blue is not, by the way, the same thing as French *pays bleu,* a favorite James phrase.)

The excruciating brilliance of such writing may remind us what an idle exercise it usually is to attempt fixing on Henry James the theological or philosophical modes of discourse in which his father and brother gam- boled and that he was always bent on avoiding. Yet on the one occasion when he was more or less invited to frame his convictions in the lan- guage of the schools – "Is There a Life After Death?" (1910), "the most interesting question in the world," as he said in his opening sentence – he did his best to go the other way and ended in what amounts to affir- mation of immortality (rather than resurrection, which is not men- tioned). In a highly obscure yet personalized essayistic style, he concen- trated on such familiar ideas as experience, change, development, diminution, disconnection, personality ("by which I mean our 'soul' "), consciousness ("it at least *contained* the world . . . it had *that* superior- ity"), and, more than anything else, *desire.* The words *Catholic* and *God,* splattered all over the rest of his work, do not appear. The word *Jesus* does not appear. (The word *Jesus* almost never appears. Lifelong, James carefully avoided writing that name.) "God" is variously denominated or euphemized as "the wisdom of the universe," "*sources,*" "the power that produced us," "our prime originator," and perhaps "the fountain of being." James makes and maintains a fascinating and apparently original distinction between "the world" (gradually disappointing) and "the universe" (increasingly rewarding): "I won't say that 'the world,' as we commonly refer to it, grows more attaching, but will say that the universe increasingly does," and again, of the "provocation offered to the artist by the universe . . . what do I take that for but the intense desire of being to get itself personally shared, to show itself for personally sharable, and thus foster the sublimest faith?" But if the universe is a being and a person who creates and reveals and shares, you might as well say God in the first place.

The argument finally turns on the relation of desire and belief, their difference maybe more linguistic than substantive. Does "she" (consciousness, now God is female)

> mean nothing more than that I shall have found life, by her enrichment, the more amusing here? But I find it, at this well-nigh final pass, mainly amusing in the light of the possibility that the idea of an exclusively present world, with all its appearances wholly dependent on our physical outfit, may represent for us but a chance for experiment in the interest of our better and freer being and to its very honor and reinforcement. . . . That conception of the matter rather comes back, I recognize, to the theory of the spiritual discipline, the purification and preparation on earth for heaven, of the orthodox theology – which is a resemblance I don't object to, all the more that it is a superficial one, as well as a fact mainly showing at any rate, how neatly extremes may sometimes meet.

And then as he moves toward conclusion, "It isn't really a question of belief – which is a term I have made no use of in these remarks [except now]; it is on the other hand a question of desire," which James first says is more important than belief and then that it is operationally the same: "If one acts from desire quite as one would from belief, it signifies little what name one gives to one's motive. . . . I can't do less if I desire, but I shouldn't be able to do more if I believed. . . . There again, I recognize[,] extremes 'neatly meet'; one doesn't talk otherwise, doubtless, of one's working out one's salvation. But this coincidence too I am perfectly free to welcome – putting it, that is, that the theological provision happens to coincide with (or, for all I know, to have been, at bottom, insidiously built on) some such sense of appearances as my own."[32]

In that same essay James tells us that death and immortality meant little to him in youth. His fictional handling of these topics bears him out:

Fictive death in the early tales is conventional, sentimental; in "The Story of a Year" (1865), "This world was the riddle; the next alone would be the answer" ("There came to his lips the commencement of that strange moribund smile which seems so ineffably satirical of the things of this world. O imposing spectacle of death! O blessed soul, marked for promotion! What earthly favor is like thine?"); in "A Passionate Pilgrim" (1871), "the side-light of that great undarkening of the spirit which precedes – which precedes the grand illumination of death"; as late as 1884, in "Georgina's Reasons," "Mildred [forerunner of Milly Theale] sank to her rest, or rose to fuller comprehensions, within the year."

More representative passages begin to appear earlier than that and continue to the end, as in "Longstaff's Marriage" (1878): "[W]hen I am dead it [his idea of a deathbed marriage] will seem less importunate, because then you can speak of me in the past," as in a tale or novel, a narrative: "It will be like a story"; as in "The Aspern Papers" (1888): "His early death had been the only dark spot in his life" – death not as clôture but as interpolation; as in "The Liar" (1888): "The proper time for the likeness [having your portrait painted] was at the last, when the whole man was there – you got the totality of his experience"; as in "The Death of the Lion" (1894): "Dead – passe encore; there's nothing so safe. One never knows what a living artist may do"; as in "The Real Right Thing" (1899): "He had broken short off – that was the way of it; and the end was ragged and needed trimming"; as in "Maud-Evelyn" (1900): "[T]he way death brings into relief even the faintest things that have preceded it" ("Marmaduke was a gentleman to the end – he wasted away with an excellent manner"); as in "The Abasement of the Northmores" (1900), which also ridicules the same themes: "His work, unencouraged and interrupted, failed of a final form . . . fragments of fragments." Overall what we see is Henry James almost completely in control of death as a working and worked element of aesthetic, and specifically literary, form. In the Notes for one of his two novelistic fragments, The Ivory Tower, he amusingly reveals the near identity in his mind between death in the real world and represented death in the practice of narrative art: "After Book 2 he [Mr. Betterman] is no more," represented death being nothing other than the handy disposal of a fictional personage no longer essential to sequential progression. "It's too lovely," says Rosanna Gaw of this particular solution, "so there indeed and indeed we are."

Speaking more personally, the deaths of his parents (both in 1882) and of William (1910), traumatic as they were, appear to have had no literary consequences of note. The death of Constance Fenimore Woolson (in 1894) precedes but is not demonstrably the cause of a flurry of literary Catholicizing that commenced with "The Altar of the Dead" in the following year (but it does not include Guy Domville, already underway).

On the basis of present, published evidence, no closer connection than the chronological coincidence can be made out. In his 1887 essay on Woolson, James had remarked on "that somewhat evasive and shifting line [in her works] which divides human affairs into the profane and the sacred," that line in which he had shown so much interest in his early religious reviews, and he had poked gentle fun at her American Episcopalianism. These various deaths, and others, with James' reactions to them, are handsomely discussed by Leon Edel in his biographies, and to those discussions I have nothing at present to add.

I do, however, have something to say about the death of Minny Temple on 8 March 1870, which is, of course, for Henry James the death *of* deaths. In his letters to his mother (26 March) and to William (29 March) we have the soul of our comparatively young author as bare and helpless as we shall ever find it, or should, in decency, want to. The letter to his mother reveals a Henry James for once in his recorded life hysterical, platitudinous, contradictory, confused, and preponderantly irreligious. A quick selection of phrases must represent the tortuous currents of tone, "such a breathing immortal reality that the mere statement of her death conveys little meaning," "the poignant sense of loss and irremediable absence," "old recollections and associations flow into my mind – almost *enjoying* the exquisite pain they provoke," "No attitude of the heart seems tender and generous enough not to do her some unwilling hurt," "Oh dearest Mother! oh poor struggling suffering *dying* creature!", "balm in the thought of poor Minny and *rest* – rest and immortal absence!", "the thought of her being in future a simple memory of the mind – a mere pulsation of the heart: to me as yet it seems perfectly inadmissible," "unchained from suffering and embalmed forever in all our hearts and lives. Twenty years hence what a pure eloquent vision she will be," "What a pregnant reference in future years," "I felt for her an affection as deep as the foundations of my being," "Poor Minny! how much she was not to see! It's hard to believe that she is not seeing greater things now," "life – poor narrow life – contained no place for her," "Let me think that her eyes are resting on greener pastures than even England's." The letter is painful and human and natural and almost entirely secular. What had happened to that Protestant Christianity James had been vaunting in the *Nation* and other periodicals? ("We are all of us Protestants.")

Three days later, to William James, Henry had his answers, religious and literary. Equating Minny Temple with Jesus Christ, not previously mentioned and only indirectly hinted at now, James thinks she must have died to save his soul, as a writer, that is: "It's almost as if she had passed away – as far as I am concerned – from having served her purpose, that of standing well within the world, inviting and inviting me onward by all the bright intensity of her example," and not, surely, to an early grave.

"The more I think of her the more perfectly satisfied I am to have her translated from this changing realm of fact to the steady realm of thought," which is maybe how you write to an older brother already suspected of philosophical propensities, but philosophically is precisely how Henry James was *not* going to deal with Minny Temple; he was going to deal with her according to his own special rapprochements. In a sentence that reflects his habit of prayer, as we have seen it in letters and especially in the *Notebooks,* he shifts pronouns: "Poor living Minny! No letters would hold you. It's the *living* ones that die; the writing ones that survive." And finally, the Jamesian act of secularized (aestheticized) consecration: "In exchange, for you, dearest Minny, we'll all keep your future." Not a word of God or Christianity. But wait – the tale is not all told.

We have each of us read with considerable emotion the concluding chapter to *Notes of a Son and Brother* (1914), that elegy for "the end of our youth." Some of us may even have noticed in her quoted letters Minny Temple's own failed efforts to comprehend and accept the Christian revelation. It is probable that her difficulties were the same as James', typical of enfeebled Protestantism in a dreary epoch of scientized skepticism. That the letters were written to John Gray and came into the possession of Henry James late in life for the purposes of this particular publication makes no great difference. Presumably, he would have known, had he known anything at all; presumably, he and Minny Temple would have talked. Everyone knows how Henry James' vow to commemorate Minny Temple's life was magnificently redeemed in *The Wings of the Dove* (1902) and elsewhere. What no one seems to have noticed at all but what is strikingly clear from my "Calendar: Chief Items of Catholic Interest in Henry James" is that the death of Minny Temple in March 1870 leads in at least a chronological way to literary results the most curious, specifically to the publication eight months later of "Travelling Companions," first in that series of ambiguous documents which I call "The Narratives of Catholic Conversion." In these we find a train of young men and young women, mostly the latter, who in one or another situation of confrontation with a world more Catholic than their origins do or do not "go Catholic," with appropriate fear and trembling, possibly more social than religious, on the part of a narrative text presumably in turn representing a readership chiefly but not exclusively Protestant. It is almost as if James were asking himself, fictively, of course, why Minny Temple didn't do *that* instead of dying in frustration and disappointment.

In the interest of scholarly scrupulosity I have given the lapsed time between the death of Minny Temple and the publication of "Travelling Companions" as eight months, but of course the real lapsed time would have been much less than that: For a tale to appear in print in month z it must have been submitted in month y and written in month x. We will never know the date of month x, but we may be confident that it was after the death of Minny Temple and probably after James' return to the United States end-of-April/early May. "It's a good deal like dying," he wrote Grace Norton from London on 28 April 1870.

The news of the death reached him in Great Malvern, England, after he had "done" Catholic Italy. Having Italy and Minny Temple in his pocket – one single pocket, wonderfully ample – it made no difference where he might henceforth reside. At home or abroad, he could easily run Minny Temple through her posthumous religious paces, as nice marriageable proto-Catholic Miss Brooke in "Travelling Companions," as orphaned and Romish-tempted-but-tried-and-true Protestant hold-out Nora Lambert in *Watch and Ward,* as the no-named flamboyant Italian Catholic heroine of "At Isella," as the superfluously agreeable pro-Catholic American wife in "The Last of the Valerii," as ex-Protestant Catholic-converting Miss Waddington in "Adina," and even as Catholic-convert illegitimate international Christina Light in *Roderick Hudson* – where else can she derive that combination of religious impetuosity and girlish charm?

In later years, Minny Temple would reappear, much modified but still discernible, as Francie Dosson in *The Reverberator;* projected backward as Maisie Farange in *What Maisie Knew;* perhaps even a little as the delightfully mad Anglican governess in *The Turn of the Screw.* Only at the very last would she turn her fact to the wall as Milly Theale, about whose religious identity there will in due course be a word or two to say. Minny Temple is finally resurrected and returns as sweet Nan in James' Notes for *The Sense of the Past* – some forty-odd years later! "*The* thing, at this ragged edge, is to keep hold of the clue, as tight as possible, that I have grabbed for my solution in the line of her *making* the sacrifice; making it all with a sublime intelligence *for* him, on account of what he has told her of his own epoch – which she stares at in her deprivation." What Minny Temple did for Henry James was exactly what sweet Nan did for Ralph Pendrel: sacrificed her future. And behind these obvious parallels looms another parallel almost too obvious: Minny Temple was Jesus Christ and the literary career of Henry James her Church.

PART THREE

The Narratives of Catholic Conversion

1. *Watch and Ward* (1871)

The term that is the title of Part Three means to imply a narrative by Henry James, short or long, early or late, in which the topic of Catholic conversion figures significantly. Catholic conversion is seldom or never the only topic, and it is almost always a minor topic, and still it is an important topic, inattention to which makes for incomplete or skewed interpretation. The matter of Catholic conversion may be quite openly represented, as in *Watch and Ward, Roderick Hudson,* and *The Reverberator,* or it may be merely implied, as in *The American,* or it may be almost invisible in the depths of its submersion, as in *What Maisie Knew* and *The Turn of the Screw.* The Catholic conversion may or may not take place – with Adina Waddington and Christina Light it does, with Nora Lambert and Rowland Mallet it does not – but it is enough that it be put forward as a possibility. Then there ensues, doubtless to the author's fiendish delight, a world of doubt, distaste, and fear, justified and unjustified alike, but mostly the latter, the idea of Catholic conversion being observed (naturally, James being James), from a sort of Protestant or post-Protestant yet partly pro-Catholic point of view, with a deal of cosmopolitan Catholic sophistication and a deal of Catholic local color deriving from what I have called the sacred seculars. Henry James is personally detached; he is not in the least himself upset by prospective or actual changes of religious belief and loyalty. He takes them seriously but he is not undone by them. What he seems mainly aware of is their grand utility for fictional representation of a somewhat melodramatic kind. For James, religious conversion meant not only change but change abrupt and disjunctive, as he explained in his 1866 essay on George Eliot: "I believe it to be very uncommon for what is called a religious conversion merely to intensify and consecrate pre-existing inclinations. It is usually a change, a wrench; and the new life is apt to be the more sincere as the old one had less in common with it."

For *Watch and Ward* and many another Jamesian document, the two salient aspects of Catholicity and associated ambience are conversion, or, more accurately, conversion versus non-conversion while subject to temptation, and convent or monastery. (Convent "means" sequestration and celibacy, both unnatural.) In this his first novel, these aspects parallel, in a loose sort of way, Nora Lambert's "incarceration" in Roger Lawrence's adopt-your-own-wife-while-she's-still-a-little-girl-and-bring-her-up-right masculine fantasy (pre-*Pygmalion,* pre-*Lolita*) and the changeover or "conversion" of Nora from ward to wife, consequent upon Roger's changeover or "conversion" from guardian to secret-husband-to-be to outright suitor and, finally, to married mate. These parallels are never explicitly stated; I infer them, with some trepidation. The Catholic theme is never very clearly worked out in the text, and it is unevenly spread, mostly clumped in chapters 5 through 8 (in a total of eleven). After chapter 8, Catholicity as even a possible topic disappears. The range of Catholic tone is bewilderingly, if at first glance conventionally, inclusive, from horrified fascination to righteous repulsion. Yet oddly enough, an alternative – an almost opposite – tone is furnished *Watch and Ward* by Mrs. Keith, a Roman Catholic convert who retains all her previous virtues and attractions and who mediates, as best she may, between the discordant ecclesiastical claims, while she also mediates between "the church" and "the world," an updated Anne Sophie Swetchine who is also, be it noted, an American.

There is a certain literary flavor to all this Catholicizing, and all this standing pat, this clinging to your tried-and-true American Protestant rectitudes, lest they be reft from you in the dead of night and you wake forlorn, and this literary flavor is signaled in chapter 7, where Hubert Lawrence, the attractively villainous Unitarian minister, and Nora discuss an aesthetically disreputable novel. Obviously it is a conversion novel, as we begin to suspect *Watch and Ward* of also being, even if it shall never prove possible to identify which, if any, exemplar young Henry James may have had in mind. " 'Heaven preserve us! what a hotch-potch!' cried Hubert. 'Is that what they are doing nowadays?' " Neither is it possible to know if Hubert means the doings of the novelists or the doings depicted by the novelists. These latter, are, in brief: A young Protestant clergyman is in love with a beauteous young Catholic thing who declines to abandon her faith for love; the clergyman nearly "goes over" to Rome but stops just short (it would put him out of a job), and instead, miraculously, no details vouchsafed, he converts her out of Papistry to Protestantism, as I believe never once happens in a James fiction, baptizes her – superfluously, of course – and, far more important, marries her. Hubert contends that the minister should have married the woman first and converted her (not himself) second. (In *Roderick Hudson,* the Cavaliere reports to Rowland Mallet that Catholic Prince Casamassima, who proposes to marry Christina Light, at the time a Protestant, "will handle that point after marriage.")[1] Discussion of this doubtless imaginary novel trails off, but we are left with a trio of distinct impressions: that conversion from Protestant to Catholic was, or was held to be, a serious and perhaps even a frequent occurrence and was thus an acceptable topic for popular fictions contrived for an Anglo-American readership and set in an Anglo-American social and cultural milieu; that in this context romantic love transcends Christian piety in about the degree that matrimony (legal) is valued over religious faith; and that these preferential attitudes are congruous with a Protestantism of waning zeal.

As a move from the thin to the thick, the simple to the complex, the recently reductive to the historically huge, Catholic conversion was *picturesque* as well, thus additionally rendering it an attractive question for James, especially if the Catholic contagion, if one may put it so, might be seen as geographically intensified in Europe; and in Europe, especially in Italy; and in Italy, especially in *Rome* – that place, that name, that implication![2] Italy was the country James always loved most, Rome the city he knew best at that time. Even in "De Grey: A Romance," which antedates *Watch and Ward* by three years, Father Herbert has become a priest in Rome. Not only in *Watch and Ward* but in "Travelling Companions" (1870), "The Last of the Valerii (1874), "Adina" (1874), and *Roderick Hudson* (1875), not to mention *The American* (1876–7) and *The Reverberator* (1888), the potential threat of Catholic conversion while in Europe hangs over the innocent American tourist or expatriate head, that threat perhaps lingering down even unto Isabel Archer in Rome and Lambert Strether in Paris. As for *Watch and Ward,* where the centralizing experience of conversion more or less begins – somewhat more delicately, the previous year, in "Travelling Companions" – it appears that although it can happen to you anywhere, a Catholic conversion is most likely to happen to you in Rome. At the very least, Rome is the perfected picturesque setting for your so fascinating yet rather grotesque change of heart.

The chief Roman Catholic *event* in *Watch and Ward* is paradoxically the appropriate, permanent, and even benign conversion of Mrs. Keith *at Rome.* Whatever significance that conversion may be felt to involve must depend on our apprehension of her "character," which is unexceptionally estimable, chiefly in her not trying to convert other people – *the* predominant and conspicuous Catholic sin, according to Henry James.

It also depends on her role in the familial fabulations, which is "central." She is the indispensable nexus for Roger and Nora, between whom there exists not only the highly desirable difference of gender but the somewhat more intractable difference of seventeen years. Mrs. Keith is of the right sex and the right age to serve as duenna, traveling companion, substitute mother, and pivot, being, for these functions, about the same age as Roger, whose matrimonial suit she long since rejected but whose lifelong friend she remains. In the final paragraph of *Watch and Ward,* she and Nora are also "very good friends," even while Mrs. Keith continues in her blithe and blameless Catholic course and Nora continues in her own faith, presumably Roger's, Roger's in turn being presumably Protestant, though not necessarily the Unitarianism of that irresponsible Hubert. Nora has attended an Episcopal school.

Again paradoxically, "Mrs. Keith had long been for Nora an object of mystical veneration" who yet obligingly also says to Roger, "Let me take her to Europe and bring her out in Rome. Don't be afraid; I'll guard your interests." Among those interests must be presumed watching and warding against a Catholic conversion, even though Mrs. Keith is herself a Catholic convert and therefore always (her example) a potential threat to Protestant continuance. The religious behaviors of these two wonderful women are worth following in some detail, and indeed they constitute the novel's major religious, moral, and social points, that is, pluralism, tolerance, and charity. The complicity of the love plot and the religious plot begins at the close of chapter 2, when Roger suddenly realizes that he is bringing up Nora so as to marry her; when he naturally postpones telling her this (she is too young); and when, instead, he informs Mrs. Keith, by letter, of his changed intention. Mrs. Keith is in Rome, that hotbed, where she *did it* – "she had done as the Americans do, and entered the Roman Church." (How many Americans, in fact, did any such thing?) The provenance of the letter is quite extraordinary. "I am told," he writes, what we have just been told, "you have become a Roman Catholic. Perhaps you have been praying for me at St. Peter's. This is the easiest way to account for my conversion" – the key term that blends the plots – to what? only this: "a worthier state of mind." Also inexplicably, he adds, "Pray for me more than ever," sounding like Henry James in his letters. Even if we are not entirely sure of the nature of the connections, love, maturation, marriage, St. Peter's, the city of Rome, prayer, the one holy catholic apostolic church, and Mrs. Keith's practice of it *in that place* are all fictively conjoined.

But no sooner are these items conjoined than division appears in two distinctly different forms of threat, convent and conversion. Convent first. Roger deplores his lacking "that charm of *infallibility,* that *romance of omniscience,* that a woman demands of her lover" (emphasis added).

The First Vatican Council, with its declaration of papal infallibility, took place the preceding year. Very wrongly, Roger fantasizes: "If I were only a good old Catholic, that I might shut her up in a convent and keep her childish and stupid and contented!" (Like Pansy Osmond, in effect.) Later, Nora is with Mrs. Keith for a year's stay in Rome, where are all the marvels and the perils. Nora makes friends with a German lady, religion not given, who has a twice maltreated sister (seduced and sequestered) in "the convent with the dreadful name, – the Sepolte Vive," fictive precursor to Claire de Cintré's lockup in Paris: "The inmates are literally buried alive; they are dead to the outer world." The German lady and Nora do not know the sister's conventual name. They do not know but that she may even have died. They assume her to be "immured" from the living by "a dead stone wall." The visiting ladies weekly deposit flowers "in the little blind wicket of the convent-wall. . . . [W]e put in our bouquet and see it gobbled up into the speechless maw of the cloister," as is the way with cloisters. "It's a dismal amusement, but I confess it interests me" – all this in a letter from Nora to Roger, who ought to be horrified, especially if he connects this actual cloistering with his own fantasies. It interests James, too, quite obviously, and we presume his readership. The tonal treatment of the convent idea in *Watch and Ward* is simple and clear, and there is a word for it: *Gothic*.

On the question of conversion, the novel assumes a tone appropriately lighter, subtler, and more complex, for although you (the reader) might imaginably become a Catholic (you might even *be* one!), the chances of your being eternally immured in such an ecclesiastical dungeon as the Sepolte Vive must be accounted slender. And if you were a Catholic in the ordinary lay sense – that is, not a religious – your life mightn't be half bad, as the happy social existence of Mrs. Keith reminds us. In the same letter to Roger, Nora gaily goes on to say that she "can drop a little bow to a good old cardinal as smartly as you please," more easily, we are to infer, than in Boston. And then to the main point (even if it is with his entire approval that Nora is with Mrs. Keith in Rome, such a picturesque spot to "come out"): "Mrs. Keith has presented me to half a dozen [good old cardinals], with whom I pass, I suppose, for an interesting convert. Alas, I'm only a convert to worldly vanities." All is saved. At least for the moment.

Earlier in the same letter, Nora says that Mrs. Keith "keeps pretty well *au courant* of the various church festivals," a mode of behavior presumably acceptable to Protestant American readers desiring to be au courant. "Just don't convert *me* or shut me up in a convent," we can almost hear those readers of 1871 muttering. "I couldn't care less what else you do." Thus before sailing for Italy, Mrs. Keith and Nora attend mass in Boston. "The reader will perhaps remember [how could the reader not!] that

Mrs. Keith was a recent convert to the Roman Catholic faith; as such, she performed her religious duties with peculiar assiduity," as other religious types, converted or no, perchance did not, but of course her "assiduity" is "peculiar" and maybe her "duties" as well. "Her present errand was to propose that Nora should go to church and join in offering a mass for their safety at sea." Then well-nigh perfected Mrs. Keith proffers the unasked-for (it would be rude) yet ardently desired assurance: " 'I don't want to undermine your faith, you know; but I think it would be so nice,' said Mrs. Keith." Mrs. Keith's major virtue is that she doesn't proselyte. What additionally would be so nice is going to mass without (on Nora's part) believing or even understanding a Latin word of it and without being solicited to shift her allegiance: "Appealing to Roger, Nora received permission to do as she pleased," according to the dogmatics of Protestant Americanism. What would also be and what *is* so nice is the way piety, once it gets into a literary work, itself becomes literary: "The two ladies spent an hour at the foot of the altar," where we may be certain no novelistic hour was ever better spent, "an hour of romantic delight to the younger one," Mrs. Keith's Catholic delights tastefully omitted. Later the same day Nora hears Hubert preach in his Unitarian church. "She thought of her brief exaltation of the morning, in the incense-thickened air of the Catholic church; but what a straighter flight to heaven was this!" It is the rounded note of early James: Romance is awarded to Catholicity, rational realistic preference to Protestantism, offense to none.

The danger of conversion remains, despite the non-evangelizing scruples of Mrs. Keith. (Perhaps it is an aspect of genre.) A Catholic conversion is *always* to be feared, perhaps for no reason at all but in the way that art is said to be feared in *The Tragic Muse*. There must be repeated reassurance that Nora is not converting but standing firm in her birthright. Hubert gets in a last dig, rather (we think) uncalled for, "And one more request. Don't let Mrs. Keith make a Catholic of you." As if wonderful Mrs. Keith either would or could! There is, however, a problem, which begins in paranoia and ends somewhere else: If Nora has free will, she can become a Catholic any time, any place – with or without the connivance of Mrs. Keith or any other earthly influence. The idea of Nora's free will appears to be very disturbing for *Watch and Ward* – if only she were a good old Calvinist, she might well be "elect"! (but then there would be no novel). Nora's free will threatens both the denouement of the love story and Protestant American superiority. "I'll have no Pope but you," says Nora to Hubert, and we may wish to remind ourselves again of papal infallibility, perhaps not entirely a welcome reflection to our young novelist already so enamored of the ambiguous.

From that center of world threat, Rome, Nora also writes Hubert that although much frequenting churches – "picturesque," "historic," "rich with traditions" – she remains, protesting and reformed, "a barbarous Western maid, doubly a heretic, an alien social and religious, – and [I] watch the people come and go on this eternal business of salvation," as her creator was likewise fond of doing. She is doubly a heretic for being Protestant and American, which is what she is supposed to be, and to stay, even while the text of Henry James wobbles all over the lot. The main thing, surely, is the aesthetic experience: "To go into most of the churches is like reading some better novel than I find most novels." But *Watch and Ward* will be better than most novels – among other reasons, because it goes into churches and flirts with *the* Church. "Not in the least that I'm turning Papist," Nora once more explains, "though in Mrs. Keith's society, if I chose to do so, I might treat myself to the luxury of being a nine days' wonder, (admire my self-denial!) . . . [for] there is small danger of my changing my present faith for one which will make it a sin to go and hear you preach." Love of man conquers love of God. Protestantism retains its own. Henry James plays it both ends against the middle.

Watch and Ward ran serially in the *Atlantic Monthly* from August through December 1871. In a long letter of 9 August 1871 to Charles Eliot Norton, James speaks laconically but confidently about the work: "The subject is something slight; but I have tried to make a work of art, and if you are good enough to read it I trust you will detect my intention. A certain form will be its chief merit." To watch and to ward, while we the readership watch and wait (a phrase to recur in later texts), is at least one aspect of the subject, the intention, and the form. A Catholic conversion (for Nora) has been watched for and warded off. But a Catholic conversion (for Mrs. Keith) has been accepted and even admired. Henry James has written a conversion novel that is at the same time an anti-conversion novel, a revision and a rebuttal of and satire upon the general type.

2. Italian Sketches and Italian Tales (1870–5)

The illuminating difference between the Italian sketches and the Italian tales of the same period is that the sketches are distinctly more anti-Catholic. It is doubtless a difference dependent on genre and on the relation of genre to the imputed readership. The sketches are primarily designed to give the folks back home a sense of vicarious tourism and a residual conviction of their American and Protestant superiority. The tales, which are after all only fictive, are designed to give those same home-folks a deliciously wicked sense of what it might be like to be

other than their culturally denuded uninteresting nonpicturesque Protestant selves, or at least to enable them imaginatively to consort with
such others. An occasional anti-Protestant note sticks out: The cathedral
of Basel is "cold, naked, and Lutheran." But for the most part James'
Transatlantic Sketches (1875) is more directly concerned with the pros and
cons of Catholic Italy. Be sure it is picturesque! Be equally sure that just
about everything else is wrong with it!

The chief thing wrong with Catholic Italy is that it has no pertinence
for present-day Americans. The central image is that of the "ever-empty
[Catholic] churches," and the key word is *old*. *Transatlantic Sketches* is full
of such condescending phrases as "the poor, disinherited Pope," "the
shrunken proportions of Catholicism," and "the loneliness of the re-
maining faithful." St. Paul's Without the Walls is "a last pompous effect
of formal Catholicism" in a "Rome of abortive councils and unheeded
anathemas." S. Sabina, on the Aventine, prompts the expostulation "What
a massive heritage Christianity and Catholicism are leaving here!" and
yet, only two pages later, "What a crossfire of influences does Catholicism provide!" (Catholicism also provides a lot of exclamation marks.)
Mostly the tone is milder than that and is carried by such typical phras-
ings as "in the Catholic days," "old Catholic lands," and "old Catholicism and old Italy." The latter are then contrasted at length with the utter
boredom of new Protestantism in New England, "a white wooden
meeting-house, looking gray among the drifts." We seem caught between a world that stubbornly refuses to die, however superannuated,
and a world that had better not have been born.

Catholic Italy is overcast with "the dreadful double scepticism of a
Protestant and a tourist" amid many more of the same, "idly gazing
troops of Western heretics – passionless even in their heresy." In the
sketches there are no Catholic conversions going on. Convents are occasionally glimpsed, but no wonderful young ladies are immured in them.
Celibacy comes in for its lumps, "the uncleanness of monachism," but
that tough-minded sentiment by no means prevents aesthetic perception
of "a dozen white-robed Dominicans scattered in the happiest composition on the pavement" of S. Francesca Romana. As our tourist author
can "never see a leather curtain without lifting it," he naturally comes
upon a worshiper now and then and even a young priest, whose irrelevant devotions are favorably compared with the irrelevant inanities of
the Carnival crowd – "he alone knelt there for religion," furnishing "a
supreme vision of the religious passion – its privations and resignations
and exhaustions, and its terribly small share of amusement." The diminution of papal and other ecclesiastical omnipresence, visually considered, is regrettable. And still Assisi "looked like a vignette out of some

brown old missal," but of course we moderns contemplate "the passionate pluck of St. Francis" with "the sense of being separated from it by an impassable gulf – the reflection on all that has come and gone to make us forgive ourselves for not being capable of such high-strung virtue." *Transatlantic Sketches* makes good reading but less good reading than the Italian tales. Moving from comparatively hard fact to liberated fiction, James retains much local color from the sketches contemporaneous with them (as many have noted), but it is the tales themselves that speak most directly to our continuing entertainment.

"Travelling Companions" in the *Atlantic Monthly* for November–December 1870 is the first of the Catholic conversion narratives from the altar of Henry James. It was not his first Catholic narrative, however – "De Grey: A Romance" (1868) was that, and "Gabrielle de Bergerac" (1869) is also earlier – but it was his first conversion (or non-conversion) tale, a quite different matter, indeed almost the opposite, the *ménage* or family-module piece shaping itself as excessive stasis while the very word *conversion* connotes radical change. What "Travelling Companions" (1870) mainly shows to the light of prurient inquest is young Henry James commencing to play with the idea and even with the word *conversion*. Somewhat resembling *Watch and Ward* (1871) and even *Roderick Hudson* (1875), it is a tale weaving several distinct narrative threads – of love and marriage (that the companions are now man and wife is divulged in the final sentence), of amateur art criticism (frescoes, paintings, churches, mosaics, piazzas, statues, mostly real), of Italian travel appreciation from Milan across northern Italy to Venice and down to Florence (if you drew the companions' itinerary on a map it would look like a huge Arabic numeral 7). Along that already tripled narrative path the question of Catholic conversion is from time to time shyly introduced, there being no evident reason why Catholic conversion should be an issue at all except for our being in Catholic Italy, that temptress.

Narrator-hero Mr. Brooke, an American national long resident in Germany who now aspires to be "the good American," opens the religious topic, very indirectly, when in a talk about nationalism he says to Miss Evans, to whom he also aspires: "I am sure I wish with all my heart . . . to be a good American. *I'm open to conversion. Try me*" (emphasis added). Narrator refers to the patriotic sentiment, of course, and to love, not to Catholicity, and still it is *the word*. Not long after, Miss Evans obligingly remarks, apropos of nothing, "I'm glad I'm not a Catholic." But then she feels "a lingering sisterly sympathy" with certain "pale penitents and postulants," Milanese ladies, charmingly garbed, whereupon narrator inquires, "Don't you wish you were a Catholic now?" An Italian woman on her knees near the altar in prayer rises, approaches, and speaks, embodying, as narrator says, "the genius of the Picturesque. She shows us the essential misery that lies behind it," a revelation popular with non-Catholic American tourists in Italy, including James.

Subsequently at Venice, in Saint Mark's, admiring the mosaics – "To this builded sepulcher of trembling hope and dread, this monument of mighty passions, I had wandered in search of pictorial effects. O vulgarity!" – narrator espies Miss Evans a-kneel on a *prie-dieu* and "gazing upward at the great mosaic Christ. . . . Was she really at her devotions, or was she only playing at prayer?" He nears; she smiles; *she does not stand up*. She says her prayers are only half-prayers. He says half-prayers are a good deal for one who recently thanked Heaven for not being a Catholic. She assures him "I'm not a Catholic, *yet*" (emphasis added). At Scuola San Rocco the two together adore Tintoretto's *Crucifixion,* he for the painting, she for the matter represented: "Miss Evans repeated aloud a dozen verses from St. Mark's Gospel." At Padua, church of St. Anthony, "which boasts one of the richest and holiest shrines in all church-burdened Italy," she murmurs, mysteriously, "O the Church, the Church," and he makes such a little speech as we shall hear from Christina Light in *Roderick Hudson:*

> "What a real pity," I said, "that we are not Catholics; that that dazzling monument is not something more to us than a mere splendid show! What a different thing this visiting of churches would be for us, if we occasionally felt the prompting to fall on our knees. I begin to grow ashamed of this perpetual attitude of bald curiosity. What a pleasant thing it must be, in such a church as this, for two good friends to say their prayers together!"
>
> *"Ecco!"* said Miss Evans.

It is the last time Catholicity is discussed by these two good friends, although Mr. Brooke, subsequently alone in Rome, "shortly before the opening of the recent Council," manages timely and respectful remarks, however indeterminate, about "the greatness of this church of churches." Then he is in the world's cathedral, "near the brazen image of St. Peter," people-watching. A non-idolatrous lady is also watching. It is Miss Evans come to church with her French maid who "was now at confession." The tale quickly ends. No one has been converted. We are not quite sure, in retrospect, why not or what was the reason to talk about it. Perhaps it was an aspect of local color on the move, and when the couple settled down it went away.

The narrator of "At Isella" (1871) also speaks with typical American tourist *brio,* plus impertinent derogation, of "entering church-burdened Italy," his own tale being equally church-burdened, another example of romanticized ultramontane Catholicity displayed as local color or the picturesque. The second half of "At Isella," the narrative proper, features a beauteous and formidable Italian lady fleeing her very bad un-Catholic husband in order to join her lover at Geneva while the narrator is en route to meet his *promessa sposa* in a more seemly fashion at Florence, just at that place where we left the other happily married and still un-Catholic American young people at the conclusion of "Travelling Companions." The Italian lady is your representative Italian female Catholic, quite operatic, in fact. True to type, she has committed herself to God and the Holy Virgin ("They will help me"); to the latter she regularly and loudly prays, or of her she expostulates. Disdaining any the least moral compunction for her irregular romantic conduct, she proffers instead a loyal piety: "I have had faith. . . . My husband has none; nothing is sacred to him, not the Blessed Virgin herself. If you were to hear the things he says about the Holy Father!" Can they be worse than the things James wrote home in personal letters about that same Holy Father, Pius IX?

The narrator is presumably Protestant and the majority of the *Galaxy* readership even more certainly so. Agog with wonder at the luridities of religious difference and perpetually perched on the paradox of Protestant majority status in the United States for the time being but not in the world at large or perhaps over the long historic haul, the readership was doubtless equally titillated by the Catholic tone of the tale's first, introductory, tourist-fiction half. From the outset, the narrator seems obsessed with Catholic Europe and is appropriately rewarded, with, for example, "the most reckless pleasure in the fact that this was Catholic Switzerland"; with, further, as traveling companion a French priest, "young and pale and priestly in the last degree," appallingly innocent in worldly affairs, "a mere passive object of transmission – a simple priestly particle in the great ecclesiastical body"; with the Simplon Hospice and its "pious brothers" and "the true, bold, convent look" ("striving to close in human weakness from blast and avalanche"); with "benediction" and "altar-candles"; with "that peculiar perfume of churchiness – the *odeur de sacristie* and essence of incense – which impart throughout the world an especial pungency to Catholicism" – to "At Isella" not least – with "fine priestly company" and "The Prior himself . . . a priest dominant and militant" ("Heaven grant, I mused as I glanced at him, that his fierce and massive manhood be guided by the Lord's example. . . . He ought to be down in the hard, dense world, fighting and sinning for his mother Church"). A mother and child are pictured as Catholic Italy imitating Italian Catholic art: "[S]he made a picture which, in coming weeks, I saw imitated more or less vividly over many an altar and in many a palace."

There may or may not be much of "real" Henry James in these portrayals, but if we assume on his part a remarkable instinct for what his

American audience craved in the way of religious gratification, with special emphasis on how *those people* carried on *over there,* such a performance as "At Isella" tells us a great deal about an increasing fascination with, and tolerance for, the rich details of a faith and practice more passionate, more complex and more precise, and (of all things!) more tolerant than their own, however advanced, reformed, purified, up-to-date, and American the latter. It was 1871 and the aftermath of the Vatican Council, with its stunning, nearly unanimous proclamation of papal infallibility, the beginning of the end of the Tridentine Church. That, as much as anything else, must have made it exotic and even horrendous to read all about how "the other half" (putting the figure at its lowest estimate) lived – evidently with more gusto than "we," and more sensuously, too. The oddest thing of all was that by 1871 "America," that purest Protestant stronghold, was itself overrun by Roman Catholics who were also American citizens, people who bizarrely voted in elections *and* prayed to the Blessèd Virgin, not in Rome or Paris but in Chicago and Philadelphia. The readership, which had always prided itself on its religious toleration, would therefore now be in the process of changing its mind even further about certain things, young Henry James assisting at the transitions. It would evidently put up with the narrator's remark that at the magic word *Italy* we Americans "cross ourselves."

"The Madonna of the Future" (1873) features aesthetic Americans commingling with native Florentines – these latter, especially Serafina, the superannuated "Madonna," are predictably Catholic; the Americans are predictably Protestant. For Theobald, the idealistic artist *manqué,* we have the best possible evidence: He is buried "in the little Protestant cemetery on the way to Fiesole." Conversion is twice alluded to in a purely secular sense: Theobald's "high aesthetic fever" is called "a sign of conversion," and an American lady asks the skeptical narrator H—— if Theobald has made a convert of him (to Theobald's view of himself). "The Madonna of the Future" contains no real conversions (as from Protestant or unbeliever to Catholic) or threat of any. Protestants and Catholics exist as separately in the text as if they were different species. The tale is not about conversion but about contrast. Consequently an abundance of Romanism differentiates the local-color background of Florence and the local-color heroine from the American aesthetes abroad, as well as from the American readership at home, to whom "The Madonna of the Future" offers Roman Catholic exoticism secularized or distanced, anyhow *safe* (yet "interesting!"), in such phrases, images, and sentiments as these: "solemn church-feasts of the intellect"; the good old days when "religious and aesthetic needs went hand in hand" (and thanks to the Church there was a splendid market for Madonnas); "the truly religious soul is always at worship, the genuine artist is always in labor";

those who once believed in Theobald are "the faithful" (but "we fell away from the faith"); Serafina is embroidering "an ecclesiastical vest-ment," presumably not Unitarian; she has just been to confession; her hair is like "the veil of a nun"; she wears "a little silver cross" on her ample Italian bosom; she looks "like some pious lay-member of a sister-hood, living by special permission outside her convent walls"; beneath Theobald's sketch of her dead baby "was festooned a little bowl for holy-water"; according to Theobald, she might, when young, "have stepped out of the stable of Bethlehem. . . . She, too, was a maiden mother"; she alleges for him "the heart of an angel and the virtue of a saint." When last seen, Serafina tells narrator, "I've just paid for a nine days' mass for his soul." Protestant American Theobald, when still living, condescend-ingly speaks of "her simple religion," but the ascription of simplicity is belied by the details of the narrative, which seems to say that Catholicity is old, foreign, strange, complex, fascinating, comprehensive – "but not, of course, for *me!*"

As Leon Edel points out in his "Introduction" to volume 3 of *Collected Tales,* a thematic congruity of "The Last of the Valerii" and "Adina" (January 1874, May–June 1874) "is that civilized man must keep the primitive side of his nature properly buried; that it is dangerous to ex-hume dormant primeval things; that they contain the evil man has eter-nally sought to master." Each of these tales also thematizes, or just fails to thematize, Catholic conversion, even if the connection between buried evil and Catholicity be difficult – even impossible – to ascertain. In "The Last of the Valerii" the American girl enters a mixed marriage and does what she can; in "Adina" the Amerian girl "bolts" from her boyfriend and runs off to marry an Italian, "going Catholic" in the process, as in popular fictions of a previous epoch American young ladies – some, not all – went native, adopted Indian ways, and would not return to house-keeping and needlepoint.

Featuring an Italian-American love match (fine at first, then less than fine, then fine again), "The Last of the Valerii" anticipates certain aspects of *The Golden Bowl,* not including prose style: "The Conte Valerio's grandeur was doubtless nothing for a young American girl, who had the air and almost the habits of a princess, to sound her trumpet about; but she was desperately in love with him, and not only her heart, but her imagination, was touched." Unlike Maggie Verver, Martha is Protes-tant. The religious difference troubles her: "She loved him so devoutly that she believed no change of faith could better him, and she would have been willing for his sake to say her prayers to the sacred Bambino at Epiphany. But he had the *good taste* to demand no such sacrifice" (em-phasis added). The narrator – Martha's godfather – recalls meeting them at St. Peter's "in the incense-thickened air" (same phrase as in *Watch and*

Ward), more specifically near "that sombre group of confessionals which proclaims so portentously the world's sinfulness," as in Hawthorne's *The Marble Faun*. The Count thinks he might well go to confession before the wedding, but fiancée Martha dissuades him, having problems of her own (heresy, tourism):

> "I'm willing to change my religion, if he bids me. There are moments when I'm terribly tired of simply staring at Catholicism; it will be a relief to come into a church to kneel. That's, after all, what they are meant for! Therefore, Camillo mio, if it casts a shade across your heart to think that I'm a heretic, I'll go and kneel down to that good old priest who has just entered the confessional yonder and say to him, 'My father, I repent, I abjure, I believe. Baptize me in the only faith.' "

The godfather – not, obviously, of the only faith – suggests a Protestant conversion for the Count. The Count, more American than the Americans, settles the argument on the side of happy pluralism: " 'Keep your religion,' he said. 'Every one his own. . . . I'm a poor Catholic! I don't understand all these chants and ceremonies and splendors. . . . You must not be a better Catholic than your husband.' " The Count is in fact a pagan, and so we move to the tale of excavated Juno, of statue-abuse, of American (female, Protestant, but willing!) triumphalism, for which strong efficacious redemptive waters the faint flavor of potential Catholic conversion has served as a pleasant preliminary sip.

In "Adina," the American girl Adina Waddington has an English-sounding last name and a first name that can go either way, toward either of her marital suppliants, American Sam Scrope or Italian Angelo Beati. Sam gets Angelo's topaz, which ends in the Tiber. Angelo in return gets Sam's girl. At Albano, at the Capuchin convent – always, if possible, a convent – darkened, candles on altar ("for some pious reason," "a pretty piece of chiaroscuro"), narrator makes out, darkly, a young lady, sitting, "eyes fixed in strange expansion on the shining altar." It – is – Adina – Waddington! "Was she turning Catholic and" – a wonderful non sequitur – "preparing to give up her heretical friends?" It would seem so. Perhaps she has come to dislike her fellow Americans. For whatever reasons, love mainly, Adina will soon "convert" to Adina Beati. Adina Waddington is gone, never to return, never to repent, nor, one might add, to reconvert, for Protestant Adina is just as obsolete as her maiden name. "Love is said to be *par excellence* the egotistical passion; if so Adina was far gone," gone with love, gone with Italianità, gone with Roman Catholicity. We have known all along the faith of Angelo, for his uncle is a "shrewd old priest." Adina's stepmother is appalled, we can hardly tell whether by the elopement or the conversion. " 'The thing was odious,' she said; 'I thank heaven the girl's father did not live to see it.' " But the narrator thinks quite otherwise, namely, that as "mere *action,* it seemed to me really superb. . . . There has been no prudence here, certainly, but there has been ardent, full-blown, positive passion. We see the one every day, the other once in five years. More than once I ventured to ventilate this heresy before the kindly widow, but she always stopped me short."

3. *Roderick Hudson* (1875)

Roderick Hudson is Henry James' first "full-length" novel, that is, of an extent to require a volume to itself, but not two, in the New York Edition; more than twice as long as *Watch and Ward;* vastly longer than any of the tales just glanced at. It is a comparatively ample space for the development of many complex matters, and, as in *Watch and Ward,* complication is at least threefold: the line of eros–marriage–family, the line of religious affiliation (signaled by the always provocative word *conversion*), and the crisscrossing relations of the two main lines. Brevity had made for comparative simplicity of relations: In "Travelling Companions" we find one couple only; in "The Last of the Valerii" the same, and no third parties, rivals, interlopers, in either case; even in "Adina" there are only two men enamored of one woman. *Watch and Ward* managed three men enamored of one woman, one man (Hubert) engaged to another woman (Amy) and a second (Roger) formerly enamored of the novel's secondary female (Mrs. Keith) who now serves her former suitor as consultant and aide in pursuit of her replacement.

Roderick Hudson is more complicated than that – so much more that we hardly dare read the religious line until we take hold of the eros–marriage–family line, what may be called the Love-Chain. (It is just like the social erotics of the eleventh grade in that typical American high school which Henry James never had the pleasure of attending.) Linearly set forth, the Love-Chain looks like this:

Prince – Christina – Roderick – Mary – Rowland

There are five participants, alternate in gender, linked sideways by passional propinquity; you can read it in either direction, left–right or right–left, and you can "jump around," too, confronting Christina and Mary over (over the head of) Roderick. Proceeding in the left–right direction, Prince is in love with Christina, who hates but marries him under family threat and is partly and responsively in love with Roderick who is in love with Christina but formerly in love with Mary Garland to whom he is still engaged and she is in love with him and Rowland is in love with Mary.

The chief advantage of having the Love-Chain in the front of your mind is that it helps prevent misreadings of the religious conversion (or nonconversion) line. It also helps highlight certain religious configurations otherwise easy to overlook, for example, the opposition between Catholicizing and finally converted Christina Light and Protestant American Mary Garland, who comes from a family of ministers and stays that way, her faith unaffected by a trip to Rome. As an unquestioned and unquestioning Protestant, Mary Garland also stands off against Prince Casamassima, an unquestioned and unquestioning Catholic. The more interesting characters are those seeking an exit from religious quandary, whether or not that exit is ever found: The religious peaks of *Roderick Hudson* are accordingly the curious Catholic conversion of Christina Light and the proto-Catholic yet ultimately very Protestant recessions of Rowland Mallet. It may conduce to a limited revival of interest in Rowland to notice how Christina's conversion generally proceeds in his company and against his dullness.

Christina is our primary fascination (one of the greatest fascinations in the Jamesian *œuvre*). "Have you never felt in any degree," Rowland asks her at Saint Cecilia's, "the fascination of Catholicism?" For both personages the question is loaded. The scene in which it is sounded is not altogether unprepared for, however; there have been sparkles of suggestion. While sitting for Roderick to model her bust, Christina lets down her tresses; then, "with her perfect face dividing their rippling flow she looked like some immaculate saint of legend being led to martyrdom," quite Roman, in two distinct senses. She has a reasonably impressive Catholic vocabulary, as when she tells Roderick that she would respond to greatness of character, should she ever see any, "with a generosity which would do something toward the remission of my sins." The phrase immediately follows the Confiteor in the Latin mass. It is not a random collocation of words Christina Light has chanced upon, and it is not an effusion of original genius.

Rowland never passes Saint Cecilia's without a visit. Like Strether and other unmarried James males who wander into Catholic churches, he finds a woman praying. The woman is "the faithful Assunta"; with her, Christina, sitting apart, not at prayer; Rowland pulls up a chair; Assunta, who was kneeling, rises and approaches. Christina motions her off, saying (obviously in Italian but given by the text in English "translation"): "No, no; while you are about it, say a few dozen more!" The reader infers that Assunta's prayers, being Catholic, are repetitive and rote, whether in Italian or in Latin, Ave Marias, paternosters, litanies, formulas, readily repeated or extended, not ad hoc, personal, spontaneous, organic, original, expressive, "sincere." "Pray for me," Christina goes on in English. "Pray, I say nothing silly." The remark is addressed to

Assunta but meant for the Anglophonic ear of Rowland, to whom she adds, transposing Assunta from second to third person: "She has been at it half an hour; I envy her capacity!" It is in this ambivalent international bilingual context that Rowland asks about her fascination with Catholicism.

The form of his question is significant, for he might have said, "Have you *ever* felt the fascination," the simple interrogative form that anticipates no one reply more than another. "Have you *never* felt the fascination" tends to elicit one of two answers, "Yes, of course," or "No, I haven't; I don't feel things, I'm insensitive, unimaginative, bigoted." Christina naturally gives the first answer and immediately qualifies it by relegating her religious experience to the past. "Yes, I have been through that, too!" (she as well as other people? or in addition to her other tribulations?). But if Christina lacks clarity she seldoms lacks authority, as demonstrated in the details of her explanatory narrative (her mother should also be kept in mind, anything to escape such a mother!). I take her statements bit by bit, she has such a tendency to talk seriatim, constructing as she goes: "There was a time when I wanted immensely to be a nun; it was not a laughing matter. It was when I was about sixteen years old. I read the Imitation [of Christ, by Thomas à Kempis] and the Life of Saint Catherine." If her tale is entirely contrived how has she come by the names? "I fully believed in the miracles of the saints, and I was dying to have one of my own. The least little accident that could have been twisted into a miracle would have carried me straight into the bosom of the church."

We will return to Christina's conversion at a later point – its latest point for *Roderick Hudson* in the original version – but I am not sure we shall ever entirely understand it, or her, or James' understanding of it either. Yet surely it is true, as Leon Edel says, that James "was to love Christina as he loved few of his heroines."[3] To love her is to love or at least to accept, partially, provisionally, imaginatively, her Catholicity, for without it she would be a different personage – in fact, quite unimaginable save as a specimen of late adolescent fascination soon to fade. The trouble is that Christina's Catholicity, perhaps in the degree that it is "real," that is, in the degree that James is capable of representing it – chiefly as he represents her as representing it – is so minimalist and contradictious as to be virtually inexpressible, at the opposite end of the scale from a stereotype. In *The Princess Casamassima* (1886) and in the New York Edition revisions to both novels, James continued to work on her – inconclusively, as we shall see. Perhaps Christina was too real, too close to home. In all the works of Henry James she is at once the most (not the best) Catholic personage (unless Margie Verver is) and correspondingly inexplicable. She seems to compel James to analogize himself as a non–Catholic in antithesis to her, his eager outside confronting her imputed inside. She also confronts James as the hyperbole of his own heritage, the James family affluent, intellectually distinguished (more so every day), but not "old" even by American standards, Irish in origin, but, curiously, not Catholic. The "No Irish Need Apply" joke of *The American* may suggest James' occasional awareness that he was somehow defined as a member of a "minority," in the bizarre American usage, a minority *of* a minority, for as the small boy must have learned early in the streets of New York, the Irish tend to be Catholic.

Meanwhile, James has Rowland Mallet take a hand with Christina. Out of his own mechanisms of avoidance and repression, he answers Christina according to the highest conceptions of Jamesian ambiguity: "Rowland had already been sensible of something in this young lady's tone which he would have called a want of veracity, and this epitome of her religious experience failed to strike him as an absolute statement of fact." There appears to be on the part of Rowland a certain skepticism vis-à-vis Christina and a certain skepticism vis-à-vis his own skepticism. What he suspects in her is a less than perfect adequation of present state-ment (representing present memory) with "actual" past experience. But how can he know that, or how, even, can she? In any event, this "trait'" (want of veracity?) is for Rowland "not disagreeable" (double negative) because she, according to him, "was evidently the foremost dupe of her inventions." Because she once wanted to become a nun and has not? Because she isn't "even" a Catholic? Because she has been tempted to become one? And who was it that asked the question in the first place about have you never felt the fascination?

But "already" Rowland is shifting to a different set of categories, matched by a linguistic shift away from a lexicon dominated by words associated with truth and reality to a lexicon dominated by such words as *fictitious, believed, extemporized, idealize, interesting, picturesque, imagi-nation, vivacity, spontaneity*:

> She had a fictitious history in which she believed much more fondly than in her real one, and an infinite capacity for extemporized reminis-cence adapted to the mood of the hour. She liked to idealize herself, to take interesting and picturesque attitudes to her own imagination; and the vivacity and spontaneity of her character gave her, really, a starting-point in experience; so that the many-colored flowers of fiction which blossomed in her talk were not so much perversions, as sympathetic exaggerations, of fact.

In plain English, Christina and her exaggerations are virtually one. They might even be true! ("And Rowland felt that whatever she said of herself might have been, under the imagined circumstances.") It is the way she is, "impulse was there, audacity, the restless questioning temperament." Those who regard Christina Light, as I tend to do (within limits), as James' quintessential Catholic must surely admire the audacity of his impulse, for these are not traits normally attributed to Catholics by non-Catholics – quite the reverse.

Rowland's response has its own fascination, not least the way he accuses and defends himself for not being a Catholic. "I am afraid I am sadly prosaic," he begins, thus ceding to Christina's putative faith the realms of poetry and romance, "for in these many months now that I have been in Rome, I have never ceased" – another double negative, plus return to the loaded word *never (not ever)* – "for a moment to look at Catholicism simply from the outside." Suddenly Rowland's defensive elaboration of outside–inside metaphors turns obscure. "I don't see an opening as big as your finger-nail where I could creep into it!" It is not clear what he, or even James, means by an "opening," or why they should want one, or why they should feel it to be unavailable. It is equally unclear what comparison is proposed by an entity into which you would creep if you could but are prevented by no fault of your own. A building, perhaps, somewhat along the lines of a convent or prison? If so, a convent-prison curious, inside and outside reversed, not an edifice that immures but an edifice that precludes.

To her two questions, "What do you believe? . . . Are you religious?" Rowland answers the first, inclusively, "I believe in God," and ignores the second. She asks him to tell her about his religion, and he says he can't, it is too much a part of him, as it should be. She disagrees. Religion should be eloquent, aggressive, persuasive, illuminating: "*It should wish to make converts*" (emphasis added). Then she attacks him for worldliness, driving him past skepticism into near solipsism: "What do you know of anything but this strange, terrible world that surrounds you? How do you know that your faith [basically is not having one] is not a mere crazy castle in the air; one of those castles that we are called fools for building when we lodge them in this life?" From medieval homily Christina turns to Arnoldian lament (sounding very much like "Dover Beach") for the lapse of faith, specified as Catholic. She juggles three distinct meanings of the word *church* (building, institution, communion), she juggles the word *faith,* she makes unwarranted inferences about Assunta's soul (she is almost as dreadful as Mrs. Hudson in St. Peter's), she misrepresents herself as identical to Rowland, and she is only about half right about him. But who can doubt her passion and her eloquence?

> "The very atmosphere of this cold, deserted church seems to mock at one's longing to believe in something. Who cares for it now? who comes to it? who takes it seriously? Poor stupid Assunta there gives in her

adhesion in a jargon she doesn't understand, and you and I, proper, passionless tourists, come lounging in to rest from a walk. And yet the Catholic church was once the proudest institution in the world, and had quite its own way with men's souls. When such a mighty structure as that turns out to have a flaw, what faith is one to put in one's poor little views and philosophies?"

It is not possible or even desirable to adjudicate the opposing pair – they constitute a dialectic essential to the continued vitality of narrative representation. Each of them will go on, separately, yet in reference to the other.

Just before Rowland's next and last "Catholic" performance, James gives us another Christina–Rowland encounter. Christina tells Rowland that he doesn't believe in her, and she wishes he would, to which he can only murmur, "My dear Miss Light, my dear Miss Light! . . . Pray listen to me! . . . My dear Miss Light, you are a very terrible young lady!" Indeed she is, having just treated him to an outburst of Catholic hagiography applied to herself. Once again there can be no question but that the terrible young lady knows her way around certain areas of Catholic devotional practice, thus having the innocent Rowland at her mercy:

> " 'Voyons,' I say to myself, 'it isn't particularly charming to hear one's self made out such a low person, but it is worth thinking over; there's probably a good deal of truth in it, and at any rate we must be as good a girl as we can. That's the great point! And then here's a magnificent chance for humility. If there's doubt in the matter, let the doubt count against one's self. That is what Saint Catherine did, and Saint Theresa, and all the others, and they are said to have had in consequence the most ineffable joys. Let us go in for a little ineffable joy!' "

Christina has simplified the Love-Chain by dismissing Roderick and accepting the Prince Casamassima. " 'Since then,' the young girl went on, 'I have been waiting for the ineffable joys. They haven't yet turned up.' " Her reference to herself in the first-person plural is wonderfully papal.

Rowland is in Fiesole – tormenting himself with forbidden desire for Mary Garland – at the Franciscan convent, not the evil enclosure of *Watch and Ward* and *The American* where wretched Catholic women are made more wretched still but a kindly convent, vaguely prelusive of "The Great Good Place," where harassed males may find brief retreat. It appears to have its resident Roman Catholic Devil, the brother who admits Rowland "with almost maudlin friendliness," that is, the man is a proselytizer, as well as its true frate, "the good brother," to whom, unbid, Rowland tenders his "confession," which contains no accusation of sin but much self-congratulation:

> "My brother," he said, "did you ever see the Devil!"
> The frate gazed, gravely, and crossed himself. "Heaven forbid!"

"He was here," Rowland went on, "here in this lovely garden, as he was once in Paradise, half an hour ago. But have no fear; I drove him out."

It is a beautiful example of James' secularizing by psychologizing the sacred, utilizing for aesthetic ends the Catholic practices to which neither Rowland nor he himself personally subscribes, even though Rowland is said, but not shown, to feel "an irresistible need to subscribe to any institution which engaged to keep him [the Devil] at a distance." It is, in fact, the frate and Rowland who are distanced:

"You have been tempted, my brother?" asked the friar, tenderly.
"Hideously!"
"And you have resisted – and conquered!"
"I believe I have conquered."
"The blessed Saint Francis be praised! It is well done. If you like, we will offer a mass for you."
"I am not a Catholic," said Rowland.
The frate smiled with dignity. "That is a reason the more."
"But it's for you, then, to choose. Shake hands with me," Rowland added; "that will do as well; and suffer me, as I go out, to stop a moment in your chapel."

Two gentlemen at Fiesole, one of whom thinks a handshake as good as a mass. Back in Rome, the Cavaliere says to him, "I wish you were a Catholic; I would beg you to step into the first church you come to, and pray for us the next half-hour." Rowland is the typical Romeward-leaning Protestant who will never change. Whatever the attraction of Rome as actuality, his religious position is defined by anti-Rome as idea. This many years after the Reformation, a certain tourist wistfulness may be permitted, even encouraged, but conversion, real, is the Tempter, to whom you turn your back.

For her part, "the Christina," as Cavaliere calls her, has continued her wayward willful course from secular-social Rome to romantic-sacred Rome. At St. Peter's she is seen kissing "that dreadful brass toe" (Mrs. Hudson's phrase) of the famous statue figuring the first Pope. Rowland, of course, "was stupefied: had she suddenly embraced the Catholic faith?" We are given the bare fact of her conversion, but the feel of it is traduced in an irreverent conversation between Madame Grandoni and Rowland: "One day she got up in the depths of despair; at her wit's end, I suppose, in other words, for a new sensation. Suddenly it occurred to her that the Catholic church might after all hold the key," not to the truth but to the loss of her liberty. "She sent for a priest; he happened to be a clever man, and he contrived to interest her." Like a latter-day Juliet, "She put on a black dress and a black lace veil, and looking handsomer than ever she

rustled into the Catholic church," thus inordinately and unintentionally
– but this is all the interpretation of Madame Grandoni, who here in
Roderick Hudson talks Protestant, though in *The Princess Casamassima* she
appears to be Catholic – pleasing the Prince, "who had her heresy sorely
on his conscience." Rowland underlines what Madame Grandoni has said:
"The girl is so deucedly dramatic . . . that I don't know what [further]
coup de théâtre she may have in store for us. Such a stroke was her turning
Catholic." As I have tried to show, signs of her turning Catholic have
been strewn through the text. Christina had all along thought she wanted
recognition of her rectitude and integrity, to which she has not attained.
Maybe what she really wanted was disapproval – and knew how to
get it.

Roderick Hudson is quite apart from the religious considerations of
the novel – neither believer nor unbeliever, neither Protestant nor Catholic, indifferently contemptuous toward all. From the attitudes of his
mother and his cousin-fiancée, we know his background to be Protestant. Mrs. Hudson is to perfection anti-Catholic prejudice, American style.
As her son reports her to Rowland, "Rome is an evil word, in my mother's vocabulary. . . . Northampton is in the centre of the earth and Rome
far away in outlying dusk, into which it can do no Christian any good
to penetrate." The paranoia is not so much doctrinal or even organiza-
tional as it is geographical and provincial. Every once in a while Mrs.
Hudson's fear and hatred of Rome and Romanism burst forth, and she is
naturally at her best in St. Peter's. " 'Mary, dear,' she whispered, 'suppose we had to kiss that dreadful brass toe. . . . I think it's so heathenish;
but Roderick says it's sublime.' " Always the aristocratic aesthete recently of the village, Roderick perversely and ill-manneredly assaults his
mother's religious faith by invidious comparisons he hardly believes in
himself – "It's sublimer than anything *your* religion asks you to do" –
and then he goes on, turning against Mary Garland to redefine the Protestant faith as "[t]he duty of sitting in a whitewashed meeting-house and
listening to a nasal Puritan! . . . I am speaking of ceremonies, of forms."
At that moment, a "squalid, savage-looking peasant, a tattered ruffian of
the most orthodox Italian aspect," is glimpsed "performing his devotions" before and upon the Dreadful Brass Toe. He moves away, predictably crossing himself, and Mrs. Hudson delivers the novel's greatest
line: " 'After that,' she murmured, 'I suppose he thinks he is as good as
any one!' " The man is inferior because he is Catholic and because he is
un-American. That an American might be a Catholic has not occurred
to her and will not. But clearly it was much on the mind of our author
between 1870 and 1875.

As everybody knows, Christina Light the Princess Casamassima continues into the novel that bears her name, now a Catholic revolutionary.

Her conversion holds, even though she attempts to minimize it. "I'm a Catholic, you know – but so little!" – in other words, I am not a very good Catholic. In the New York Edition James has her say instead "but so little by my own doing!" – belatedly introducing the note of external duress. Revisions of *Roderick Hudson* for the New York Edition are even more spectacular. In the encounter of Christina and Rowland at Saint Cecilia's, his great question "Have you never felt in any degree . . . the fascination of Catholicism?" is taken from him, and for it is substituted " 'One envies good Catholics many things,' said Rowland with conscious breadth." We soon see why. Christina's speech about her former religious passions, largely intact, now begins: "Oh, speak to me of that! I've been through that too, though I'm not so much a good Catholic as a bad one," that is, in this 1907 version she is already a Catholic, as she was not in 1875, and worse is to follow: "Mamma's what I call a good one – *ecco!*"

Christina Light has always been a Catholic, she is a cradle Catholic, she is the very negation of a convert, she can't possibly be converted because she already *is*. She is not a Catholic convert – not, *not*, NOT. Accordingly, all traces of Christina's Catholic conversion are deleted, and her status as a hot-and-cold Romanist is substituted. It appears that Henry James in 1907 desired that no special attention be drawn to the origins of his novelistic career in the curious business of writing conversion narratives. *Watch and Ward* had long since been forgotten, he probably believed, and the Italian tales dealing with conversion were also far in the past. All that remained was to "fix" Christina Light, which he accordingly did. But if you achieve the status of a Great Writer it is no use trying to cover your tracks; your earliest publications will be brought to the light, read, studied, and pondered, and what was once there will be there still, simple matter of fact. James predicted this fate in a 19 April 1878 letter to his father about *Watch and Ward:* "I have revised and very much rewritten it. . . . If I get any fame my early things will be sure to be rummaged out; and as they are there it is best to take hold of them myself and put them in order."

4. *The American* (1876–7)

There is no direct reference to Catholic conversion in *The American,* but precious little imagination is required to know that a Catholic conversion, neither especially desired nor especially resisted, is what Christopher Newman might very well be involved with, should he succeed in his dream of marrying Claire de Cintré; as he does not so marry, his Protestantism may just as well be thought to have been a consideration with the bad Bellegardes – that possibility is not talked about either; these things are simply inherent in the textual situation. As we have seen, the lurid topic of a Catholic conversion in the writings of young Henry James by no means requires that a conversion be consummated, only that it be threatened. Like Nora Lambert and Rowland Mallet before him, like Isabel Archer after him, Christopher Newman will stick to his Protestant guns. Indeed, all the personages of *The American* will stick to their guns, Protestant, Catholic, whatever. The two main religious persuasions of Christianity (as understood in the post-Reformation Christian "West") glare at each other with a certain miscomprehension and incipient hostility. The theme of conversion remains potential, muted, subtilized, subsumed. Not so with that companion theme which normally accompanies the idea of Catholic conversion in the conversion narratives, the convent idea, a sort of second-stage or exacerbated Catholicism, almost invariably regarded by the reader, we must suppose, as barbarous, regressive, inhumane, un-American, un-English, un–Anglo-Saxon, un-Protestant, and un-modern. From the standpoint of narratology, the convent serves as a handy alternative to inexplicable death – it is terminal. For what indeed, if you are a novelist defining the novel as "of this world," can you do with a woman (for example) who is now so utterly out of it, and by her own doing?

But although conversion is not a central topic in *The American,* allegories of religious contention flicker around the edges. "If he [Newman] was a muscular Christian, it was quite without knowing it," we learn in the second paragraph, and of course we want to find out to what degree and in what respects Newman does or does not resemble Charles Kingsley, the muscular Christian man, after which we may wonder about Newman's name, normally lost in a flurry of literary-critical Americanism – Newman is "the new man," the American experience, character, charisma, destiny, calling, mystique, and so on. Quite as much to the point, Christopher (Christ-bearer) Newman shares his last name with the most famous Anglo-American Roman Catholic convert of the modern world, a fact hardly to be kept from the reader's attention (then, I mean; and now? who knows? there has been such wonderful progress in religious ignorance), especially when attention is stimulated by allusion to Kingsley, the anti-Catholic assailant whose attacks in the public prints provoked the publication in 1864 of *Apologia Pro Vita Sua.* Unlike his namesake, Christopher Newman will neither take revenge nor fight back nor even so much as apologize, and that is one meaning of the Newman–Newman name-association game. More fascinating still is James' appropriation of the real-life anti-Catholic bias of Charles Kingsley for his fictitious situation, with a twist. For Kingsley, Newman's unforgivable sin was his *being* Catholic, because for Kingsley being Catholic meant and was equal to intellectual dishonesty. Thus in advance Newman was robbed of any possible defense save apostacy or suicide. In *The American,* Kingsley's bigotry against John Henry Newman is transferred to the behavior of Europeans against Americans, of aristocrats against commercial persons, and, of course, most brilliantly and stunningly of all, of Catholics (a certain sort) against that hapless innocent all-American Protestant, our very own *Christopher* Newman.[4]

His overall course resembles Guy Domville's; it is an A–B–A structure. Each protagonist begins in a certain posture, is knocked off balance, and snaps back to his starting point. At the end of *The American* we see Newman standing outside the ultimate convent in the Rue d'Enfer, and then alone and as obdurate as ever in Notre Dame, where "[H]e said no prayers; he had no prayers to say. He had nothing to be thankful for, and he had nothing to ask; nothing to ask, because *now he must take care of himself.* But a great cathedral offers a very various hospitality, and Newman sat in his place, because while there he was *out of the world*" (emphases added). In the New York Edition, *cathedral* becomes *church,* which is more ambiguously inclusive, but in both early and late texts the portals of Notre Dame are said to be "grossly-imaged," an apparently gratuitous fleer. In the early version, Newman heard bells chiming "to the rest of the world"; in the final version, bells "chiming off into space, at long intervals, the big bronze syllables of the Word." Last of all, Newman says goodbye to Mrs. Tristram. In the New York Edition she is more clearly in love with him than ever before (is it another Catholic temptation? we must in a minute ponder her status), and her last words, the last words of *The American,* in its final version, are "Yes, a thousand times – poor, poor Claire." Poor Clares are the Second (Women's) Order of Franciscans. The word hinted at and withheld is *poverty.* So much for one American and his millions of money.

In *The American* no one is converted, but everyone is clear-cut. Benjamin Babcock, a typical early-James satiric butt, is a Unitarian minister (like the insufferable Mr. Brand in *The Europeans*). Christopher Newman is a tolerant ignorant easygoing indifferent kindly insensitive American Protestant, with no interest in religion save for a church to sightsee or a faith that might interfere with his plans. (Babcock and Valentin seem to fancy him a Methodist.) Tom Tristram, an old friend from the States, is surely another example of the same general type, only more crass. Mrs. Tristram is to be suspected of being an American Catholic convert expatriate, on the basis of her having been to convent school with Claire de Cintré and of her socializing with an abbé – that these religious connections are novelistically expedient does not relieve them of thematic significance. Lord Deepmere is also suspect on the basis of Madame de Bellegarde's indecent desire for an alliance with his family, which appears to contain a cardinal. Madame herself is English Old Catholic, "the daughter of an English Catholic earl." Everyone else except Stanislaus Kapp and Mrs. Bread is French Catholic.

Almost as if he were the protagonist of a medieval legend, Christopher Newman three times interrogates his newfound friends concerning their Catholicity. His first question occurs in a conversation with the better Bellegardes:

> "Perhaps you are interested in theology," said the young man [Valentin].
> "Not particularly. Are you a Roman Catholic, madam?" And he turned to Madame de Cintré.
> "Yes, sir," she answered, gravely.

In the New York Edition, *theology* is changed to *religion,* and Newman answers, "Not actively." Madame de Cintré's answer is then stepped up in patriarchal dignity: "I'm of the faith of my fathers."

Newman's second question is to Valentin. To the question "Are you very religious?" Valentin gives a foursquare Roman Catholic answer: "I am a very good Catholic. I respect the Church. I adore the blessed Virgin. I fear the Devil." It is just the kind of textual maneuver that will split the audience: To certain kinds of very good Catholic in 1876–7 (and even now) it must have seemed the well-nigh perfect answer, but to non-Catholics it probably sounded a bit ridiculous yet excusable on the grounds of Valentin's being a "fell European" (Henrietta Stackpole's phrase). In the New York Edition, we have "Do you attend church regularly?" – a nice stiff Protestant phrasing – and Valentin replies that he cherishes rather than respects the Faith instead of the Church and fears the Father of Lies.

Newman's third and final question, superfluous as the others, is to Mrs. Bread: "Are you a Catholic, Mrs. Bread?" followed by her ridiculous reply, "No, sir; I'm a good Church of England woman, very Low." In the New York Edition she gives substantially the same answer to Newman's more tendentious challenge, "Are you of this awful faith, Mrs. Bread?" The most spectacular – and, if you aren't careful, the most misleading – alteration from the early to the New York Edition version is the revision of Newman's first-chapter remark "I am not a Catholic" to "I'm not a real Catholic," which can't mean that he is some other kind of Catholic but probably that he is not a Catholic at all. Somewhat similarly, James in a late revision of a passage in "A Roman Holiday" (originally 1873) designates himself in St. Peter's as "a visitor not regularly enrolled" so that for a while we wonder if he is enrolled in another way. But these are only an odd sort of litotes, dangerously (deliberately?) close to being out of control. It is my suspicion that James had no very great objection to being taken for a Catholic from time to time so long as he wasn't taken literally.

The two great Roman Catholic centers in *The American* are the very good Catholic death of Valentin and the more arguable Catholic conventualization of Claire de Cintré. For most Anglo-American readers, the represented conjunction of Papistry and dueling makes a disturbing combination and was probably meant to – but one religious audience will gloat, and another will wince. Valentin's seconds are of course Catholics. The remarks of M. Ledoux (he and Valentin "served together in the Pontifical Zouaves," and he is "the nephew of a distinguished Ultramontane bishop") are evidently designed to elicit a certain disdainful superiority on the part of the non-Catholic reader: "The doctor has condemned him. But he will die in the best sentiments. I sent last evening for the curé of the nearest French village, who spent an hour with him. The curé was quite satisfied." And again, "when a man has taken such excellent measures for his salvation as our dear friend did last evening, it seems almost a pity he should put it in peril again by returning to the world." The other second "was of quite another complexion," although presumably Catholic as well, "and appeared to regard his friend's theological unction as the sign of an inaccessibly superior mind." James is as ever fond of the word *unction* as applied to Catholics. The word *theological* is odd – perhaps *pastoral* was meant. The curé duly and dutifully enters the deathbed scene carrying "an object unknown to Newman, and covered with a white napkin," that object subsequently revealed as "his sacred vessel," which is not, for once, a secular sacred; not to Catholics, at least. The fascination of James' readers, the majority of them, with such superstitious superseded forms of behavior may be imagined. Perhaps we should also wonder more than we do about the indubitably existent American and English Catholic readers, then and now. Did they sometimes ask how it was that a sacrament divinely established and indispensable should to their fellow citizens (but not their coreligionists) seem so *outré* as almost automatically to kick off a round of literary *frissons*?

The convent business, or what might be called Hurricane Catherine-Veronica (Claire de Cintré's names as a religious) arrives in full force only in chapter 24 (of twenty-six), but it is preceded by many a little symptom of wind and wet. Christopher Newman has lived with "the pressure of necessity, even when it was as irritating as the haircloth shirt of the medieval monk." The Bellegarde hôtel "answered to Newman's conception of a convent." Claire de Cintré should go out more, Valentin thinks; she has "no right to bury herself alive," and we remember the convent Sepolte Vive in *Watch and Ward* as well as the cloistered habits of the Catholics in "De Grey: A Romance" and in *The Golden Bowl,* not to mention the tales of premature burial associated with the name of Edgar Allan Poe. " 'Madame de Cintré is buried alive,' cried Newman. . . . 'The door of the tomb is at this moment closing behind her.' " Already, at Valentin's funeral, she has a look "of monastic rigidity in her dress." She explains to Newman that her family is "like a religion. There's a curse upon the house" (again as in "De Grey: A Romance"). She will therefore go *"into* a convent" which is to say *"out* of the world" (emphases added). " 'Into a convent!' Newman repeated the words with the deepest dismay; it was as if she was going into a hospital." But " 'You don't understand,' she said. 'You have wrong ideas.' "

It can hardly be doubted that Catholic–Protestant differences of opinion will affect the interpretation of *The American* at key points. What, for example, if we assumed that both Protestant Newman and the bad Catholic Bellegardes were "wrong" and that the good liberal Catholic Valentin and Claire were somehow "right": A couple of pages after the conversational contretemps between Newman and his retreating love we find narrative authority (Henry James in his most diplomatic attire) trying on a set of attitudes that perhaps might do justice to, and even mollify, all parties. The attitudes are given as from Newman's point of view, but "Henry James" clearly stands outside them, as more sophisticated, more knowing (quite omniscient, in fact), more tolerant, and more amused:

> He [Newman] had never let the fact of her Catholicism trouble him; Catholicism to him was nothing but a name, and to express a mistrust of the form in which her religious feelings had moulded themselves would have seemed to him on his own part a rather pretentious affectation of Protestant zeal. If such superb white flowers as that could bloom in Catholic soil, the soil was not insalubrious. But it was one thing to be a Catholic, and another to turn nun – on your hands! There was something lugubriously comical in the way Newman's thoroughly contemporaneous optimism was confronted with this dusky old-world expedient.

There is also something quite comical in the way the text pivots on two meanings of the word *old,* one of them being the honorific "European," so that we then realize that "contemporaneous optimism" means something more like "American modernizing mindlessness."

Mrs. Bread from her very Low standpoint naturally confirms Newman's prejudices according to her own: "They tell me it's most dreadful, sir; of all the nuns in Christendom the Carmelites are the worst. You may say they are really not human, sir." But Mrs. Bread's concurrence with Newman's prejudices adds up to no mystically definitive interpretation. It adds up to one of two major kinds of simplistic interpretation, roughly the rigid Protestant and the rigid Catholic, with many nice shades in between. The fact of the two or more readings should be evident from Newman's casuistical analysis of the situation to the bad Bellegardes: "You don't want her to turn nun – you know more about the horrors of it than I do," which is not very tactful, any more than "Marrying a commercial person is better than that." Villainous Henri-Urbain responds, "I think my mother will tell you that she would rather her daughter should become Sœur Catherine than Mrs. Newman." I do not say *The American* should be read by his (not altogether typical) Catholic lights. What I say is that there is (obviously) more than a single reading possible for the convent idea and other aspects of Catholic melodrama in *The American,* that the possibility makes for a range of response, that the range of response will more or less depend on religious assumptions, and that all this multiplicity implies on the part of the author an awareness of religiously divergent readerships together with a willingness and ability to work them.

After so much lurid preparation as we have seen, the actual representation of matters in the chapel just this side the convent is somewhat anticlimactic. And quite anti-Catholic, too, at least in Newman's view, even though his presence at the chapel has been agreeably arranged by Mrs. Tristram's abbé friend: "You shall get into the chapel if the abbé is disfrocked for his share in it," she says, a remark suiting her sense of humor more than the probable reality and yet once more reminding us of the chasm in readings of *The American* between those who are of the faith and those who are not. Chapter 24 is thus for different kinds of readers another prime temptation to misread: Even young Madame de Bellegarde, another Catholic, says that "They say" the chanting is "like the lamentations of the damned," a comparison to which she is scarcely entitled. She more reasonably goes on, "Poor Claire – in a white shroud and a big brown cloak! . . . Well, she was always fond of long, loose things." Narrative authority meanwhile maintains a tone of generous reasonableness. The place is really not half bad, and mass goes forward as usual. "And yet *he knew*" (emphasis added), Newman, "the case was otherwise." Apparently the people are all Catholics, and it is this that seems to make the difference: "[T]hey [the Catholic visitors] were better off than he, for they at least shared the faith to which the others [the nuns] had sacrificed themselves." As for the priest and altarboys, "Newman watched their genuflections and gyrations with a grim, still enmity," pure Reformation paranoia and vilification, "they were mouthing and droning out their triumph. The priest's long, dismal intonings acted upon his nerves and deepened his wrath; there was something defiant in his unintelligible drawl; it seemed meant for Newman himself." It would appear that Newman is completely unfamiliar with the Latin mass and has no missal with facing-page translation into French or English, he who was so well equipped in the opening paragraph of *The American* with his Bäedeker. Now his apprehension of the Carmelite chant as a "confused, impersonal wail" goes on for half a page, confusing many a reader as well. But as young Madame de Bellegarde also remarks, "One must not ask too much of a gentleman who is in love with a cloistered nun."

There are minor points not to fail of. Two passages in the early version (both deleted in the final text) allude to this world as "here below," a common bit of Protestant jargon that I remember from my youth in a Presbyterian conventicle.[5] Newman's innocent remark about "my language," meaning the English language, is in the New York Edition preposterously amplified to read "our grand language – that of Shakespeare and Milton and Holy Writ," almost as if Henry James were still haranguing the young ladies at Bryn Mawr. In both early and final versions, the Catholicity of Noémie Nioche appears to be given in her reference to Newman's patron saint, a point clinched in the New York Edition by the change from "in the calendar" to "such as we all have" (the obverse phrase to "We are all of us Protestants" in the early book reviews). There is much, much more, but of a somewhat smaller interest – readers who like can ferret out further particulars, and readers who wish to give *The American* a completely irreligious reading are as ever free to do so. No one should go without the grandest card in the pack. It concerns Mlle. Noémie and comes from that decent dimwitted Anglo-Irish Catholic Lord Deepmere: "They [the bad Bellegardes] got up some story about its being for the Pope," Valentin's death, as caused by the sinful Noémie – she who also destroyed her worst painting by daubing on it the sign of the cross – "about the other man having said something against the Pope's morals. They always do that, you know. . . . But it was about *her* morals – *she* was the Pope." The most ardent Catholic reader must have smiled at James' little joke about the aspirant courtesan as Holy Father – such a welcome relief from the whore of Babylon! – while non- or even anti-Catholic readers must have laughed out loud at the same joke, and then, perhaps, on further thought, have laughed at themselves for laughing.

5. Attenuations: *The Reverberator* (1888)

Attenuations in the plural suggests (a) belatedness of thematic appearance; (b) lapse of time since previous appearance (1888 minus 1877 makes eleven years, approximately); (c) general indifference of textual tone; (d) absence of serious discussion on the part of protagonists presumptively concerned; (e) absence of determinate action. That is to say, in *The Reverberator* the question of Roman Catholic conversion once again enters a Jamesian text but not to be taken very seriously (not in the way of Christina Light and Rowland Mallett, *par exemple!*) and not, that we recall, ever to be decided. That we do not know, or much care, is perhaps what we most know. Our questions take the shape of soap-opera continuities: will Protestant Francie Dosson become a Catholic in order that she and Roman Catholic Gaston Probert may have a Roman Catholic wedding? or conversely? And if neither of them seems to prefer one course over the other, why should we bother? It is quite possible that, like the author, they will elect no course at all.

How delicately may a note be sounded and still be audible to the critical ear attentive? First mention of religious matters in *The Reverberator* is nearly lost in generalized designation: "His father, a Carolinian and a Catholic, was a Gallomaniac of the old American type," an expatriated Legitimist-Ultramontane in extremis. His French nationality appears to be acquired, or re-acquired (the sojourn of the race in "Carolina" is neither given in years nor explained); about his Catholicity we are vouchsafed even less information. Subsequent reference to old Mr. Probert continues in sweet indeterminacy: "He read a great deal, and very serious books; works about the origin of things – of man, of institutions, of speech, of religion." This might be good or bad, depending. One member of the family and her husband is felt by the rest to be preeminently " 'The thing,' " that curious entity defined, or not defined, as "the legitimist principle, the ancient faith and even, a little, the grand air." The "ancient faith" of this formulation must surely be the Catholic faith (but it is not such a clear reference as James' tag "the old persuasion," as in *The Princess Casamassima, Guy Domville,* "The Altar of the Dead," and "The Great Good Place"). Poor Mr. Probert seems older by the page, tired, bored, worn out, "gentler than before," so that he cares "less for everything (except indeed the true faith, to which he drew still closer)." None of this behavior is exhibited, only asserted.

Over against all of this eastward-and-backward-tending *The Reverberator* establishes a ridiculous yet sympathetic personage, Charles Waterlow, an Impressionist painter who is quite Brooklyn U.S.A. in all but art. Waterlow exudes a distinctly Protestant air, not at all in terms of what he believes – we are not told; it is possible he believes nothing whatsoever – but in the westward-and-forward-tending terms of what he will not put up with: "The French taste was in Waterlow's 'manner,' but it had not yet coloured his view of the relations of a young man of spirit with parents and *pastors*" (emphasis added) – "pastors," not "priests." As figuring the best of two worlds – French art, American truculence – Charles Waterlow is the deus ex machina who will liberate his friend Gaston Probert from excessive *familiality* seen as caused by or at least as consonant with excessive or misplaced (un-American) Catholicity. Like

Mr. Brooke of long-ago "Travelling Companions," Gaston Probert, the man without a country, legally American but spiritually French, must be redeemed to and by and for Americanism. "Well, *are* you a Frenchman? that's just the point isn't it?" It is Francina's golden question. And his reply, indirectly: "[H]e had no wish but to be of *her* nationality."

The main religious passage of *The Reverberator* represents ingenue Francie prattling with unscrupulous George Flack; all subtly it comprises what still apparently remains to our author of lingering direct interest in a former theme, the danger of Catholic conversion as a result of proselytizing or other undue influence (all Catholic influence being undue). The conversion theme remnants must be looked for with some perspicacity, however, so easily do they lose themselves in a satiric variety that cheerfully and equally includes not only M. Probert *père* and family – they are scarcely to be distinguished – but also suspicious ignorant bigoted anti-Catholic George Flack. The following passage would seem to turn on the ambiguous misuse by Flack and Francie of the word *introduce*:

> "And now, for instance, are they very bigoted? That's one of the things I should like to know."
>
> "Very bigoted?"
>
> "Ain't they tremendous Catholics – always talking about the Holy Father, and that sort of thing? I mean Mr. Probert, the old gentleman," Mr. Flack added. "And those ladies, and all the rest of them."
>
> "They are very religious," said Francie. "They are the most religious people I ever saw. They just adore the Holy Father. They know him personally quite well. They are always going down to Rome."
>
> "And do they mean to introduce you to him?"
>
> "How do you mean, to introduce me?"
>
> "Why, to make you a Catholic, to take you also down to Rome."
>
> "Oh, we are going to Rome for our *voyage de noces*!" said Francie, gaily. "Just for a peep."
>
> "And won't you have to have a Catholic marriage? They won't consent to a Protestant one."
>
> "We are going to have a lovely one, just like one that Mme. de Brécourt took me to see at the Madeleine."
>
> "And will it be at the Madeleine too?"
>
> "Yes, unless we have it at Notre Dame."
>
> "And how will your father and sister like that?"
>
> "Our having it at Notre Dame?"
>
> "Yes, or at the Madeleine. Your not having it at the American church."
>
> "Oh, Delia wants it at the best place," said Francie, simply. Then she added: "And you know father ain't much on religion."
>
> "Well now, that's what I call a genuine fact, the sort I was talking about."

When Francie is summoned by the Proberts to be punished for her sins, Delia Dosson and Mr. Dosson indulge vague anti-Catholic jokes suggesting, in a vague way, the impertinent presumptiousness of certain kinds of Catholic, the ignorant mindlessness of certain kinds of Protestant, and the exceeding unimportance of the whole religious question. *Our* interest, consequently, is in the trivialization of an old theme into something almost too ridiculous for words: " 'I know what it is,' said Delia. . . . 'They want to talk about religion. They have got the priests; there's some bishop, or perhaps some cardinal. They want to baptise you.' 'You'd better take a waterproof!' Francie's father called after her as she flitted away." So the Catholic conversion theme flits aways and seems to be no more. A little less than a decade later it will come to life again in forms so obscure that it is nearly impossible to make it out – nearly impossible, but not quite.

6. Supersubtlety One: *What Maisie Knew* (1897)

There are other supersubtleties – see Part Six – but *What Maisie Knew* in 1897 and *The Turn of the Screw* in the following year are specialized supersubtleties, long late lingering fragrances of the Catholic conversion thematic, coming down from as early as "Travelling Companions" way back in 1870. The term *supersubtlety* itself of course connotes the effect of a literary construction too subtle for its own good, as may be thought, too subtle, or almost, for detection. And it is just as obviously an adjunct of supersubtlety, regardless of what matters are being supersubtly insinuated, that it shall be obscured to the point of near invisibility for most readings and most readers, and that it shall be so without ruination of literary pleasure; other interpretations will more immediately abound, other interpretations will suffice, the supersubtlety will simply go unnoticed. Clearly it will somewhat depend on just who does the noticing. For a certain kind of reader, in quest, let us say, of certain things, and thereby likely to pounce on what another reader might gladly pass by, there may well be little facets of function and form asking to be moved a bit this way or that, disengaged from circumambient matter, however fascinating, brought into a brighter light.

There are two such Roman Catholic matters in *What Maisie Knew,* closely related: (1) the very conceivable Catholic conversion of Mrs. Wix, with the implication of a comparable conversion for Maisie herself, and (2) Sanctorum Communio, the communion of saints, the prayerful unitive connection of the living and the dead, whether in purgatory or in heaven. This distinctly Catholic teaching is also centered on Mrs. Wix and Maisie, but it includes, as the other Catholic emphasis does not, a number of other personages, all of them, as it happens, female. This communion of mothers and daughters is alternatively cause and effect of the religious conversion possibility. Both conversion and communion are narrational structures as well as thematized topics – form and content alike.

The possibility of religious conversion is asserted by the first of a series of passages in which Mrs. Wix and Maisie, at Boulogne-Sur-Mer, sit on a bench and gaze "at the great dome and the high gilt Virgin of the church," French Catholic of course, "that pleased them by its unlikeness to any place in which they had worshipped." It is apparently this contrast between the picturesque and its prior evangelical antithesis that at least partly explains why, in the church beneath the dome and the gilt Virgin, "Mrs. Wix confessed that for herself she had probably made a fatal mistake early in life in not being a Catholic. Her confession in its turn caused Maisie to wonder rather interestedly what degree of lateness it was that shut the door against an escape from such an error." What indeed Henry James' Mrs. Wix might "mean" can be opened up only in the logic of analysis. A person who makes the kind of remark we have just read must be a person who is considering now or in the future an act that she regrets not having performed in the past, for had she done so then she would have had in the meanwhile all the benefits that she now believes herself to be without. What I meant about the implied Catholic picturesque and the Protestant anti-picturesque is just this passage, much earlier (and in England): Sir Claude "had of late often come with her [Maisie] and Mrs. Wix to morning church, a place of worship of Mrs. Wix's own choosing, where there was nothing of that sort [as the paintings in the National Gallery of sacred subjects; as, by inference, the Catholic interior of the Boulogne church]; no haloes on heads." With her change of venue to France, Mrs. Wix seems to be having second thoughts about the church of her own choosing, second thoughts going as far back as her first choosing.

Mrs. Wix does not – obviously – "become a Catholic" in the course of *What Maisie Knew*. It is only that she seems to change course so as to head in that direction. She is mixed throughout – Catholic images laid over her Protestant bias, which is unusually (for James) vulgar, moralistic, and bibliolatrous. Still we should note the beginning of a process, cut short at novel's end, represented by the recurrent language of alteration or transcendence on the part of Mrs. Wix, and by the equally recurrent allusion to the Catholic church with its gilt Virgin atop: "This was a new tone – as new as Mrs. Wix's cap"; "She had begun in fact to show infinite variety"; "She [Maisie] watched beside Mrs. Wix the great golden Madonna" ("this prospect of statues shining in the blue"); "a certain greatness had now come to Mrs. Wix"; "her friend had risen to a level which might – till superseded at all events – pass almost for sublime"; "[T]hey gazed once more at their gilded Virgin; they sank once more upon their battered bench; they felt once more their distance from the

Regent's Park"; "an old woman and a little girl seated in deep silence on a battered old bench by the rampart of the *haute ville*"; "[S]he was a newer Mrs. Wix than ever, a Mrs. Wix high and great." The language of alteration or transcendence is perhaps best heard in dialogue; here Maisie speaks first to Sir Claude:

> "I'll go up to the old rampart."
> "The old rampart?"
> "I'll sit on that old bench where you see the gold Virgin."
> "The gold Virgin? . . . While I break with Mrs. Beale?"
> "While you break with Mrs. Beale."

Or Mrs. Beale herself addresses the other three:

> "We're representative, you know, of Mr. Farange and his former wife. This person [Mrs. Wix] represents mere illiterate presumption. We take our stand on the law."
> "Oh the law, the law!" Mrs. Wix superbly jeered.

And trots Maisie back to England, to what subsequent religious or other adventures we shall never learn. Clearly it is a fragile and indeterminate account, but those who have mastered the shades and shadows of James' religious discourse in its secularized concealments will find here much to ponder. It remains only to add that Mrs. Wix, repeatedly referred to in James' *Notebooks* as the frump, is as lower class as any Catholic-tending personage in the *œuvre* of Henry James; at the same time, she has, or is in the process of acquiring, a dignity superior not only to her previous self but also to the other personages of the novel, as well as to her social status (quite unimproved), almost certainly because of the literary Catholicizing to which she is treated.

"The ninth article of the Apostles' Creed declares the spiritual union that exists between the saints in heaven, the souls in purgatory, and the faithful living on earth. This union is one of grace and good works, and in recognition of this the faithful imitate, venerate, and pray for the intercession of the saints in heaven and for the souls in purgatory."[6] The relevant persons for *What Maisie Knew* are the Blessèd Virgin (heaven, assumed), Mrs. Wix (earth), Clara Matilda Wix (purgatory, let us suppose), conceivably Susan Ash (earth, "a lone orphan of a housemaid"), Maisie (earth), and even, again conceivably, "French Lisette," Maisie's doll (earth, artifact), a toy that stands for and in the little girl's mind really is one more young lady in narrative operation and spiritual need. The communion of saints metaphor appears to have been brought in as a counter to the idea of family, not only as impertinently defined by British laws and divorce courts but also as proved inefficacious by the lack of parental loyalty among the four or more most involved adults.

The *teaching* of the novel, as distinguished from its *metaphor*, is that people possess no natural feeling for their offspring. In certain cases, something else must fill the vacuum. Here that something else is the communion of saints metaphor, the Catholic doctrine aestheticized, secularized, and novelistically rendered.

Maisie's "little unspotted soul," "her little gravely-gazing soul," is given "even at first to understand much more than any little girl, however patient, had ever understood before," and chiefly what the unnumbered opening chapter has already made us privy to, that "the only link binding her to either parent was this lamentable fact of her being a ready vessel for bitterness." Maisie is literally shoved into the arms of Mrs. Wix, who, "Maisie felt the next day, would never let her go." Almost immediately (in chapter 4) we are told that Mrs. Wix "had been, with passion and anguish, a mother," and then we are told that Maisie is "deeply absorbed in the image of the little dead Clara Matilda, who, on a crossing in the Harrow Road, had been knocked down and crushed by the cruellest of hansoms." And then we are given Mrs. Wix's luscious remark "She's your little dead sister" – *is,* not *was; little dead,* not *dead little.* Finally we are given Maisie's response to Clara Matilda's "little mutilated life," so differently mutilated from her own: "Maisie, all in a tremor of curiosity and compassion, addressed from that moment a particular piety," the usual sacred secular of Henry James, "to the small accepted acquisition. Somehow she wasn't a real sister, but that only made her the more romantic," and the more religious too in the degree that she is the less biological. Most interestingly, Clara Matilda "was never to be spoken of in that character [of little dead sister] to any one else – least of all to Mrs. Farange, *who wouldn't care for her nor recognize the relationship"* (emphasis added). Clara Matilda, we are further informed, via Mrs. Wix, is "in heaven and yet, embarrassingly, also in Kensal Green, where they had been together to see her little huddled grave." (*Huddled* because made carelessly and in haste, given the circumstances of her death; *huddled* also because of the physical condition of the corpse.)

Maisie is as it were "[E]mbedded in Mrs. Wix's nature as her tooth had been socketed in her gum." Clara Matilda is also there embedded. She and Maisie are socketed together. Clara Matilda serving as intercessor, and if not quite in keeping with the very best Catholic interpretation then at least not according to occulted superstitiousness or mere authorial assertion, there ensues for Mrs. Wix and Maisie, and marginally for the others I have mentioned, a new relation transcending consanguinity. Even while "Parents had come to seem vague . . . Maisie's faith in Mrs. Wix for instance had suffered no lapse from the fact that all communication with her had temporarily dropped." In the next sentence Mrs. Wix is identified as "Clara Matilda's mamma." It is easy enough to see that in the course of the narrative Mrs. Wix is more and more Maisie's mamma – mammas is as mammas does. What additionally deserves attention, and seldom gets it, in connection with this process of virtual, not legal, adoption, is the spiritual efficacy of Clara Matilda, by Mrs. Wix remembered, by Maisie venerated. It is her earthly death and analogized resurrection in mutilated-by-society-even-by-her-own-parents Maisie Farange that drives the tale of gradual recovery and secular salvation. However aestheticized and psychologized, first by James, and then by the reader, the communion of saints is the life of the narrative shape. It leads to, as it leads from, the suggestion, however faintly drawn, of a Catholic connection among the lot of bereft women. The image that pulls the two themes together is the gold Virgin contemplated by Maisie and Mrs. Wix – and Clara Matilda? It is roughly what theologians call, in French, the *réversibilité des mérites*.

7. Supersubtlety Two: *The Turn of the Screw* (1898)

"It's *there* – the coward horror, there for the last time!"

As must be clear by now – and if it is not, it will become so in Part Six – the primary problem of hermeneutic criticism, especially when the matter at hand happens to be for one reason or another occluded (in which case we can hardly proceed without an unveiling), is that of overinterpretation versus underinterpretation, "reading in" versus "missing the point." God knows there are in certain works by Henry James plenty of points to miss and plenty of lacunae into which you may be sorely tempted to insert your own wishful thinkings. A secondary problem, extreme in the case of Henry James, although not unique with him, is the great spread in hermeneutical difficulty between such texts as seem all too transparent and such texts as appear to propose a defiant obstructionism, a real impossibility of interpretation, not to mention works that fall into the easy category until a more sensitive reading reassigns them to the opposite end of the scale.

The Turn of the Screw is notoriously open to a variety of interpretations. It is so, I should say, because of its very nature, as a textually and tonally coordinated bundle of multiple disjunctive allegories (using that word in a loose sense). By *multiple* I mean that there is more than a single strand of meaning to governess' tale. By *disjunctive* I mean that it is comparatively easy to isolate one strand from the other strands, reversing the compositional method of governess: "if I can put the whole thing at all together." Here we are of course to isolate the strand of conflicted religious allegiances, or, more exactly, the horror of Roman Catholic conversion from a Protestant point of view so excessive as to be psychopathic. But before attempting to isolate that theme, we need to remind ourselves that the text of this mad novella, however brilliant its prose style (which is decidedly not the usual prose style of Henry James), is simultaneously reliable (by definition; we have little or nothing else to go by) and unreliable (we are seldom sure about its credibility – but its authenticity, another matter, is perfect). Take, for example, governess retrospectively reporting one of her more amazing conversations with Mrs. Grose ("She" refers to Flora):

> ". . . She has taken the boat."
> ". . . Then where is it?"
> "Our not seeing it is the strongest of proofs. She has used it to go over, and then has managed to hide it."
> "All alone – that child?"
> "She is not alone, and at such times she's not a child: she's an old, old woman. . . ."
> "Laws!" cried my friend again; the chain of my logic was ever too much for her.

"Laws!" we too may cry, only to be refuted: "[W]e found the boat to be where I had supposed it." Or so governess says (writes). Take an earlier passage (chapter 7) where governess again reports herself reporting to Mrs. Grose:

> "No, no – there are depths, depths! The more I go over it, the more I see in it, and the more I see in it the more I fear. I don't know what I *don't* see – what I *don't* fear!"

That statement can obviously be taken in two quite different but equally suggestive senses, the colloquial and the literal. Governess continues:

> Mrs. Grose tried to keep up with me. "You mean you're afraid of seeing her [Miss Jessel] again?"
> "Oh no; that's nothing – now!" Then I explained. "It's of *not* seeing her."

In both passages, the curious logic of governess depends on negation and absence. When we come to realize what it is that she is most determined to negate, or deny, what, or who, according to *her,* is *not there,* we will have our chief clue to what *is* there.

What is unquestionably there, to begin with, is more than anything else authorial *tone* (of governess, not of Henry James). Whatever other virtues or vices governess is possessed of, governess has a *tone,* a fearful, irrational, inimical tone. Governess, we observe, is a parson's daughter, a daughter of the Church of England, that church which is, or was, a national Protestant communion legally "established" and virtually insep-arable from the "government" (so that Catholics must be excluded from public office). Politically, her Protestant paranoia differs from that of the anti-Catholic Americans represented in James' earlier conversion narratives – hers is more acute as she has more to lose; psychologically, it is the same. We may also remember *Watch and Ward* (against Catholic conversion) back in 1871, an odd novel and an odd title. That title is thrice echoed in *The Turn of the Screw*. Toward the end of chapter 8, governess says "I must watch" and two paragraphs later she says "I must just wait." In chapter 12 she reminds Mrs. Grose, and us, "I've watched and waited." In the final chapter, she describes her vision of Peter Quint outside the window as "the scoundrel fixed as if to watch and wait."[7]

Mrs. Grose and the children are also Church of England – but only governess is paranoid – and the nearby church is clearly an Anglican church. Peter Quint and Miss Jessel, who have the run of the house and the grounds, do not seem to frequent the Anglican church. For the others, two churchgoing (or nonchurchgoing) episodes (chapters 4, 14–15) stimulate narrative development. Governess' first close look at *that man* – who bears the name of the first Pope, a name rare in the texts of James, and who is looking in the window *at her* ("[I]t was as if I had been looking at him for years and had known him always") – occurs in the context of her desiring to attend with Mrs. Grose late service, their having missed morning service on account of the rain. It does not appear that either she or Mrs. Grose gets to church that day, but we have instead a quite spectacular reward, the glimpsing of Quint, the identification of Quint, and best of all at the end of chapter 5, the news that Quint has previously died. " 'Died?' I almost shrieked. . . . 'Yes. Mr. Quint is dead.' " Quint's being dead makes him in certain respects quite impossible but in other respects better than ever. A further conversation that night yields the following: " 'He was looking for little Miles.' . . . 'But how do you know?' 'I know, I know, I know!' My exultation grew." Consequently she, governess, will, as she says, accept, invite, surmount, "and absolutely save." She will do so "as an expiatory victim." Miles and Flora she will "fence about."

The second churchgoing episode is even more thrilling and its reward correspondingly even richer. Mrs. Grose and Flora enter the church together, Miles follows later, governess not at all. Since the first churchgoing episode, she has seen Miss Jessel, "My predecessor – the one who died." Miss Jessel, described by Douglas in the prologue as a "most respectable person," is described by governess as "a horror of horrors," motivated by "a kind of fury of intention" ("[T]o get hold of her," Flora, that is), dressed in "rather poor, almost shabby, mourning," and yet "But – yes – with extraordinary beauty." Returned to the house alone, and remembering her earlier sight of "the most horrible of women," governess discovers Miss Jessel "[s]eated at my own table" (i.e., altar) and writing! "She rose, not as if she had heard me, but with an indescribable grand melancholy of indifference and detachment, and, within a dozen feet of me, stood there as my vile predecessor. Dishonoured and tragic, she was all before me; but even as I fixed and, for memory secured it, the awful image passed away." Here is our first indication that governess is equally disturbed if Miss Jessel is *present* or if Miss Jessel is *absent*. The rest of the scene needs to be clarified in outline form. In sequential order:

1. governess speaks of Miss Jessel's "haggard beauty and her unutterable woe";
2. governess appears to believe that Miss Jessel looked at her as if to say "that her right to sit at my table was as good as mine to sit at hers";
3. but then, contrariwise, governess has "the extraordinary chill of a feeling that it was I who was the intruder";
4. governess addresses Miss Jessel "as a wild *protest*" (emphasis added), calling her "You terrible, miserable woman!"
5. governess then utters some other kind of sound, *not narrated;*
6. as a result, or at any rate consequently, "I had recovered myself and cleared the air." Clearing the air means: "There was nothing in the room the next minute but the sunshine and a sense that *I must stay*" (emphasis added).

These several behaviors are obviously in contradiction with one another and indeed quite mad as applied to a single dead woman, and perhaps mad still if applied to better than half (far better than half) of Christendom, but mad in a different way, historical mad rather than personal mad, ideological mad rather than petty personal pique mad. However "[d]ishonoured and tragic," Miss Jessel, whoever she is, must have done more and worse than sit writing at one's own writing table or even corrupt, sexually or otherwise, small children – indeed, the sexual interpretation of *The Turn of the Screw* has little to recommend it save the *ideés fixes* of twentieth-century interpreters. Most curiously of all, governess is able to cause Miss Jessel to disappear temporarily, to go out of existence.

Why must governess stay? Not so much because she is sex-starved or in love with the Master as because of progressive doctrine. Governess is *successor* (Protestant) to Miss Jessel who is *predecessor* (vile); Miss Jessel has gone, or ought to have gone, and she must not return. In chapter 16, governess adds, for the illumination of Mrs. Grose, that Miss Jessel said – Miss Jessel has of course "said" nothing at all – "That she suffers the torments——! . . . Of the lost. Of the damned. And that's why, to share them—— . . . She wants Flora." Occultly or otherwise, Miss Jessel means to possess and corrupt – that is, to convert and to keep converted – little innocent helpless souls. It is recognizably the view of Waymarsh in *The Ambassadors* (1903) with respect to "the recruiting interests of the Catholic Church. The Catholic Church . . . that was to say the enemy, the monster." Governess' suspicion of what little Miles may be or may have been up to is more delicately put. Owing to his silence about his "previous life," governess entertains an "absolute conviction of his secret precocity (or whatever I might call the poison of an influence that I dared but half to phrase)." James doesn't phrase it even half. After all, as she is always saying, governess knows what she knows. And how does she know it? By a "dark prodigy" (her words).

Surely what we have here is an exacerbated instance of the classic Jamesian Protestant–Catholic confrontation, point of view Protestant, verdict insane. In governess' third encounter with Peter Quint, the two are yet more reciprocal: "He knew me as well as I knew him." Confronted, like two hostile religious communions, "we faced each other in our common intensity. He was absolutely, on this occasion, a living, detestable dangerous presence" – how often that last word recurs! – but "there was nothing in me that didn't meet and measure him." Another thing governess knows is that she need only maintain her position (law of progress again): "[I]f I stood my ground a minute I should cease – for the time, at least – to have him to reckon with." For the time, at least – how pathetic, how delusory. As for the children, "They haven't been good – they've only been absent." Quint and Jessel want them (governess still and of course). Why? "For the love of all the evil that, *in those dreadful days,* the pair put into them. And to ply them with *that evil still,* to keep up the work of demons" (emphases added). Transubstantiation perhaps. " 'Laws!' said my friend under her breath." Governess goes on to point out how there had been a "bad time," "a worse even than this!" The historical dimension peers from behind the allegory. "But what can they now do?" ("Don't they do enough?") What they can chiefly do is exist. Their existence, in itself, is insufferable, and sanctimony will take it the rest of the way: "things terrible and unguessable and that sprang from dreadful passages of intercourse in the past." Maybe monasteries.

The diffuse paranoia that afflicts *The Turn of the Screw,* causing its prose so brilliantly to coruscate, may be more precisely read in terms of inclusion–exclusion among the dramatis personae. Not counting servants and villagers, there are seven personages. Master is in absentia, and that makes six. Two of the six are our Anglican observers. There remains a highly dubious quartet of two children plus two wicked *and* dead revenants who are held to have exercised undue, excessive, evil influence on the children in the past – even Mrs. Grose admits to this much – and who are held, by governess, to seek a continuation or restitution of that influence in the present and future. The threat to the children suggests – stands for and points to and represents? – the historical threat of return by the presumptively rejected and destroyed (by penal laws) pre-Reformation Roman Catholic English past, or even, more dreadful yet, recognition that that horrific past, the Catholic past of England, was by some fluke not altogether persecuted out of existence but had deviously managed to survive all this while in surreptitious and even tolerated minority fashion – in fact, Pius IX had reestablished the Roman Catholic hierarchy in England back in 1850, not far from the time of the tale. No more Vicars Apostolic after 1850, but in the time of Henry James Catholic England, what survived of it and what was now increasing through Irish immigration, was in the process of dispossessing itself of missionary status.

In "De Grey: A Romance" and in *The Golden Bowl,* James reveals a penchant for arranging his Roman Catholics in handy groups of four (conceivably corresponding to himself, his parents, and dreadful desirable William). In *The Turn of the Screw,* governess provocatively remarks to Mrs. Grose, "The four, depend on it, perpetually meet," meaning Flora and Miles, Miss Jessel and Peter Quint, and of course excluding themselves. Miles and Flora, governess goes on to say, are "steeped in their vision of the dead restored" (to *reform* is good, to *restore* is bad). In the following chapter (chapter 13), governess adds the apparently innocuous remark that "all roads lead to Rome," with further obscure, portentous sayings about "Forbidden ground," namely, "the question of the return of the dead in general and of whatever, in especial, might survive, in memory, of the friends the little children had lost," and whom governess is now so zealously and so hopelessly committed to exterminate in order to "save" her charges. Peter Quint and Miss Jessel bear in the mind of governess and through her in the mind of the reader, however subliminally, some vague general sense of being threateningly "Catholic," that is to say at once obsolete and totalitarian, "like Catholics" oppressive and devious and potentially tyrannical (the Inquisition), inciting to the same kind of fear in governess – it can hardly be *her* fault! – that the country parson's daughter associates with both pre- and post-Reformation Catholicity in England, of all places. In that same vague general sense, the children are, by her, and by us, through her, felt as likewise being, or of having been, or of being about to become "Catholic."

Linguistically and ineradicably embedded in the very notion of the Protestant Reformation are the central intentions "to protest" and "to reform" (*ecclesia reformata sed semper reformanda*). Protestantism is unavoidably a secondary dependent adversarial communion, a movement upon, or against, or away from, or apart from, a prior communion. One may therefore easily imagine the consternation in Protestant circles should the Church of Rome, according to its own best enemies, itself reform itself to the point where protest and reform were no longer profitable, an unlikely event. Using our imaginations even more boldly, let us ask what would happen to Protestant Reformism if the Catholic Church should cease to exist, or, stretching our imaginations even more boldly, if it could be somehow felt, and even *proved,* that it never did exist? Where would Protestantism be then?

It would be at Bly, with governess in her plight, particularly at those junctures when the reality of Miss Jessel is most fiercely challenged, when governess feels that if Miss Jessel does not exist then neither does she, governess, exist. In chapter 20 governess, like the apostles, sees Miss Jessel standing "on the opposite bank" (John 21). Her elation ("my thrill of joy at having brought on a proof!") is evident; her reasons are tolerably clear: "She was there, and I was justified; she was there, and I was neither cruel nor mad." *How* Miss Jessel is there is equally gratifying: She is there as a "pale and ravenous demon." And Miss Jessel's imputed intention further proves governess' premise: "[T]here was not, in all the long reach of her desire, an inch of evil that fell short." She is "the hideous plain presence," that word again. She ought not to be there. She ought not to be. She ought to have died and to have stayed dead. There can be only one governess. Yet there Miss Jessel is, the vile predecessor, mighty strong language, we feel, applied to an ex-governess but apt enough for nearly nineteen centuries of Christ-betrayal on the part of the Holy See. By another turn of the screw, Mrs. Grose and Flora do not perceive Miss Jessel, and governess' position begins to crumble: "I felt – I saw – my livid predecessor press, from *her* position, on my defeat" (emphasis added). Miss Jessel's position is, in brief, *presence* and *absence* combined and conflated. She is "there" and she is "not there." She has died and she lives. Her survival or her return may not be tolerated. Mrs. Grose, not desiring to go mad with governess, neatly solves the problem. She says to Flora: "She isn't there, little lady, and nobody's there – and you never see nothing, my sweet! How can poor Miss Jessel – when poor Miss Jessel's dead and buried?" At least some people, many of them in England, had thought she was dead and buried. It was all they ever wanted. ("It's all a mere mistake and a worry and a joke – and we'll go home as fast as we can!") Henry James devotees will recall with pleasure of irony that the mad Irishman from New York now frequenting the higher circles of English life and letters first had the germ of what became *The Turn of the Screw* from the Archbishop of Canterbury himself.

In view of James' attempts to cover up the conversion of Christina Light in *Roderick Hudson,* thereby covering up his early addiction to the tale of Catholic conversion, I find wonderfully intriguing his quite otherwise inexplicable evasiveness about *The Turn of the Screw* – what he seems to say, over and over, is that *The Turn of the Screw* has neither intention nor meaning. James' first *Notebooks* entry (12 January 1895) is vague but not yet evasive (no one else was supposed to read it), related in tone and movement to that excessive fear of Catholic proselytizing found in the early religious book reviews and in the early conversion narratives: "[S]o that the children may destroy themselves, lose themselves by responding, by getting into their power. So long as the children are kept from them, they are not lost; but they try and try and try, these evil presences, to get hold of them. *It is a question of the children 'coming over to where they are' "* (emphasis added).

Evasiveness proper begins three years later, in 1898, during and after publication. The scandalous tale was still in the process of serialization when James wrote to A. C. Benson, son of the Archbishop, on 11 March 1898, explaining that it was from his father he had had the germ. "I wrought it into a fantastic fiction," he writes in his best butter-wouldn't-melt-in-your-mouth fashion. Later the same year, questions apparently having been asked, James put his heart into his obfuscations; to Edmund Gosse on 12 October 1898, "The difficulty, the problem was of course to add, organically, the element of beauty to a thing so foully ugly," which is in effect to say nothing while hinting a great deal; on 21 October 1898 to Dr. Louis Waldstein, "[A]s regards a presentation of things so fantastic as in that wanton little Tale, I can only rather blush to see real substance read into them," as blush he well might though not for the reason alleged; on 9 December 1898 to H. G. Wells, "[T]he thing is essentially a pot-boiler and a *jeu d'esprit";* on 19 December 1898 to Frederic W. H. Myers, "The *T. of the S.* is a very mechanical matter, I honestly think – an inferior, a merely *pictorial,* subject and rather a shameless pot-boiler." What is common to all these statements is the consistent denial that *The Turn of the Screw* was written with any specific purpose in mind other than simply to *be* written, coupled with the strange assertion that it possesses no discernible content.

The treatment of the *T. of the S.* in the preface to volume 12 of the New York Edition is evasive as ever but more talky: "I find here a perfect example of an exercise for the imagination unassisted, unassociated – playing the game, making the score, in the phrase of our sporting day, off its own bat." It isn't, that is to say, "about" anything, which perhaps helps explain James' idle, irrelevant maunderings about ghost stories, fairy tales, psychical research. Among the many gems of Jamesian subterfuge, a few brief selections must suffice: "[T]his perfectly independent and irresponsible little fiction rejoices, beyond any rival on a like ground, in a conscious provision of prompt retort to the sharpest question that may be addressed to it," "a piece of ingenuity pure and simple, of cold artistic calculation, an *amusette* to catch those not easily caught," "Otherwise expressed, the study is of a conceived 'tone,' the tone of suspected and felt trouble, of an inordinate and incalculable sort – the tone of tragic, yet of exquisite mystification," "I cast my lot with pure romance." The most famous and most frequently quoted statement is of course that which claims that the tale presents only blanks for the reader to fill in, so that, whatever the meaning imputed, it is all the reader's fault. Thus, by the cunning contrivance of Henry James, I stand convicted – but of what it might not be easy to say.

Postscript. "She was my sister's governess," the outside narrator has Douglas say in the prologue. "She was the most agreeable woman I've ever known in her position; she would have been worthy of any whatever. It was long ago, and this episode was long before." Between "this episode" (*The Turn of the Screw* proper) and the much later date of Douglas' acquaintance with her, governess has obviously rid herself of whatever threatening fear and pain it was that was turning her screw – and she has written an obscure allegorical account of that fear and pain, presumably therapeutic. How else her cure may have proceeded is a matter of conjecture, but aside from the writing itself the number of ways by which she might have recovered her sanity is limited to not more than a couple, as may be imagined.

PART FOUR

Pas de quatre

1. Catholicity Neat: "Gabrielle de Bergerac" (1869)

"Catholicity Neat" denotes a literary work representing Roman Catholicity undiluted either by represented circumambient contextual Protestant-secular matter or personages or significant authorial interference, be it only through manipulations of style and tone (irony, sarcasm, horrendous exaggeration, deliberate contradiction). "De Grey: A Romance" and *Guy Domville,* although I have chosen to take them in a different category, are other examples of the type. *The Golden Bowl* is or is not, depending on what you think of the role played by the Assingham couple in isolating and defining the curious Catholicity of the four major personages. "The Altar of the Dead" is probably not, because of Henry James' eccentric albeit "picturesque" misrepresentations of the Catholic world ostensibly delineated. James' first known extant published bit of fiction, "A Tragedy of Error" (1865), is imaginably another such instance of Catholicity Neat if only in the most marginal and peculiar way. All its personages are French. *If* they are by the reader presumed to be Catholic, they may be so somewhat along the lines suggested by James' essay on Balzac a decade later: "A magnificent action with him is not an action which is remarkable for its high motive, but an action with a great force of will or of desire behind it . . . a magnificent lie, a magnificent murder, or a magnificent adultery." James' first tale boasts all three magnificences.

"Gabrielle de Bergerac" is of course James' only fictional treatment of the *ancien régime.* Seen as it usually is from the standpoint of political history, the tale features conflict and change, old versus new, past versus future, nobility versus the people, obsolescent autocracy versus the realism of modernity, all in transit through the funnel of the French Revo-

102

lution, culminating in the Terror, and in somewhat distant relation to the American Revolution as well. Seen from the religious standpoint, the tale appears in a somewhat different light – conflict and change recede. Everyone in "Gabrielle de Bergerac" is Roman Catholic, and as we know from outside "Gabrielle de Bergerac" the Roman Catholic church in France did survive the French Revolution, even if certain personages in this particular tale did not. For there, to the reader of 1869, it was. And, indeed, there it is still.

Catholicity Neat is not necessarily Christian. You can be a very good Catholic without being Christian at all, and such would appear to be the spiritual condition of more than one personage here. But at a minimum Catholicity Neat gives you local color of a reliable if modest sort. People say *"nom de Dieu!"* and "Holy Virgin!" and are thus defined for the reader as not us (of Protestant race), while narrative voice inserts from time to time such favorite words as *sacred* and *consecrate*. Prayer is a frequent topic, even if it be only a flamboyant emotional explosion – "For the love of God, Gabrielle," says her impious brother, "or the fear of the Devil, speak so that a sickened, maddened Christian can understand you!" On other occasions, prayer has a simple dignity: "I have the misfortune to have no mother [for marital advice]. I can only pray God." Or, in response to physical fear, "She buried her face in her hands, like one muttering a rapid prayer." Or, in response to physical love, "It is more than enough to watch you and pray for you and worship you in silence." There is predictably a parish church and an abbé (alluded to) and a curé "who had apparently just discharged the last offices of the Church" to a dying peasant.

As in the early religious reviews and in the fictions of Roman Catholic *ménage* (to be dealt with in Part Five), it is strongly implied that a Catholic group, however constituted, has as the price of its cohesion a corresponding alienation from the world. The tone of "Gabrielle de Bergerac" will occasionally remind the sensitive reader of "De Grey: A Romance" or even of *The Golden Bowl:* "We gave no entertainments, and passed the whole year in the country . . . a simple, somnolent sort of life. . . . But the little town is there, and the bridge on the river, and the church where I was christened." There is also the reciprocal desire to break out in the direction of the world. "She had a passion for the world" is one aspect of the Baronne, as, in a slightly different sense, young Henry James had said of Madame Swetchine. Hero Coquelin, consequently, is of paramount importance: "Marked as he was . . . with the genuine plebeian stamp, he opened a way for the girl's fancy into a vague, unknown world." The "bad" suitor tells Gabrielle: "You are not made for solitude . . . you are not made to be buried in a dingy old château. . . . You are made for the world." The world of Paris is what Gabrielle and Coquelin achieve but at an unfortunate moment: "They both went to the scaffold among the Girondists."

Old M. de Bergerac, as hitherto hinted, is an indifferent Christian – he is barely civilized. The other personages are distinctly better, though scarcely saints. Their education, social tone, and general assumptions are according to the best Roman Catholic trappings, and the secrets of their inmost souls go entirely unexamined. Coquelin knows Latin and Greek, thus qualifying as a tutor: "[H]e had been put to study with the Jesuits," but to his eternal credit "he had incurred their displeasure by a foolish breach of discipline, and had been turned out into the world. Here he had endeavoured to make capital out of his excellent education." In various moods, none of them excessively devout, he imagines himself as he might have been in the old days, "a trembling, groaning, fasting monk, moaning my soul away in the ecstacies of faith" or as "having gone into the Church. If I hadn't died from an overdose of inanition, very likely I might have lived to be a cardinal." Coquelin, who has served in the American Revolution, is Americanized and modern. But Catholic nonetheless.

Gabrielle, his aristocratic mate, has for her part been perpetually threatened with failure to marry "in the world" so that "nothing would be left for her but to withdraw from it, and to pledge her virgin faith to the chilly sanctity of a cloister." ("I shall never marry; I shall go into religion," she remarks on a gray day.) Already she had, before Coquelin, a predisposition of that sort: "Once a year she spent six weeks with certain ladies of the Visitation, in whose convent she had received her education, and of whom she continued to be very fond." Even though *The Portrait of a Lady* is thirteen years in the unforeseeable future, it is warm-up time for Pansy and Gilbert Osmond: "Several of them are excellent women, charming women. They read, they educate young girls, they visit the poor – ." But despite an occasionally querulous tone, as some of these quotations attest, "Gabrielle de Bergerac" is on the whole a sterling example of Catholicity Neat, the old persuasion rendered on its own terms and yet curiously unthreatening – even, perhaps, reassuring. We can hardly fail of the observation that all this, enchanting as it may be, was some place else, and a long time ago.

2. Secularizing Catholicity: "The Altar of the Dead" (1895)

Guy Domville had concerned itself with one group of English Catholics, the rural gentry, often referred to as – James must have relished the term – Old Catholics. In "The Altar of the Dead" he shifts attention to the more numerous and more important (from the standpoint of nineteenth- and twentieth-century church history) mass of English Catholics, the middle-class and working-class industrial and urban poor. The proletarian strength of modern English Catholicity is only hinted in the unnamed heroine's labor as a literary hack, "writing under a designation that she never told him in magazines that he never saw," but the urban sociology is clear enough in her residence and in the general locale of the church that contains the altar of the dead. There is also a class difference between George Stransom, a marginal Catholic if Catholic he be, and the unnamed woman, so subtly stated as almost to escape our notice in such observations, made entirely in passing, as this: "Her debt, however, of course, was much greater than his, because while she had only given him a worshipper he had given her a magnificent temple." Half the irony of that statement resides in the words *however, of course,* and *only;* the other half in the alleged superiority of a building to a person. The moral difference is that between such a phrase as "the warm centre," which seems to refer less to the church than to the woman, and such a phrase as "His own life," Stransom's, with "its central hollow."

Late-twentieth-century readers are apt to miss or misinterpret the significance of the setting in "The Altar of the Dead." Especially the word *suburb* does not connote a secluded refuge of the rich but nearly the opposite: "She lived, as she said, in a mere slum" ("her dim suburban world").[1] Her ascription may be exaggerated, but it points to the metropolitan differentiations that in turn point to the other differentiations structuring the tale: "As much as himself she knew the world of London, but from an undiscussed instinct of privacy they haunted the region not mapped on the social chart. . . . For long ages he never knew her name, anymore than she had ever pronounced his own." She lives near the church, and he does not. She and the church are located in a "suburb" not far from the cemetery where Stransom's fiancée is buried. It is in a "desert" where no cabs intrude, not because there are no people but because the people have no money for cabs, "the great [big, not wonderful] grey suburb . . . one of those tracts of London which are less gloomy by night than by day" – at night there are lamps – largely inhabited by the urban poor and in which we appropriately find the "temple of the old persuasion," the Catholic church with the mortar between its bricks still wet, the building in winter "unwarmed." James' *Notebooks* entry shows him reluctantly driven to the idea of a *Catholic* church, he, too, having his need for certain particular items of setting, a side-chapel with an altar broad and deep enough to sustain an array of multiplied and multiplying candles. Finding the Catholic church, James almost inevitably found it in a London suburb, among the metropolitan Catholic poor, most of them, no doubt, of Irish extraction.

In this church, Stransom descries, a little like Strether descrying Madame de Vionnet in the glamorous gloom of Notre Dame, "the only worshipper . . . a woman . . . who had sunk deep into prayer. He wished he could sink, like her." Up to this point, Stransom's religion of the dead has been mental only and entirely secular, as James first conceived it in the *Notebooks*. Now Stransom begins to realize, as James evidently had, that his merely intellectualized image had a "great original type, set up in a myriad temples, of the unapproachable shrine," that is to say, in plain English, a Christian and specifically a Catholic altar. Stransom asks himself "if he shouldn't find his real comfort in some *material* act, some *outward* worship" (emphases added). The possibility of Catholic conversion is carefully excluded – as it is excluded from virtually all James performances except those I have called the narratives of Catholic conversion – and, in the meantime, "the black-robed lady continued prostrate," James' pet term for Catholic females at their devotions.

For "The Altar of the Dead," the word *liberal*, with all its various and for the most part favorable significations in the writings of earlier James, seems mainly to connote the dispensing of money along with attitudes of condescension adjunctive to such largesse. Chapter 1 (of nine) ends with word play on *poor* and *liberal*, each word to be taken at least doubly in a material and in an inward sense: "The poorest could build such temples of the spirit – could make them blaze with candles and smoke with incense, make them flush with pictures and flowers. The cost, in the common phrase, of keeping them up fell entirely on the liberal heart." Liberal Stransom works out his liberal deal: "Even for a person so unaffiliated the thing would be a matter of arrangement." There follows a year of negotiation – even more than "The Beast in the Jungle," which it so much resembles in style and tone and thematics but not in religious reference, "The Altar of the Dead" largely consists of time passing while little or nothing happens – with "bland ecclesiastics," including the bishop; in general, there are "concessions in return for indulgences" (not in the ecclesial sense of the term); in conclusion, "the attitude of those whom it concerned became liberal in response to liberality. The altar and the small chapel that enclosed it, consecrated to an ostensible and customary [i.e., Roman Catholic] worship, were to be splendidly maintained," and, it must be presumed, the ostensible and customary worship neither interrupted nor desecrated. Readers will probably differ on how far they think the bishop is stretching a point. The bishop is of course no bishop at all but a mere *ficelle*.

Thus at length George Stransom, even if himself no Catholic and no convert either in the usual acceptation of such terms, enters the one holy catholic and apostolic church by the side door, as you might say, there, if not earlier, to be met head on by the Lord's Prayer and its unmitigated insistence on forgiveness. Stransom is bent on not forgiving Acton Hague, a former colleague, dead since chapter 2, and a powerful public personage with a distinctly English Catholic name (that of Lord Acton, the famous historian, 1834–1902); Acton Hague was also the lover of the nameless lady in black. Acton Hague has plainly maltreated them both, but the lady forgives, as Stransom does not (though he says he does); then she can hardly forgive Stransom his nonforgiveness. Stransom is finally admitted to her house and finds it a veritable domestic shrine to the memory of Acton Hague, for whom she then wants a candle on Stransom's ecclesiastical altar. He refuses. They part. More time passes in vain, except as "Acton Hague was between them, that was the essence of the matter. . . . Stransom, even while he wanted to banish him, had the strangest sense of desiring a satisfaction that could come only from having accepted him."

In the ninth and final chapter, "The Altar of the Dead" is increasingly (more than in chapters 1 through 8, even) secularized – psychologized and aestheticized. First, the altar and its candles are subjectivized, the prose becoming more resplendent as it becomes more solipsistic and unaffiliated:

> His altar moreover had ceased to exist; his chapel, in his dreams, was a great dark cavern. All the lights had gone out – all his Dead had died again. He couldn't exactly see at first how it had been in the power of his late companion to extinguish them, since it was neither for her nor by her that they had been called into being. Then he understood that it was essentially in his own soul the revival had taken place, and that in the air of this soul they were now unable to breathe. The candles might mechanically burn, but each of them had lost its lustre. The church had become a void; it was his presence, her presence, their common presence, that had made the indispensable medium.

Second, the altar and its candles are deprived of whatever sacred meaning they may still have after that romantic-love reduction and further restricted to a relevance altogether of this world, and now the prose grows more resplendent still and the content still more banal – transcendence defers to infantility:

> He lost himself in the large lustre, which was more and more what he had from the first wished it to be – as dazzling as the vision of heaven in the mind of a child. He wandered in the fields of light; he passed, among the tall tapers, from tier to tier, from fire to fire, from name to name, from the white intensity of one clear emblem, of one saved

soul [!], to another. It was in the quiet sense of having saved his souls that his deep, strange instinct rejoiced. This was no *dim theological rescue, no boon of a contingent world;* they were saved better than faith or works could save them, saved for the warm world they had shrunk from dying to, for actuality, for continuity, for the certainty of human remembrance. (emphasis added)

(James has his contingencies backward.) Third, the altar and its candles are even further aestheticized, and, so, secularized – but all these processes amount to a process of secularization that some readers may feel sails close to blasphemy but is probably no more than ineptitude in the handling of "dim theological" concepts; now it is as if the candles were elements in a do-it-yourself sculpture of multiple and movable parts:

> Symmetry was harmony, and the idea of harmony began to haunt him; he said to himself that harmony was of course everything. He took, in fancy, his composition to pieces, redistributing it into other lines, making other juxtapositions and contrasts. He shifted this and that candle, he made the spaces different. . . . There were subtle and complex relations, a scheme of cross-reference. . . .

Finally, after further bursts of descriptive and narrative virtuosity on James' part, George Stransom, ailing long since, and older by the sentence, has a vision of his long-dead fiancée: "She smiled at him from the glory of heaven," whereupon, psychologically if not actually (or only from the pen of Henry James), descending like the dove of the Comforter alight on the head of Jesus at the Jordan, "the descent of Mary Antrim opened his spirit with a great compunctious throb for the descent of Acton Hague." These descents seem to mean, among other things hard to make out, a return, or a reversal in time, plus a conciliating conflation of memories. She, Acton Hague's loyal lover, has for her part been the beneficiary of a comparable narrational, if not exactly substantiated, supernatural beneficence: "This afternoon, by a miracle, the sweetest of miracles, the sense of our difference left me. . . . It's my confession – there it is." Her confession is in fact James' denouement and clôture. Still muttering about candles, George Stransom droops and dies. (He can scarcely be said to have left this world in God's friendship.) Or so we must infer from a final sentence that looks back to the conclusion of Edgar Allan Poe's *Narrative of A. Gordon Pym* (1838) and forward to the purported extinction, by governess, of little Miles in the final sentence of *The Turn of the Screw:* "But alone with him in the dusky church a great dread was on her of what might still happen, for his face had the whiteness of death."

In their edition of James' *Notebooks,* F. O. Matthiessen and Kenneth B. Murdock observe, "It is puzzling . . . [that] he thinks of it as so slight and so empty [James had characterized his "conceit" as "a little fancy which doesn't hold a great deal"]. . . . Certainly his inclusion of it as a title-story to a volume in the New York Edition, and his preface to it, suggest no dissatisfaction, and it has often been counted among the best of his tales."[2] Not knowing about the curious relations between Henry James and Constance Fenimore Woolson, Matthiessen and Murdock were unable to get the significance of the address where the *Notebooks* entry was made, Woolson's former address at Oxford. Leon Edel, who "discovered" Fenimore, has supplied the missing link.

But there must be more than biographical and psychological reasons for James' divided mind about "The Altar of the Dead," and I think the explanation may be simply that, on the one hand, the central emphasis of the story, the anguish over modern disrespect for the dead, was in real life James' own feeling, as we find it expressed in a variety of contexts, mostly personal letters (but perhaps best in the New York Edition preface) from 1890 to 1909, and that, on the other hand, James may have been aware that he had failed to "do" anything very nearly resembling a Catholic view of death. In other words, James tried in "The Altar of the Dead" to write as an insider and an outsider both, and the contradiction tended to tear the tale in two. Certainly Matthiessen and Murdock are right in their impression that it has often been counted as among the best of James' tales, but not, I suspect, without certain reservations on the part of Catholic and other seriously Christian readers, who can hardly be expected to overlook its inadequacies and even its impertinences vis-à-vis the religious faith allegedly represented. For all his skill in the depiction of externals, and for all his liberal and charitable tolerance, James was by his own conviction too remote from that faith to figure it convincingly at the point where it most called for figuration, at the point where human fear and divine revelation collide and hopefully coalesce.

That is perhaps too scrupulous a judgment. James is not Dante, and "The Altar of the Dead" is not the *Paradiso*. James gets by well enough in his own way, chiefly by ranges of style, as, for example, "Stransom had entered that dark defile of our earthly descent in which some one dies every day. It was only yesterday that Kate Creston had flashed out her white fire" over against "There were hours at which he almost caught himself wishing that certain friends of his would now die, that he might establish with them in this manner a connection more charming than, as it happened, it was possible to enjoy with them in life." Whatever else, the prose of Henry James may always be listened to.

3. Protestantizing Catholicity:
"The Great Good Place" (1900)

The narrative line of "The Great Good Place" is as simple as the simplicity the tale worships. "George Dane had waked up to a bright

new day" that is neither bright nor new, and then he falls asleep again
and dreams himself into, and at, and finally home again from the great
good place, "all right" once more. There are a couple of dozen analogues
of the place itself, including "a happy land – far, far away!", "the new
consciousness," a bath, a brotherhood (normally with a capital B), a convent, a villa, Italy, a monastery, death, the world redeemed, the English
countryside, a country-house, a hotel, a club, a garden, a temple, a silver
bowl, a German or other water-cure, "a poem of Goethe, a dialogue of
Plato, a symphony of Beethoven," liberty-hall, a convalescent home, a
kindergarten, a mother's breast, a Swiss pension, a respite from armed
conflict: "[T]hey wondered proportionately whether to return to the front
when their hour should sharply strike would be the end of the dream."
The front is the world, modern life, especially if you are a celebrity. But
none of these analogues of the great good place is absolute or binding,
and there is in the dream desultory talk of their inadequacy: "Why should
we call it names?"; "we may really call it, for that matter, anything in
the world [!] we like"; "It simply stands quiet . . . and let's us call it
names?" It certainly seems to.

The chief analogue is that of a Roman Catholic place of spiritual retreat
redesigned for Protestant use – the form and its psychological effects are
retained and the religious content is deleted. Exactly as in his early reviews of religious books, James (or his protagonist) in the dream designates himself gregariously as "we of the great Protestant peoples." What
we great ones lack, he says, is what "they" (Catholics) have, and so we
must naturally have it too in our own inimitable way. George Dane more
or less knowledgeably refers to "the break that lucky Catholics have always been able to make, that they are still, with their innumerable religious houses, able to make, by going into 'retreat.' . . . The place, the
time, the way were, for those of the old persuasion" (James' fond but
mildly condescending term for Roman Catholicism, as also in *The Princess Casamassima, Guy Domville,* and "The Altar of the Dead") "always
there – are indeed practically there for them as much as ever. They can
always get off – the blessed houses receive."[3]

Now the deprived Protestants, wistful and even a trifle envious, need
it (retreat) more than they (Catholics) do, "still more congested with
mere quantity and prostituted, through our 'enterprise,' to mere profan-
ity," that is to say, it is Protestants rather than Catholics who are the
poor hounded (rich and famous) personages of the modern world. Their
retreat must, of course, be appropriately secularized: "I don't speak of
the pious exercises; I speak only of the material simplification." James'
Protestant version of a religious retreat resembles a bland vacation,
perhaps under continuous hypnosis or continuous intoxication. It is the
architecture, rather than the intention, that recalls "some great abode of

an Order, some mild Monte Cassino, some Grande Chartreuse more accessible," without demands, theological or other. And there are no women or children either, nothing but Brothers, adult males, important ones, in flight from being too much sought after according to their just deserts.

"The Great Good Place" is a dream vision, a fairy tale, a ghost story in which the protagonist and his young double (to all intents and purposes a secretary for the day) seem to exchange identities, somewhat along the lines of *The Sense of the Past,* but more briefly, more simply. "What he had yearned for was to *be* you," says the Brother, and so George Dane responds, "It meant that he should live with my life, and think with my brain, and write with my hand, and speak with my voice. It meant, above all, that I should get off." James' vicarious atonement is altogether of the worldly sort, not in the least salvific, and even the exchange of identities is one-sided: " 'And who were you?' the Brother continued. 'Nobody. That was the fun.' " The fun of "The Great Good Place" is precisely its satiric absences and negations. To the question "What *was* the general charm?" the answer is immediate, abundant, and vague: "[S]uch an abyss of negatives, such an absence of everything." The golden key to it all "was simply the cancelled list. Slowly and blissfully he read into the general wealth of his comfort all the particular absences of which it was composed. One by one he touched, as it were, all the things it was such rapture to be without."

"The Great Good Place" is one of Henry James' periodic anathematizings of worldliness, but unlike *Guy Domville* it suggests no involvement with any serious alternative to worldliness, no taking of orders, for example, only an intermission from "the world [which] was everywhere, without and within, and, with the great staring egotism of its health and strength, was not to be trusted for tact or delicacy." Worldliness is too much social life, mail, newspapers, publicity, advertising, visitors, parties, interviews – invasions of privacy rather than temptations to idolatry. The tone is from time to time mildly embattled. George Dane refers to his young double as "My substitute in the world," which is Civil War talk. Tone also veers back and forth between one world and another. Before the intervention of the young man, Dane says he seemed "to have lost possession of my soul," which is satanic or psychiatric (but also New Testament) talk. Later, "he had got his soul again," not from the Devil but from "the hubbub of the world." Back there, in the world, "in its place, *was* life – with all its rage." And because "life" is so ambivalent – desired yet often too much of a good thing – "death" is correspondingly ambivalent. When George Dane first wakes, at the beginning of the narrative, the trouble is that "Nothing had passed while he slept – everything had stayed; nothing, that he could yet feel, had died – many things had been born." Death is oblivion, but only temporary and selective; death as the reduction of a list of chores is consequently an object of playful desire:

> "Ah, don't speak as if we were dead!" Dane laughed.
> "I shan't mind death if it's like this," his friend replied.

It was life itself that was death by overplussage. Dane says he feared that the "wild waters would close over me, and I should drop straight to the bottom where the vanquished dead lie," which sounds like Dante but is almost its antithesis.

It is not the Christian Hell James has in mind but the *fin de siècle,* as clarified by a friendly and helpful Brother, "The wild waters, you mean, of our horrible time." There *is* no other time (secular atheist talk), we are assured, " 'any other is only a dream. We really know none but our own.' 'No, thank God – that's enough.' " These are not, obviously, theological but satiric emphases, literary and aesthetic positions. And almost needless to add, the imputed God of "The Great Good Place" is the Perfect Artist of a recognizably Jamesian type. The whole show is, Dane says, "so exquisitely personal!" ("Precisely – it rests, like all good things, on experience.") God is the maker of the dream, and God is by the same token one's very own self: "[T]he wise mind was everywhere – the whole thing, infallibly, centred, at the core, in a consciousness. And what a consciousness it had been, Dane thought, a consciousness how like his own!" God is thus made in man's image, yet the adverb *infallibly,* so cunningly included in that definition of "God," is Roman Catholic talk. "The Great Good Place" goes by the good old argument that anything made implies a maker, in this case a strikingly eclectic maker: "It had been born somehow and somewhere – it had had to insist on being – the blessed conception." But the conception is not by any stretch of the imagination the infant Christ in his manger, much less his mother, nor even the Holy Spirit hovering. Neither does "The Great Good Place" permit any possibility of the Real Presence. We are specifically warned off: "There was no daily miracle."

4. Satirizing Secularity: "The Birthplace" (1903)

Satire in "The Birthplace" is directed against bardolatry, Shakespeare worship, idolatry in general, and at bottom the ambivalent worship of fiction and even of lies:

> "Don't They want then *any* truth? – none even for the mere look of it?"
> "The look of it," said Morris Gedge, "is what I give!"

"They" (capitalized) is alternatively the trustees and the gullible public. The trustees culminate in Mr. Grant-Jackson, who has a "broad, well-fitted back, the back of a banker and a patriot." The Birthplace (capitalized) is "to *his* piety and patriotism, the most sacred [spot] on earth." The collocation is of literature, mendacity, money, nationalism, and sacrilege of several sorts. The Birthplace is of course the Shakespeare shrine, five of them, in fact, administered to this day at Stratford-Upon-Avon by the Shakespeare Birthplace Trust Properties, presumably as ridiculous as ever. At the sacred location "Shakespeare" is simply "God" ("more than their author – their personal friend, their universal light, their final authority and divinity"). There is, however, some question whether he ever existed; if he did, he was perhaps Jesus Christ, not literally of course, but according to textual innunendo:

> "There should really, to clear the matter up, be no such Person."
> ". . . There *is* no such Person."
> ". . . But *wasn't* there——?"
> "There was somebody. . . . But They've killed Him. And, dead as he is, They keep it up, They do it over again, They kill Him every day."

Here and throughout comedy depends on James' wicked hyperbolic conflation of Shakespeare's nativity at Stratford with that of Our Lord at Bethlehem. All jokes seem to depend on at least provisional belief in the basic Christian doctrine of Jesus as both man and God, the point of subtraction being that Shakespeare is *not God,* but was man only, about whose private life we blessedly know almost nothing, as is only proper, but whose Works (also capitalized) we should *adore.* His Works are spoken of as a Set (again, capitalized), such as the New York Edition, upcoming in the years immediately to follow.

Much textual hilarity, as these citations suggest, derives from the improper use of capital letters referring to persons and places and objects secular at best, trivial or ridiculous or nonexistent at worst, a stylistic mannerism at one time more frequently found in religious writing than it is now, especially among evangelical Protestants. We are regularly regaled with such insipidities as this excerpted bit of conversation between the guardians, man and wife, of the sacred shrine:

> "I mean *Him* . . . We shall just live with Him."
> ". . . The more we do the more we shall love Him."
> ". . . The more we *know* Him . . . the more we shall love Him. We don't as yet, you see, know Him so very tremendously."

In such a context of deliberate and mindless idiocy, sacred seculars of the satiric sort may happily flourish. From Islam we have Mecca, from Judaism the Holy of Holies, from paganism the centralizing concept of "idol." Most of the sacred seculars are for thematic reasons Christian, many of them more particularly Catholic: "laid up treasure," temple (several times), shrine (several times), sacred (often), key (possibly Petrine by analogy), mystic presence (secular, fake), priestess (the previous guide lady), enshrined Presence (secular, fake, perhaps Catholic as well through the capital P), sanctities (unverifiable and improbable "facts"), pilgrims (those who come to be bilked), priest (several times, the new guide, the showman, the chief liar), Casa Santa (the Birthplace Catholicized and Latinated), a sacred doll in a Spanish church that you're a blasphemer if you "touch," altar of sacrifice, votive offerings, a pulpit-edge, a *presence* (now italicized) diffused, "the clerical unction, demanded by the priestly character," the usual Catholic word *unction*.

It is of course conceivable that "The Birthplace" also insinuates dubiety about Jesus being God, or our knowing anything whatsoever about *his* birthplace, its conditions and implications; if so, then we have satire of two parallel idolatries rather than satire of one single sacralized secularity; perhaps we have in the most indiscriminate reading a satire of the human habit of sacralizing anything and everything (especially if not true), even a barely hinted satire of Henry James Himself. However the tale be read, it mainly holds up to literary ridicule the religious (and other) habits of unthinking sanctimony: "There can only be *one* way, and . . . I'm sure it's quite enough!" If "it" is that way, or that kind of way, it is surely more than enough, given that the one way in question happens to be untrue and that it is for that reason cherished as if it came down direct from the Father when in fact it is only another instance of human fatuity asserting itself in its customary rites of delusional self-admiration.

PART FIVE

The Catholic Ménage
as Literary Space

1. "De Grey: A Romance" (1868)

"God be with you!" and the old man crossed himself. Involuntarily, Margaret did the same.

The term *ménage* may include a family, a household, a tightly knit neighborhood or comparable community such as a parish, or even certain combinations of these, for example, the extended family situations of *Guy Domville* or the unusually interchanging households of Portland Place and Eaton Square in *The Golden Bowl*. In both those works, and in "De Grey: A Romance" as well, Roman Catholic *ménage* serves the aesthetic purpose of defining and delimiting a literary space, within which the unities of action and setting may swell to their limits and not beyond. In all three works there is also stated or implied a religious, cultural, and sociological comment along somewhat the same lines: Roman Catholics in the United States and in England, in basically Protestant countries, are either through their own fault or the fault of others or both (or even nobody's fault) unusually and inordinately bound up with one another as consequence and subsequent cause of their alienation from the rest of the world. From time to time there will be in the text a faint trace of anti-Catholic assumption, such as Mrs. De Grey's neighbor ladies' thinking her odd because of "the circumstance that she was a Catholic, and kept a priest in her house." The neighbor ladies are wrong and right, by turns, and still it is notable how little anti-Catholic prejudice emanating from the circumambient community is directly represented in James' narratives, or his one drama, of American and English Catholicity. Meanwhile, as I said, the chief merit of the term *ménage* lies in its flexibility. It covers a variety of cases without prejudice, as in the way the word itself means variously a household, strictly speaking, but may easily be stretched to cover a *ménage à trois,* and at least twice in the Jamesian *œuvre* a *ménage à quatre.* Indeed the Roman Catholic *ménage à quatre* is quite a specialty with Henry James.[1]

Ménage and Catholic are so closely related as to be virtually inseparable for the extent and purpose of this tale. " 'Margaret,' he [Paul De Grey] said, 'my mother found you in church, and there, before the altar, she kissed you and took you into her arms. I have often thought of that scene. It makes it no common adoption.' " Indeed, "It makes it sacred and everlasting," typical Jamesian sacred secular talk and maybe even more, as this is a Catholic character represented as saying so. But readers searching for direct evidence of incest will find themselves frustrated. James' Catholics often give off an air of incest, but little or nothing can ever be proved against them. (Think of the Ververs.) And yet, Paul again, to Father Herbert, that house priest, echoing St. Peter to Our Lord in the Gospels: "Where should we [Margaret and he] go? As long as you live, as long as my mother lives, we shall make but a single household." All this inbreeding, whether in fact or by way of figuration, makes for or is made by cultural alienation owing to religious difference, especially blatant in the case of Mrs. De Grey, "who at times was acutely sensible of her own isolation in society"; even her house (which is also her family, her line, her genealogy, her "race," as in Edgar Allan Poe's "The Fall of the House of Usher") is "steeped in repose and physical comfort, rescued from the turbid stream of life, and placed apart" from 1820–1 New York as ordinarily construed. And at least for Mrs. De Grey, isolation leads to a certain mindlessness vaguely resembling that so delicately attributed by the young James in his religious book reviews to European Catholic women writers (Mademoiselle Eugénie de Guérin, Madame Anne Sophie Swetchine). Mrs. De Grey "was fond of her son, of the church, of her garden, and of her toilet. She had the very best taste; but, morally, one may say that she had no history," a statement heavily ironic. She whiles away her time "reading a pious book or knitting under-garments for the orthodox needy."

As we learn in due course from Father Herbert, "The De Greys are an ancient line; they keep their records." These go back to the Crusades, but the De Greys, and Father Herbert, and Margaret Aldis (*and* her dead family, it may be presumed) are as Catholic now as De Greys ever were in the Middle Ages. Roman Catholic background and local color abound, preponderantly picturesque. Father Herbert is "a younger son of an excellent Catholic family" and "an Englishman by birth," who has given up a legal career and "repaired to Rome" (literally and religiously), where he "obtained admission into a monastery, studied theology, and finally was invested with priestly orders." Later, in order to join the now-married De Greys in New York, he "succeeded in obtaining an ecclesiastical mission to the United States," where he loses interest in parish and pulpit and becomes Mrs. De Grey's house priest, somewhat as in Thackeray's *Henry Esmond* but innocent of political complication. Father Herbert has "composed a large portion of a History of the Catholic Church in America," unpublished, "written, not from a sympathetic, but from a strictly respectful point of view" – with "a fatal defect," narrator says, "it lacks unction." In certain respects, Father Herbert is Henry James. Margaret Aldis (with Catholic duenna) is by Mrs. De Grey seen at mass two Sundays in a row and then midweek "apparently just leaving the confessional." The rites of sacred adoption referred to by Paul De Grey consequently take place "within the sacred precinct," Mrs. De Grey entirely forgetting to make her own confession. On one occasion, Father Herbert "went and laid one hand [his left hand, we are to infer] on her head [Margaret's], and with the other made over it the sign of the cross, in the manner of a benediction, – a consecration of the passionate gratitude," Margaret's "which had finally broken out into utterance."

Now all together as family – positively stuck, positively glued together; the *ménage* thickens – Margaret of a Sunday evening "sang in a clear, sweet voice the chants of their Church," not ours, we are gently reminded, the pronominal adjective distancing the narrator and (most of) the readership from any too inappropriate Catholic communing; the readership does not so much participate or assist as it overhears and observes from the outside, decidedly the place to be, given such heterodox goings-on. Narrator also treats us to the worldly wisdom (presumably Catholic) of "Women and priests, as a general thing, like a man none the less for not being entirely innocent." Once Father Herbert asks Margaret to abstain from mass and gives her "absolution" (James means dispensation). Much is made of a De Grey heirloom, an illuminated missal, later called "the quaint old missal . . . the grisly register of death" and a "prayer-book." It contains much De Grey family history of the sort belonging in the family Bible among normal people, and we shall come back to it. In the same missal Margaret more happily finds "a familiar orison to the blessed Virgin," not so invariably chanced upon in Protestant Bibles – more local color, more laying in of the picturesque; the same reference to the Mother of God inspires Margaret's resistance to the alleged family curse. The text of "De Grey: A Romance" abounds, but less than in later James, with sacred seculars, such words as *glory, pious, soul, spiritual* vaguely connoting much sacral mystery and denoting things we are never quite sure of. What, for example, is a reader to do, confronted with young Margaret said to be "in a sort of earthly halo" or shown as "the immaculate person of the sweetest and fairest of women"? It is romantic excess, to be sure, perhaps partly covered (explained, excused) by the Catholic ambience, excessive in its own right. *Basta così.*

"De Grey: A Romance" is a wild, wild story. It is appropriately controlled and contained by numbers, historical dates and the ages of personages. The first and last sentences of the tale tell all, or nearly all. The first sentence reads: "It was the year 1820, and Mrs. De Grey, by the same token, as they say in Ireland (and, for that matter, out of it), had reached her sixty-seventh spring." The last sentence is a remark, to her, by Father Herbert: "Yes, madame, it's the survivors [who are to be pitied], – even after fifty years." The missing or occluded number is of course the year 1770–71. What happened that year we are never quite told, but we are virtually certain that it involved Mrs. De Grey, then a sprightly seventeen or so, and Herbert, about five years older, and that it happened in England (her father is English, and that is surely where she also came from). We may be just as virtually certain that it was somehow "not very nice" or "the sort of thing you might expect of those Catholics" – whatever. Meanwhile, the tale deluges us with many other numbers, and even the months of the year are regularly insisted on.

The dates in the illuminated missal carry us back to 1587. Allusion by Father Herbert carries us back all the way to the Crusades, when "One of the race, they say, came home from the East . . . infected with the germs of the plague." Surely we are to think, however imprecisely, of some Roman Catholic kind of syphilis that kills off the first lover (female) but spares the next, so that each male may subsequently procreate another infecting procreating Catholic male, except that in the present and in one previous generation it is the males who (also?) die, George De Grey, for example, father to Paul, "reduced to a shadow of his former self by repeated sensual excesses," and then Paul De Grey, who suddenly ages – one minute he is twenty-five, the next he feels like sixty – and expires. We are doubtless to note that Mrs. De Grey reports to Father Herbert that she fears she is going blind and that Margaret goes insane. Earlier, Margaret is described as "soulless," in a "prolonged stupor," and "sitting like one whose soul had detached itself and was wandering through space." Father Herbert is, so far as we know, the only one uninvolved; paradoxically, he is the only one who consistently believes in the family curse.

Mrs. De Grey, sixty-seven in 1820, was born in 1753. She says Herbert is about five years older. He was born, then, around 1748. In the family annals we find that one generation back, "John De Grey married, April 4th, 1749, Henrietta Spencer. She died May 7th." George De Grey marries in his thirty-third year. Mrs. De Grey would be about forty-two at the birth of her only child. It is all a trifle atypical, to say the least, and except for repeated echoes of Poe ("Ligeia" in addition to "The Fall of the House of Usher") and Hawthorne (Margaret Aldis is not only Charlotte Stant in the making but Beatrice of "Rappaccini's Daughter" and Phoebe Pyncheon from *The House of the Seven Gables*), it is quite apart from the normalities of "American life," American respectable Protestant life, that is. Despite all the English-American family connections, neither of the two chronologically pertinent Anglo–American wars is alluded to. "De Grey: A Romance" was published in July 1868 in the *Atlantic Monthly*. The effect of the tale must have been about 10 percent to remind the readership that Catholics are people, after all, and about 90 percent to remind them how blessèd they were not to be of this awful faith.

Those who enjoy their vistas may relish the way that Paul De Grey, before his disasters, is an "ardent American" and that Herbert, before his priesthood, is to the elder De Grey, in France and Italy, a "travelling companion." And when Paul De Grey says to his family, "I don't mean to bury you alive," he may be taken as inadvertently pointing us to the Sepolte Vive of *Watch and Ward*. S. Gorley Putt notes in "De Grey" a germ of *The Sacred Fount* and perhaps of "The Beast in the Jungle" too, so that it hardly defies credulity to imagine that "De Grey" may also contain germs of *The Golden Bowl*.[2] One mightily convincing germ is Paul De Grey recommending to a stultified Catholic household such worldly recreations as thirty-six or thirty-seven years later Charlotte Stant will be got in for:

> He declared that he would set their habits to quite another tune, and that the family should no longer be buried in silence and gloom. It was an absurd state of things, and he marvelled that it should ever have come about. They should begin to live like other people, and occupy their proper place in society. They should entertain company, and travel, and go to the play of an evening.

Before Margaret providentially appears, Mrs. De Grey herself has been looking for "some nice, fresh young girl, who would laugh once in a while, and make a little music, – a little sound in the house." A miniature of Paul abroad shows Paul as a newly elegant figure: "In what the change consisted it was hard to tell; but his mother declared that it was easy to see that he had spent two years in the best company in Europe." That figure will likewise reappear years later as Chad Newsome, apparently de-Catholicized but all too evidently "involved" with a married woman, older and Catholic.

2. *Guy Domville* (1893, 1895)★

In "The Art of Fiction" (1884), attempting to rein in the rampaging notion of incident, James gave as his minimalist example: "When a young man makes up his mind that he has not faith enough after all to

★ The play, written in 1893 and produced in 1895, was unpublished during James' lifetime.

enter the church as he intended, that is an incident, though you may not hurry to the end of the chapter to see whether perhaps he doesn't change once more." The hero of *Guy Domville* changes once more, and it is still not much of an incident. In Act I he is about to become a priest, in Act II he has abandoned his vocation in order to marry and perpetuate his "race," and in Act III he is about to become a priest. It goes without saying that different spectators of this back-and-forth indecisiveness will respond to it differently: "[I]t is far better to be a priest (if you can) than to be anything else whatsoever" versus "being a priest is the worst thing in the world imaginable, especially a *Catholic* priest." Neither of these views, nor any gradations in between, necessarily underwrites any great fascination with *Guy Domville* as a dramatic performance.

Despite *Guy Domville*'s being James' most purely Catholic work – in a minute we will need to make a head count of the Catholics on and off stage, there are that many of them – *Guy Domville* is not directly about Catholicity except as Catholicity sacerdotal, ascetic, and celibate, and, on the other hand, Catholicity familial and communitarian, may be useful in the antithesis God (Art) and worldliness. How useful it was should already be clear from the fact that for James' dramatic purposes Catholicity and worldliness are so closely related as virtually to be one and the same thing. There are no Protestants in *Guy Domville,* indeed no particularized non-Catholics or anti-Catholics. The same religionists "do" both the spiritual and the worldly act. Everyone, practically speaking, in *Guy Domville,* is Catholic, and the conflict occurs among them rather than between them and "the outside." In fact, as we shall see, there *is* in *Guy Domville* no outside. *Guy Domville* is all *ménage.*

The curious and virtually indefinable concept of worldliness, even more indefinable in Henry James than elsewhere, was lifelong a topic of his intermittent interest, yet hardly what you would call a passionate interest, except theoretically, James himself being in so many respects worldly. Still, readers of these pages will recall his guarded encomia of Madame Swetchine for being such a worldly *dévote*. And readers of James' other pages will recall many an additional passage ostensibly on the same topic, perhaps most of all his unqualified remark in the preface to *The Tragic Muse:* "[T]he conflict between art and 'the world' striking me thus betimes as one of the half-dozen great primary motives." As *Guy Domville* all blatantly shows forth, religion, especially in its ostensive Catholic form, and "the world," the antithesis from which the conflict of art versus the world came in the first place, and where it continues to run its course, quite as if Henry James *et alia* had never thought to redesign it for primarily literary use, will also serve, only it will now be a question, perhaps never to be answered, whether art is an emblem of religion or religion an emblem of art, or maybe they are the same jewel, glancingly aglitter.

However that may be, the age-old topos of *contemptus mundi* is frequent in James during the Gay Nineties (and both earlier and later,
too); for example, in "Louisa Pallant" (1888), the self-accusatory bad
mother, "I have been punished by my sin itself. I have been hideously
worldly" ("It relieved her to warn and denounce and expose," and all
three actions she attributes to "God"); in "The Pupil" (1891), Morgan
Moreen to Pemberton, "They're [his family] so beastly worldly. That's
what I hate most"; in a charming Captain Jay–Rose Tramore conversational exchange in "The Chaperon" (1891), concerning another
woman:

> "She's too worldly," he murmured, while he held Rose Tramore's [hand]
> a moment.
> "Ah, you dear!" Rose exclaimed . . . .

in "Glasses" (1896), the narrator's curious reference to "my mother, who
had not much left in life but the quiet look from under the hood of her
chair at the things which, when she should have quitted those she loved
[that is to say, died], she could still trust to make the world good for
them"; in *The Ivory Tower* (1914, unfinished), the protagonist's "after-
sense" of the deathbed interview with his uncle as "an impression of one
of those great insistent bounties that are not of this troubled world," and
if they are not then we want to know of what world they are, and of
course and as usual what we find is the aestheticization of the divine,
"the anomaly expressing itself in such beauty and dignity, with all its
elements conspiring together, as would have done honour to a great page
of literary, of musical or pictorial art."
  On the other hand, there can be little doubt that James fondly cherished and occasionally adopted (when he was fed up with social life) a
certain artist-ascetic-priestly equation, apparently derived not only from
a high estimate of his own vocation but from fanciful analogues discovered beyond the bounds of Protestantized Anglo-Saxon boredom. And
of course he will have it two or more ways, changing sides as the mood
takes him. In his long 1873 essay on Théophile Gautier, James is severe
in his disapproval of worldliness, as if it might never be a temptation for
him. The next year he praises Turgenev for his "apprehension of man's
religious impulses, of the *ascetic* passion, the capacity of becoming dead
to colours and odours and beauty, never dreamed of in the philosophy
of Balzac and Flaubert." But James had delighted in picturing Balzac
dressed up like a Benedictine monk. In "The Lesson of the Master" (1888)
James appears to have shifted over to the opposite position (but who can
ever believe one word from the mouths of James' fictionalized "writers"?). As for Flaubert, in the 1893 essay James quotes him with evident
approval and, I suspect, self-identification: " 'I have in me,' he writes to

the imperturbable Madame Sand, 'a *fond d'écclésiastique* that people don't know' – the clerical basis of the Catholic clergy."

Stimulated by all this ambivalence and by the further impossibility of determining whether Guy Domville intends to become a monk or a diocesan priest – it makes some difference, and the text of the play has it both ways – biographical criticism has naturally been fertile in proposing a variety of Guy Domville–Henry James equations. My favorite fancy is Henry James fancying that to be a priest is almost automatically not to be a dramatist, whence we may infer that he *is not writing this mediocre play*. As for James' *fond d'écclésiastique,* H. G. Wells was probably right in saying that "Guy Domville was one of those rare ripe exquisite Catholic Englishmen of ancient family conceivable only by an American mind."[3] Or only, it might be even better to say, by one particular American mind. That mind was evidently having quite a little Catholic flurry. F. O. Matthiessen and Kenneth B. Murdock observe that the long 3 and 7 November 1894 *Notebooks* entries concerning *The Wings of the Dove* were written "at about the time *Guy Domville* went into rehearsal," and Leon Edel remarks that James' visit to the Archbishop from whom he had the idea for *The Turn of the Screw* was five days after *Guy Domville's* disastrous opening night.[4] The main entry for "The Altar of the Dead" is dated 29 September 1894. The first *Notebooks* entries for *Guy Domville* and *The Golden Bowl* are two years earlier, in August and November, respectively. The *Guy Domville* note shows James envisaging a denouement exactly the reverse of what he ultimately wrote. A later *Notebooks* allusion to *The Golden Bowl* occurs on 14 February 1895, just after *Guy Domville* closed. These various Catholic items appear to be connected, if only by date and association.

"I delight in a palpable imaginable *visitable* past" James memorably wrote in the *Aspern Papers* preface. But because Catholicity was "old," James' incursions into the Catholic world are often more decidedly backdated than that – for example, "De Grey: A Romance," "Gabrielle de Bergerac," and of course *Guy Domville.* "Period – 1780" we are told is the time of the action – *period* rather than *year,* and, even so, a particular year is given. James would have remembered from his Dickens (*Barnaby Rudge*) that 1780 was the year of the No-Popery riots in response to some very feeble gestures toward Catholic Emancipation (1829 is the real year for Catholic Emancipation in England). But it seems certain that James is thinking neither of riots nor of emancipation, only that the pre-1829 setting enables him to oblige his priest-to-be to repair to Douai for theological training. Perhaps all he had in mind for 1780 was a nice old date breathing a certain sentimental-aesthetic ambience, and what that ambience was we may guess from "The London Theatres" (1881), in which James toys with the notion of a homogenized eighteenth-century pre-

industrial attitude (or tone): "It appears to be generally conceded that
there was formerly a style in England. In the last century, the English
theatres went hand-in-hand with a literature which sprang substantially
from the English mind itself."[5] Dating his play in the late eighteenth
century, James would hopefully tap into that mind and that literature
and that theatre, blithely ignoring the facts of his own un-English nationality and the anti-Catholic foundations of the post-Reformation English mind. As so often, he was writing against the grain of his audience.
The resident alien would force an alien topic with its alien values on a
doubly alienated audience. In 1780 the American Revolution was still in
progress, another little matter that goes without notice in *Guy Domville*.
If it is not a masterpiece of the drama, it is at least a masterpiece of New
World aggression.

Catholic counting, at which we finally arrive, inevitably involves consideration of *ménage* and of plot (as plots go). No priests appear in the list
of characters because they never appear on stage – no great loss perhaps,
considering the already stupendous problems of costume – and, as we
shall see, there are plenty of lay Catholics. The stage directions are vaguely
and teasingly ecclesiastic (Old Catholic), a garden, an old house named
Porches in the West of England (for Acts I and III), complete with sun-
dial "formed like a table" (thus like an altar). Sacred seculars, doubles
entendres of the usual divine-worldly sort, continue throughout – but it
is hard to tell if they are really sacred seculars, these people are *Catholics;*
they might even mean what they say (unlikely, however), jokes on the
word *call,* remarks about *fishing.* Frank Humber informs Lord Devenish
that Guy Domville goes into retreat tomorrow. Guy Domville is Catholic One. Humber adds, "as we Catholics call it." Humber is Catholic
Two. Lord Devenish raises his hat and says, "The true and only Church!"
and identifies himself as Catholic Three. Humber next reveals that the
local Romanists are "protected by my Lord Edenbrook," who makes
Catholic Four (although invisible) – and how many others does he pro-
tect? Lord Edenbrooks's private chapel and chaplain (Catholic Five, also
invisible) "are precious comforts to us" ("The centre, of course, of your
little cluster of the faithful"). This community our hero will now for-
sake, to "enter a religious house" (another *ménage*) as a "preparation for
holy orders." He will proceed from Bristol to Douai "and the good Fathers [Benedictines] who brought him up," Humber too. Domville, not
Humber, "has what they [Benedictines, and Catholics in general] call the
vocation."

Mrs. Peverel, mistress of Porches, niece of my Lord Edenbrook, is
Catholic Six; as Lord Devenish says, "Very good [Catholic] blood!" Lord
Devenish delivers a letter from his mistress, Maria Domville, another
branch of the family and another Romanist – Catholic Seven (she will

appear in the flesh during Act II). Guy Domville's own mother, who bred him up to be a priest, is Catholic Eight, if the departed faithful be allowed – and why not? Mothers, including "our Mother-Church," are quite the dominant factors in this play, as they tend to be in James' representations of Catholics. Guy says he will give up his name and take another, which sounds monastic, and then that he enters the Church because "there are people everywhere to help," which sounds more pastoral. The Domville estate and line go back to the Conquest; the Domvilles are "Old Catholics" in more than a single sense. It is the split between two of these senses that constitutes such conflict as constitutes the play:

> GUY. (*Quietly, firmly.*) I was bred up, my lord, to be a priest.
> LORD DEVENISH. You were not bred up, I suppose, not to be a Domville!
> GUY. The very Domville that, in our branch, was always given to the Church.

Lord Devenish soon inquires if Guy Domville has never imagined "*another* possible life – the natural, the liberal [!], the agreeable, the life of the world, of men – and of women"? (*Hamlet* tone.) So we come to hear of Maria Domville's daughter, Mary Brasier, "a Catholic, a beauty, and a fortune," she also to figure in Act II – Catholic Nine. By her Guy Domville is to be tempted and ultimately to reject temptation, returning to the point where he set out. As Guy remarks, "I know no pride so proper as that of the office I've been appointed to fill," and as Lord Devenish responds, "The more little Domvilles the more good Catholics!" As if the stage were not already filled with good Catholics! Guy Domville still insists on going to Bristol with Father Murray, probably the same as Lord Edenbrook's chaplain and not to be counted twice.

In Act II, we learn that George Round, engaged to Mary Brasier, daughter of Maria Domville and her first husband – who is, in fact, a coverup father, Lord Devenish being the real one, and she another of James' Catholic bastards – is also Mr. Brasier's nephew, hence, we may scarcely doubt, another very good Catholic: Catholic Ten. Round and Mrs. Domville exchange knowing remarks about "fidelity to the old persuasion." Like Lord Edenbrook, Lord Devenish has his chaplain, the same, I make out, as Father White – Catholic Eleven (but Catholic Twelve if Father Murray and Lord Edenbrook's chaplain are not the same). And that, I also make out, is all the Catholics there are in *Guy Domville*. It is a stage crowded with Catholics, James' largest assortment, his amplest *ménage*. As usual, these Catholics are closely connected by religion and family both and correspondingly discriminated from society at large.

James' conception of Catholics isolated in a surrounding world is at least admirably suited to theatrical concentration.

But unlike "De Grey: A Romance," "The Altar of the Dead," and even *The Golden Bowl,* there is in *Guy Domville* no luridity, no hint of inherited disease, no mental and moral eccentricity, no suspicion of incest, nothing at all *peculiar* unless you insist on holding that Roman Catholicity is itself peculiar, especially in its celibate priesthood, but that is your problem, as it were, James' play being Catholic romanticism unadulterated and in extremis. "GUY. I was dazzled by life! MARY. You see what life is." Later, "I've seen it," the world, "and it doesn't answer!" Later still, "I looked at life as you showed it, and then I turned away my face," a phrasing that may or may not shed new light on Milly Theale. (The tone of these remarks also resembles that of the last conversation between Ralph and Isabel in *The Portrait of a Lady*.) And thus Guy Domville returns from the world to his vocation, and with a little cleaning up in Act III the play is done.

The overwhelming problem with *Guy Domville,* as James apparently never saw with any clarity, is a problem of genre. *Guy Domville* is not especially dramatic – the resolution of its conflict is predetermined. Nor could it ever have been a successful narrative for its want of any possible development. The plain fact is that *Guy Domville* is in its thematology and structure basically lyric, the presentation of a Catholic problem, to be sure, but mainly an evocation of the spiritual and social quality of Catholic lives. *Guy Domville* is a fantasy, a mood poem, a daydream, an idyl. It distantly resembles "The Great Good Place," but in *Guy Domville* James' wistful sense of Catholic beauty is in no way Protestantized. *Guy Domville* represents at least one occasion in his life when Henry James not only wrote about Roman Catholics, all favorably in this case, but when he also wrote as if he were himself a Catholic, almost as if he were trying it on to see how it felt (*The Golden Bowl* may make a second such occasion). It seems to feel quite easy and tranquil. As James modestly wrote Henrietta Reubell on 31 December 1894, five days before opening night, "It is a little 'romantic' play of which the action is laid (in England) in the middle of the last centry." ("I beg you heartily to indulge for me, about 8.30 o'clock on that evening, in very fervent prayer.")

Indeed, James wrote some of his best letters on the subject of *Guy Domville,* a fistful. He was never able to leave it alone or to let it go. "Don't worry about me: I'm a Rock," he wrote brother William on 9 January 1895, thus lining himself up with the wonderful Honorine Carré of *The Tragic Muse* and with what Catholics are sometimes prone to call the Petrine element. "If the play has no life on the stage I shall publish it; it's altogether the best thing I've done." He didn't. It wasn't. Why was he so determined to think it was? It seems not to have entered his mind that something might be wrong with the genre or that the audience was anti-Catholic. And yet he was sure that the trouble lay in the relation of subject and audience. As he said in the same letter: "[M]y subject – an episode in the history of an old English Catholic family in the last century – militates against it, with all *usual* theatrical people, who don't want plays (from variety and nimbleness of fancy) of different *kinds,* like books and stories, but only of *one* kind." More lightheartedly he wrote the same day to W. Morton Fullerton about his "harmless and ingenious little play," as if he had been accused of nefary, and about "the purity and lucidity of one's motives (mine are worthy of Benjamin Franklin)." Why should there have been any question about his motives? And if James blamed the subject, while at the same defending it, why did he then write Mr. and Mrs. William (James) on 2 February 1895 that "this little drama has brought me in two or three weeks twenty-five times more letters than a career of refined literary virtue has brought (about my books) in twenty-five years." Does he wish to imply that *Guy Domville* is somehow *not* "refined"? *not* "virtuous"?

In the same letter he quite predictably reminds his correspondents, and himself, that all he has on his hands is "a little old-time story, far enough off to have a certain 'Henry Esmond' quality and yet near enough for all reality." A few lines later, he quite unpredictably acts as if it were his characters' religion rather than his play that is being scorned and rejected: "I saw they couldn't care one straw for a damned young last-century English Catholic, who lived in an old-time Catholic world and acted, with every one else in the play, from remote and romantic Catholic motives," which is surely to lay on the adjectives. Even more strangely, two days later, to William again, he wishes the theatrical season were more advanced so there would be more Americans in the audience. They would keep *Guy Domville* running, he is sure, "and not merely *as* compatriots, but as feeling the play better." Why should they? we wonder. Because Americans are more aesthetic? more imaginative? more tolerant? (three unlikely conjectures). Because more of them are *Catholic*? (even if they are only, poor dear things, *American* Catholics, a mixed matter to which James would a decade later turn a mild attention in *The Golden Bowl*). But around 15 March 1895, when he writes to Mrs. Edward Compton, James appears to have given up: The play is "an unmitigated disaster." And there, except for Leon Edel, who has been "after" *Guy Domville* for four decades, the poor sad ashes lie neglected. James criticism has not been much interested in it, as James criticism has shown little or no interest in his religious content either.

3. *The Golden Bowl* (1904) The Crown of His Career

The Golden Bowl is indisputably Henry James' Roman Catholic masterpiece. If it could hardly have been predicted, it can be retroactively traced and, in part, understood. Way back in 1892 (28 November) we have the chief *Notebook* entry, with not a direct word of *ménage,* not a direct word of Roman Catholicity, not a direct word of "De Grey: A Romance," itself a quarter of a century further back. And yet we may easily find the nub, or hub, of all these concatenated matters in such observations as "The whole situation works in a kind of inevitable rotary way – in what would be called a vicious circle." Fanny Assingham echoes this language, explaining to Colonel Bob how it was Maggie who "*began* the vicious circle":

> "It's their mutual consideration, all round, that has made it the bottom-less gulf; and they're really so embroiled but because, in their way, they've been so improbably *good.*"
> "In their way – yes!" the Colonel grinned.
> "Which was above all Maggie's way." No flicker of ribaldry was anything to her now.

The link back to "De Grey: A Romance" subsists in James' perdurable habit of regarding Catholics as deplorably cut off from the world, especially in non-Catholic countries, and proportionately too bound up with one another (*ménage*). At some point he must have reasoned it out that if these people were so peculiar, and in just these ways, why, then, they must be Catholics! We shall soon come to the passages in the novel in which James somewhat deviously establishes the religious faith of his major personages. The oddity of their behavior requires no special demonstration.

And yet it will bear a closer look so that we may more clearly fix in our minds the really unacceptable nature of these queer people before we come to James' virtual identification with Maggie Verver. It is the centralizing contradiction of *The Golden Bowl* – and doubtless the chief cause of the antithetical excesses in its interpretation – that James simultaneously insists on the eccentricity of his *ménage* while also insisting that he is somehow one *of* them, or vice versa. "A necessary basis for all this," he had observed in that *Notebook* passage, "must have been an intense and exceptional degree of attachment between the father and daughter." That is a complication indeed but by no means the whole complication – not even when we add the premarital and extramarital exploits of the daughter's husband and the father's new wife. There are also Maggie and Charlotte, as the Prince meditates upon them and "what the friendship had been for Maggie. It had been armed with the wings of young imagination, young generosity; it had been, he believed – always counting out her intense devotion to her father – the liveliest emotion she had known before the dawn of the sentiment inspired by himself." Here is powerful bisexual libido playing quite freely and in almost every conceivable direction among the four major personages – adultery is not all that is going on here. Almost incredibly, the Prince is said to "believe" all that I have just quoted while looking into the eyes of Charlotte. And he and Charlotte have just performed one of their almost-as-incredible little Roman Catholic erotic-hypocritical-delusionary conversational exchanges:

> "Only it's almost terrible, you know, the happiness of young good generous creatures. It rather frightens one. But the Blessed Virgin and all the Saints," said the Prince, "have her in their keeping."
> "Certainly they have."

Therefore, the Prince and Charlotte seem to assume, they need not.

Incest is never openly charged, but it is several times insinuated by textual maneuvers. Adam Verver's relations with his daughter are said to be, by him, conceived as "their decent little old-time union," where the word *union* hints more than we have any warrant for daring to imagine, and the words *decent* and *little* and *old-time* moderate our prurience. The Principino is not so much "a new link between a wife and a husband, but Maggie and her father had, with every ingenuity, converted [!] the precious creature into a link between a mamma and a grandpapa . . . the place of immediate male parent swept bare." Maggie literally and bare-facedly speaks of having been her father's wife, but of course we are not to take her literally: "It was as if you couldn't be in the market when you were married to *me*. Or rather as if I kept people off, innocently, by being married to you." The word *innocently* stands out, no matter how we discount the substance of her remarks, no matter how many times we insert the phrase "as it were." One practical consequence of all this excessive togetherness, one euphemistic way of putting it (Fanny Assingham's), is that the foursome are "too much taken up with considering each other. You may call such a mistake as that by whatever name you please; it at any rate means, all round, their case. It illustrates the misfortune," said Mrs. Assingham gravely, "of being too, too charming." And too rich. And too idle. And too American (all but Prince Amerigo, who is trying to live up to his name). And too Catholic.

Mindless blither about such Catholic types as too, too charming regularly signals in *The Golden Bowl* James' anti-Catholic bias, which will subsequently be crossed by, and come under the control of, his pro-Catholic bias. It is not, it would seem, a matter he cares either to leave alone or to clarify. Here it is Adam Verver quite fatuously describing the Roman Catholic social and psychological formations that I have been calling *ménage:*

> "I don't say it's me particularly – or that it's you or Charlotte or Amerigo. But we're selfish together – we move as a selfish mass. You see we want always the same thing," he had gone on – "and that holds us, that binds us, together. We want each other," he had further explained; "only wanting it, each time, *for* each other."

That may be what *he* thinks, but it is not what we *know,* which is that Amerigo and Charlotte want each other and not at all *for* their respective spouses. What we may also know, if we have been following James' Catholic act from the beginning down to its present glorification, is that what holds them, what binds them, is not only the illicit crisscross of libidinal transgression but the fact that they are all Catholics together – indeed, it may be inferred, however unreasonably and salaciously on James' part, that the libidinal crisscross is caused by their Catholicity, or, if *cause* be too strong a term, then that, in a general sort of way, Catholics are like that, strange, unreliable, perverse, centripetal, molecular. And yet, as we shall see, they are sometimes wondrously aesthetic. These divided views go all the way back to James' early book reviews of religious topics, perhaps even back so far as to his early Newport friendship with John La Farge, American Catholic aesthete.

If it is not Adam Verver fatuously discoursing then it is narrative authority with comparable insipidity declaring with contemptuous sarcasm the glamour of all this apparently inescapable stupidity and pain, in ostensible reference to "that wonderful reunion of the couples" – *which couples?* – "in the interest of the larger play of all the virtues of each, which was now bearing, for Mrs. Verver's stepdaughter at least, such remarkable fruit." Impatient readers sometimes find themselves wishing that James would solve his problem with a nice quick divorce, while careless readers jump to the conclusion that the Verver foursome can't divorce because they are Catholics and will therefore put up with unlimited amounts of adultery, having no choice in the matter. That is a trivial consideration at best, and James, elsewhere tolerant about divorce – for example, in "The Siege of London" – blocks it off here, not so much in a Catholic as in an anti-American way. Playing on the doubtful fact of Mrs. Rance "having" a husband, he gives us this magnificent passage:

> She had him, it was true, only in America, only in Texas, in Nebraska, in Arizona or somewhere – somewhere that, at old Fawns House in the county of Kent, scarcely figured as a definite place at all; it showed somehow from afar as so lost, so indistinct and illusory, in the great alkali desert of cheap Divorce.

The Golden Bowl immediately precedes James' Grand Tour of his home-land, which is also to be the fictive fate of Adam Verver and Charlotte Stant Verver. Fanny Assingham once again serves as sufficient prophet; "I see the long miles of ocean and the dreadful great country, State after State – which have never seemed to be so big or so terrible." For *The Golden Bowl*, the United States of America is, or are, Hell – figuratively, of course. They *are*, metonymically, "the great alkali desert of cheap Divorce," antithesis not of marriage but of everything.

The Roman Catholic adulterous talk of Prince Amerigo and Charlotte will also bear a further look, it is so much the best of that papist local color that James always finds ready to his hand, and that he gladly shovels in, so soon as he begins to sniff, from however far off, *the church*. Charlotte does most of the talking, and here she is again on the subject of Maggie's virtue and its implicit impact on her relations with Maggie's husband. Her syntax and references are a little hard to follow, but Maggie's excessive generosity appears to be the topic. Doubtless Charlotte has her devious reasons for speaking as someone outside the faith, even though we know, or will soon know, better: " 'It takes stuff within one, so far as one's decency is concerned, to stand it. And nobody,' Charlotte continued in the same manner, 'is decent enough, good enough, to stand it – not without help from religion or something of that kind. Not without prayer and fasting – that is without taking great care. Certainly,' she said, 'such people as you and I are not.' " Charlotte's secularistic reductions are extraordinary: The true faith is equal to "something of that kind," prayer and fasting are the same as being, or seeming to be, cautious. In a later conversation, when the Prince points out that she's of the same race (nationality) as the Ververs, whereas he is not, she replies that "you're not . . . too different from *me*," meaning, I think, to draw his attention to the fact of their both being human and then to the difference of her being female and his being male. A few remarks later Charlotte concludes that they must trust each other, and now it is the Prince's turn to chime in with the good old Catholic note: "Oh as we trust the saints in glory," and in another moment they are falling all over each other, saying, each to each, "It's sacred." Later yet, Charlotte informs the Prince that "one's decency and one's honour and one's virtue," specifically her own, or the credit of them, "are my rule of life, the absolute little gods of my worship, the holy images set up on the wall." She means that behind the respectable appearances of her conformity to the four-way *ménage* she and her lover may regard themselves as sufficiently free and safe. The subtlest and perhaps the most sinister Catholic adulterous passage conflates Charlotte's sense of the Prince's face ("of temporising kindness"), which she wears, presumably concealed, around her neck, "like a precious medal – not exactly blessed by the Pope." Prince Amer-

igo is of course an Italian Catholic said to be the descendant of a certain
Pope, not named. He and Maggie are married at the Oratory where Merton Densher sought refuge in *The Wings of the Dove.*

Charlotte Stant, we have long since been informed, is a Florentine-
born American national and like many of her Jamesian sisters a convent-
flower. She is full of early Italian memories, including that of "the good
sisters of the poor convent of the Tuscan hills"; in a "subsequent phase"
she and Maggie attend a "much grander institution" – but equally Catholic, we think – in Paris. Fanny Assingham *is* the Pope, in a manner of
speaking, when (*ex cathedra*) "in her seat of infallibility." She speaks,
with what James is fond of referring to in Catholic contexts as *unction* (to
Maggie, the most Catholic of them all), of "that little silver cross you
once showed me, blest by the Holy Father" and of the "little innermost,
say this time little golden personal nature of you – blest by a greater
power I think even than the Pope." Had she not spoken thus, I should
have taken her for Protestant Episcopal (Church of England in her ex-
patriation), and now I shall never be sure.

There are two dominant Roman Catholic passages in *The Golden Bowl,*
one fairly early, one quite late; they are polar; the novel's dirty linen
hangs between them; they define the *ménage* according to its religious
constitution; they establish the Catholic ambience and even furnish the
raison d'être of the novel. The first of these is in the second chapter of
Book Second of the first half (*The Prince*):

> The Assinghams and the Miss Lutches [visitors] had taken the walk,
> through the park, to the little old church, "on the property," that our
> friend [Adam Verver] had often found himself wishing he were able to
> transport, as it stood, for its simple sweetness, in a glass case, to one of
> his exhibitory halls; while Maggie had induced her husband, not invet-
> erate in such practices, to make with her, by carriage, the somewhat
> longer pilgrimage to the nearest altar, modest though it happened to
> be, of the faith – her own as it had been her mother's, and as Mr. Verver
> himself had been loosely willing always to let it be taken for *his* – with-
> out the solid ease of which, making the stage firm and smooth, the
> drama of her marriage mightn't have been acted out.

From that passage we immediately draw several inferences, some of which
are borne out elsewhere in the text, as, for example, that Adam Verver
has not this day been to mass – he has not been the previous Sunday,
either, nor will he go the following Sunday, nor will we have any evidence of his ever going, even though, on the other and, we will have no
further evidence of his not going – and as, for example, that Prince
Amerigo, typifying Latin male, is "not inveterate in such practices," but
that at least this once he goes to please his wife. We may by the same

token infer that Maggie is a better Catholic than her husband; and we are directly informed that she is not a Catholic through him but that she inherits her faith from her dead mother, as in *Guy Domville* dead Catholic mothers had a continuing efficacy. What is hardly borne out either in *The Golden Bowl* or in the rest of Henry James is the implication carried by that part of the passage which follows the second dash, viz., that you have to be a Catholic to marry one. The implication is contradicted by the case of Christina Light (as originally conceived). It is contradicted in the passage itself by the lack of inveteracy in the Prince. It is most of all contradicted a hundred or so pages earlier in *The Golden Bowl* by the declaration that the prince's brother has married a woman "of Hebrew race, with a portion that had gilded the pill." In short, there is no reason in the world why Maggie must be Catholic to marry the Prince and even less reason why her father and mother should be. Other looming issues raised by that passage must also be reluctantly passed over (who built that sweet little old church? in whose possession is it now? why is the other church farther away and modest?).

Here is the second polar passage, Charlotte, Maggie, and Maggie's priest, who appears also to be Charlotte's priest, Father Mitchell, fat and hungry, who "prattles," typical churchman of literary satire, yet of whom James says, *after* the passage I am about to quote, "priests were really at the worst, so to speak, such wonderful people," another curious lapse of tone and attitude for which I have no explanation save a reminder that James had no dire personal stake in such jaunty sentimental generalities, the unqualified wonderfulness of priests being once again a good-natured outsider's view, for that reason, and others, suspect. The second polar passage is in Book Fifth (of six), the second half (*The Princess*). As the passage is so seldom featured in James criticism, I quote it at some length. We are once more at Fawns, at lunch, at "three o'clock of a canicular August" afternoon:

> A consensus of languor, which might almost have been taken for a community of dread, ruled the scene – relieved only by the fitful experiments of Father Mitchell, good holy hungry man, a trusted and overworked London friend and adviser, who had taken for a week or two the light neighboring service, local rites flourishing under Maggie's munificence, and was enjoying, as a convenience, all the bounties of the house. *He* conversed undiscouraged, Father Mitchell – conversed mainly with the indefinite wandering smile of the entertainers, and the Princess's power to feel him on the whole a blessing for these occasions was not impaired by what was awkward in her consciousness of having, from the first of her trouble, really found her way without his guidance. She asked herself at times if he suspected how more than subtly, how

perversely, she had dispensed with him, and she balanced between visions of all he must privately have guessed and certitudes that he had guessed nothing whatever. He might nevertheless have been so urbanely filling up gaps, at present, for the very reason that his instinct, sharper than the expression of his face, had sufficiently served him – made him aware of the thin ice, figuratively speaking, and of prolongations of tension, round about him, mostly foreign to the circles in which luxury was akin to virtue. Some day at some happier season she would confess to him that she hadn't confessed, though taking so much on her conscience; but just now she was carrying in her weak stiffened hand a glass filled to the brim, as to which she had recorded a vow that no drop should overflow. She feared the very breath of a better wisdom, the jostle of the higher light, of heavenly help itself. . . .

A paragraph intervenes and then it is Maggie imagining the reactions of Father Mitchell to this frozen company, and then imagining Father Mitchell with Charlotte, earlier the same day, in the course of which imagining the reader is given, thus late in the text, well toward the end of the novel, conclusive revelation about the Catholicity of *that* doomed creature, subject as she is to a pincer action on the part of the Ververs, her stepdaughter and husband, wife and father-in-law of her lover:

> . . . the good priest as he finally sat back with fat folded hands and twiddled his thumbs on his stomach. The good priest looked hard at the decanters, at the different dishes of dessert – he eyed them half-obliquely, as if *they* might have met him to-day for conversation better than any one present. But the Princess had her fancy at last about that too; she was in the midst of a passage, before she knew it, between Father Mitchell and Charlotte – some approach he would have attempted with her that very morning perhaps to the circumstance of an apparent detachment recently noted in her from any practice of devotion. He would have drawn from this, say, his artless inference – taken it for a sign of some smothered inward trouble and naturally pointed the moral that the way out of such straits was not through neglect of the grand remedy. He had possibly prescribed contrition – he had at any rate quickened in her the beat of that false repose to which our young woman's own act had devoted her at her all so deluded instance.

So now it is all quite clear how even the fourth member of our matrimonial quadriplex is a Roman Catholic, although she seems to be dodging her devotions, about which James continues to be indistinct, except as to "confession," that grand remedy. It is a curious business, as well, James' insistence on Maggie's not consulting Father Mitchell. If Maggie has aught to confess, beyond her justified lies, the reader does not know it. She is a victim of sin rather than a sinner (like Hilda in *The Marble Faun*). It is as if James regards his fictive priest – sufficiently fattened and ridiculed, one would think – as some sort of rival. Why should the woman confer with *him,* he seems to suggest, when she has *me?*

Long ago I quoted James in his preface to the *Lady Barbarina* volume in the New York Edition, 1908, four years after *The Golden Bowl,* slyly reminding us, or at least appearing so to do, that he may be a master of more than one "sharp antithesis," granted the perpetual interest to the writer and reader of fiction of *"contrasted* things." For many pages, including those of the present chapter, I have been attempting to discern, to understand, to explore, to show forth, and even at times to "explain," the Catholic–Protestant antithesis that structures and decorates much, though by no means all, of James' writing, and that has been so generally overlooked in the criticism, bent as it has naturally been on the antithesis between "the distinctively American and the distinctively European outlook," not to mention – we have seen plenty of this, too – the antithesis between male and female ways of thinking, feeling, and doing. Now is the time to approach the Catholic–Protestant and the American–European antitheses the one to the other and see how at least on this occasion they are related and perhaps even reconciled. And after that reconciliation, we may even be privileged to behold the genders reconciled.

The peril of the path is of course to line up Protestant America against Catholic Europe. Those equations are easy and obvious and tempting (to some), but they are reductive and simplistic and factually false. James knew better, and we also know better, or should. If not, *The Golden Bowl* may instruct us. Here we have staring us in the face, positively demanding critical attention, one Roman Catholic Italian (Roman in two or more senses, including the downright and outrageously papal), multiply interrelated, both rightly and wrongly, with three American (Roman) Catholics (Charlotte and the two Ververs), one of these American Catholics (Maggie) devoutly and vigorously Catholic, virtually sponsoring her home-away-from-home English parish ("local rites flourishing under Maggie's munificence," the Roman Catholic faith of Great Britain in this instance supported by American Catholic money), and if anyone wants Fanny Assingham to boot that merely increases the pile-up of Roman Catholics who are *also* citizens of the United States, regardless of their current residence in England, whether for art collecting or just for the worldly pleasure of living someplace else.

The Golden Bowl, is, for one last great occasion, and even if James could not have known this, the international theme cast on a large canvas, and perhaps it is also, as many have felt, a final resolution of difficulties. My best suggestion for a fresh rereading of the novel (apart from the idea of the Catholic *ménage* and other matters already dealt with) is the notion that our author, rounding age sixty, was in the course of composition unusually aware of something quite peculiar and potentially misleading in his previous big international novels that it was never too late to adjust. Given the agglutinated Catholicity of the *Golden Bowl* cast, prompted in the first place, I am convinced, by that ever-ready conception of Anglo-American Catholic alienation, opportunity was available. In the previous international novels, the chief protagonists were Protestants, however gentled in their heresy, presumptively more or less to match James' own. Might it not be inferred by unwary readers that their intellectual-moral superiority was owing to religious causes when in fact it was owing to their expatriated Americanism? Were we to have adored them for flaunting their Protestant value and virtue all over a Europe considerably less Protestant? How could we, when their Protestant faith was so feeble and so benign, so tolerant, so prone to complete indifference, so accommodating, especially *when on the grounds,* to the old persuasion? The misleading religious inference James subverted, indeed deleted, by Catholicizing his mainly American characters. Now we have Roman Catholic Americans abroad not in a Catholic but in an easygoing (compared with what it used to be) ecumenical setting within which their own rites may freely flourish in communion with those of the natives who share the same faith and amid the predominant majority of citizens who happen to be Protestant Church of England communicants instead and who peacefully on Sunday traipse off to their own dear little church (stolen from the Catholics centuries ago) from the Catholic hospitality of Adam Verver – and not a harsh word said.

Bizarre as it may seem, Maggie Verver, an American Roman Catholic, is James' most fully developed and most powerful fictive personage – and no wonder she is a bit frightening! To her father's perception, if not invariably to ours, Maggie resembles both a nymph and a nun (she is a little like a gender-reversed Donatello resurrected from *The Marble Faun*). Even more stunningly, she is the heiress of an American Protestant Puritan line that apparently turned Catholic in an earlier generation. There is "some probable reference in her American blood to dusting and polishing New England grandmothers," but *now* "she looked as if she had been carried there prepared, all attired and decorated, like some holy image in a procession, and left precisely to show what wonder she could work under pressure." Fanny Assingham *accordingly* feels as if she herself were "the truly pious priest" (another gender reversal) confronting "his miraculous Madonna." Maggie is even said to feel that she possesses "by miraculous help, some advantage." She is said to be "living with eternity; with which she would continue to live." She is, in one configural extension, the Mother of God.

Maggie *malgre lui* is the one who works under pressure, works miraculously, with utterly laudable Balzacian duplicity, to right a wrong situation, to untangle a confusion, to sort out and reassign roles. You can equally well say that in effect she *writes* the novel or that she *is* the novel. The first half of *The Golden Bowl* is almost all situation, the second half almost all action. The action is almost all hers. She not only inhabits the shaped receptable of novelistic space but she shapes and informs it; without her, that space would hardly come to exist in the form that it does. And you can say that she writes the novel and that she is the novel by virtue of the realization that in effect she *is* Henry James. She and her maker alike began empty – dull, innocent, minute, victimized – and ended in the posture Napoleonic. Maggie Verver is the small boy be-skirted and Catholicized, alienated from origin *deux fois* and at least that many times triumphant past limitation. Finally, she is Henry James having escaped and transcended both his inherited Protestant American beginnings and that debilitating sort of Americanism which tends to see things in certain perspectives – Protestantly, as who should say.

Perhaps best of all, James has managed these escapes and transcendences without having to do one single thing about them in his "real" or "personal" life, but just as the Ververs got in Charlotte Stant to live certain aspects of their lives on their behalf while they remained at home, so James gets in Maggie to "do" Catholicity for him while he remains outside, in rapt ironic admiration at what he has wrought. In *Guy Domville* (I have argued) Henry James was trying to imagine himself as a Roman Catholic – what would it feel like? In *The Golden Bowl* (I am arguing) he was trying to imagine himself as a Roman Catholic novelist. What would *that* feel like? especially if at the same time that novelist happened to be a woman. Supernaturally almost, but in fact through the most literary means, we have our answer: It would feel like *The Golden Bowl*. Of Adam Verver, a multimillionaire wizard (also of course Catholic), it is strangely (or not) said: "He had never spoken of himself as infallible – it wasn't his way." It wasn't James' way either: "[T]he difficulty was here of course that one could really never know – couldn't know without having *been* one's self a personage; whether a Pope, a King, a President, a Peer, a General, or just a beautiful Author." If, as I long ago remarked, the Works of Henry James are in a sense Minny Temple's "church," why should he not, at their apogee, be her, and his own, Pope?

PART SIX

"Prove That I'm Not!": Toward the Impossibility of Interpretation

I might push it away, but I couldn't really get rid of it; nor, on the whole, doubtless, did I want to, for to have in one's life, year after year, a particular question or two that one couldn't comfortably and imposingly make up one's mind about was just the sort of thing to keep one from turning stupid.

"Maud-Evelyn," 1900

"I'm not a prophet or a soothsayer, and still less a charlatan, and don't pretend to the gift of second sight – I only confess to have cultivated my imagination, as one has to in a country [the United States] where there is nothing to take that trouble off one's hands. Therfore perhaps it is that things glimmer upon me at moments from a distance, so that I find myself in the act of catching them, but am liable to lose them again, and to feel nervous, as if I had made a fool of myself, when an honest man like my cousin Perry looks at me as if he thought me a little mad. I'm *not* mad, cousin Perry – I'm only a mite bewildered by the way I seem to affect you. . . ."

"I like your free talk – I like it, I like it!" Molly broke in at this. "I wouldn't have it a bit different, though we have certainly never heard anything like it in all our lives. I'm not afraid of you now," the girl continued, "or else I'm no more so than I want to be. . . ."

The Sense of the Past, unfinished

Certain literary works by Henry James clearly intend that the perceptive reader shall take all, or most, of the personages and behaviors for Roman Catholic and interpret them in that light, however variously – "De Grey: A Romance," "Gabrielle de Bergerac," *Guy Domville,* "The Altar of the Dead," *The Golden Bowl.* Other works quite as clearly intend that the same perceptive reader shall take all, or most, of the personages and behaviors for Protestant, with an appropriately various response –

Washington Square, The Bostonians, "The Great Good Place." A third set of works presents Protestants, Catholics, and Unaffiliated Persons in patterns of comparatively easy differentiation – *The American, The Princess Casamassima, The Ambassadors.* And yet still other works are either more mixed or more obscure in their intentions regarding religious affiliation; they may contain, or even feature, personages probably or certainly Protestant but with Catholic leanings or tendencies (never the opposite; that would not be picturesque) – *The Portrait of a Lady* is a prime example. Carried a little further, and a little further still, and finally to exasperating extremes, James' penchant for personages or tendencies in the Catholic way produces works so uncertain as to religious affiliation and at the same so provocative as virtually to proclaim: "I defy you, reader, to say that this or that personage, this or that behavior, is *not* Catholic; and the burden of proof is on *you!*"

Of James' twenty-odd novels, I have already dealt with *Watch and Ward, Roderick Hudson, The American, The Reverberator, What Maisie Knew, The Turn of the Screw,* and *The Golden Bowl.* There is no Catholicity to speak of in *Confidence, Washington Square, The Tragic Muse, The Other House, The Sacred Fount, The Outcry, The Sense of the Past,* and *The Ivory Tower.* Catholicity in *The Bostonians* is minimal and marginal. That leaves seven of the greatest James novels in which Roman Catholicity *is* something of a problem and on the whole an increasing problem, and so I take them in the chronological order of composition, which is also, given some backing and filling, the order of their noninterpretability: *The Europeans, The Portrait of a Lady, The Princess Casmassima, The Spoils of Poynton, The Awkward Age, The Ambassadors,* and *The Wings of the Dove.*

In the cunning with which he represents religious affiliation in some of his novels, Henry James may well remind us of the Baroness Münster in *The Europeans: A Sketch* (1878): "[T]here was what she said, and there was what she meant, and there was something, between the two, that was neither." It is not always certain that the reader can get at the second or third of these – *The Europeans* in the aggregate furnishes a splendid opening instance of such uncertainty – but at least what the text says is available to scrutiny and bewilderment. At the end, Felix Young and Gertrude Wentworth are married by Mr. Brand, a Unitarian "ecclesiastic," as he is several times called, and that should settle the matter of Felix Young, and perhaps, by implication, of his sister too, were it not for the young man's perpetually tolerant obligingness to please all and sundry in every conceivable connection; and were it not for his previous characterization of Mr. Brand as "a sort of lay-priest . . . I don't exactly make him out"; and were it not for his overriding secularistic desire, reminiscent of Mr. Brooke in "Travelling Companions" (1870) to demonstrate his questionable Americanism, even if in his view the demonstration involves a superfluous conversion – when his sister asks, "[D]o you mean to turn American?" he simply replies, "I am a very good American already" (but permanently resident in Europe save for the New England interlude of the narrative).

His nationalistic and other desire to please does not, however, render him unequivocally Protestant. And indeed, insofar as he may be presumed of the same persuasion as his sister, he may be presumed quite un-Protestant, that is to say according to the Jamesian calculus quite Catholic. In the opening chapter we are informed of Eugenia's passionately disproportionate and irrational feeling at the mere sight of a Boston church-spire – "She hated it, she despised it. . . . She had never known herself to care so much about church-spires" – and that she has been educated in a convent. The mother of Eugenia and Felix (we learn in chapter 2) had, like other early Henry James women, "turned Roman Catholic," *turned* being a regular James synonym for *converted,* that fact of conversion presumably settling the question of her children's religious upbringing – if it needed settling (it did and it does, and it may fail of a final settlement). Eugenia and Felix talk an identifiably Catholic line, marked by a blissful ignorance of provincial and heretical ways:

> Her glance fell upon young Mr. Brand, who stood there, with his arms folded and his hand on his chin, looking at her. "The gentleman, I suppose, is a sort of ecclesiastic," she said to Mr. Wentworth, lowering her voice a little.
> "He is a minister," answered Mr. Wentworth.
> "A Protestant?" asked Eugenia.
> "I am a Unitarian, madam," replied Mr. Brand, impressively.
> "Ah, I see," said Eugenia. "Something new."

Later she seems to think that the Wentworths must be Quakers. Another ludicrous conversation shows Felix in a naïvely relaxed attitude of Catholic assumption, wishing to paint Mr. Wentworth's portrait in a style, and describing it to him in a manner bound to be unacceptable to the prejudices of a New England post-Puritan:

> "It's an interesting head; it's very medieval.". . .
> Mr. Wentworth looked grave. . . . "The Lord made it," he said. "I don't think it is for man to make it over again."
> "Certainly the Lord made it," replied Felix, laughing, "and he made it very well. But life has been touching up the work. . . . I should like to do you as an old prelate, an old cardinal, or the prior of an order."
> "A prelate, a cardinal?" murmured Mr. Wentworth. "Do you refer to the Roman Catholic priesthood?"

That conversation was in chapter 5 (in a total of twelve); thereafter, textual interest in Catholic–Protestant relations is virtually nonexistent or, when present, virtually impermeable to intelligence. Is it the ignorance of Eugenia or of Henry James which assures us that the Reigning Prince of Silberstadt has the power to annul her morganatic marriage? And when she makes, "as it were, a great many stations," going through Robert Acton's house, are we to understand a significant religious metaphor (heavy irony) or only a casual locution? (But what other kind of stations are "made"?) Is it significant of anything but good will, on the part of Felix, and indifference, on the part of Eugenia, that he does, and she does not, go to church (clearly Protestant; most likely Unitarian) with the Wentworths ("She had, however, never been, during her residence in the United States, what is called a regular attendant at divine service")? – but it is equally obvious that we have never seen her going to mass. Is it aught more than the most obvious and conventional fictive contrivance that Mr. Brand should perform the wedding ceremonies that serve as effective clôture of all? Are we to think that Felix has "turned" Protestant? If so, Felix is one in a million. In Henry James, conversions go in the opposite direction, that is to say, against and across the convictions of the majority readership. Surely that readership might have been pleased to have its convictions gratified. The Jamesian novel does not gratify Protestant convictions, however: Either it leaves them alone or it contradicts them, which is surely a curious thing, James in real life being so evidently Protestant and a fortiori so uninterested. But by now we should be accustomed to how curious James is in his representation of religious affairs.

The Portrait of a Lady (1881) is James' masterpiece of inclusive graciousness. There is something in it for everyone – and many of these things are indeterminate and ambiguous. At the end, Henrietta Stackpole tells Casper Goodwood that Isabel Archer Osmond has "started for Rome," not, we are virtually certain, to enter the Roman Catholic church, and yet she may – and we never to know. This novel is not a conversion novel, and still it cherishes as it retains certain tonalities and effects from that curious genre, for example the convent. The Portrait of a Lady is not otherwise particularly concerned with religious differences. Rather, the personages and their behaviors are presented as somehow mixed and between (Catholic and Protestant, Christian and secular), hovering, hung up. And all or most of this ambience comes upon us unawares, the first or English third (chapters 1 through 21) being nearly as secular as Henry James criticism takes all Henry James to be. There are, of course, sacred seculars; "It was in her disposition [Isabel's] at all times to lose *faith* in the reality of absent things; she could summon back her *faith*, in case of need, with an effort, but the effort was often painful, even when the reality had been pleasant. The past was apt to look dead, and its revival to wear the *supernatural* aspect of *resurrection*." Even with emphasis added, this is not religious prose. The ostensible reference is to suitors out of sight and out of mind. The secret message is that if certain pages (of *The Portrait of a Lady*) are not as clear to memory as memory ought to like, you may go back and read them again.

Overall *The Portrait of a Lady* exudes a vaguely Anglican or Protestant Episcopal air: It is forever moving in two opposite directions at once. Lord Warburton, his sisters, and his brother the Vicar (the muscular Christian) are obviously Church of England, the Touchetts perhaps so, and Mr. Bantling too (Henrietta won't mind). Isabel is much offended by her husband's insulting allegation that "she had no traditions, and the moral horizon of a Unitarian minister. Poor Isabel, who had never been able to understand Unitarianism!" And why should she? It is not "picturesque," one of her favorite terms. Yet Isabel is in her origins generically Protestant, and her Protestantism lingers, "The old Protestant tradition [vis-à-vis the horror of convents] had never faded from Isabel's imagination." The "old" (!) tradition is the assurance that a convent is tantamount to a prison and that a convent-prison is tantamount to the Catholic church – once you are in you can never get out, and therefore you must never begin, as in drug addiction. Even a kindly remark by Madame Catherine falls "with a leaden weight upon Isabel's ears; it seemed to represent the surrender of a personality, the authority of the Church." She and Osmond are married in the American chapel at Firenze.

But already at Firenze and later in Rome Isabel frequents Catholic churches, over and above St. Peter's, which is tourist Catholic and not necessarily to count. As in *The Marble Faun,* Isabel Archer's Rome is the Rome of ruins, of loss, of pain, of sorrow: "[S]he had come to think of it chiefly as the place where people had suffered." And thus we have the confused nexus of secularized Roman Catholicity for Isabel:

> This was what came to her in the starved churches, where the marble columns, transferred from pagan ruins, seemed to offer her a companionship in endurance, and the musty incense to be a compound of long-unanswered prayers. There was no gentler nor less consistent heretic than Isabel; the firmest of worshippers, gazing at dark altar-pictures or clustered candles, could not have felt more intimately the suggestiveness of these objects or have been more liable at such moments to a spiritual visitation.

Isabel Archer will not, while in our purview, go further than that; on the question how far that is, different kinds of readers will entertain different kinds of opinion. Other matters are more certain: There is in the text of the novel no word of Crucifixion and Resurrection, of Apostolic Succession and Tradition, of the Real Presence – and no one in the entire novel is ever caught going to mass or to any other religious service except a wedding or a funeral. Isabel Archer's Catholic sympathies, whatever they may be, tend toward the aesthetic, the impersonal, the touristic, the literary, and in this she is at one with her creator and with most of her creator's audience. But she or narrative authority or both acquiesce in the designation "heretic," a category proceeding from the Catholic rather than the Protestant understanding of her status, and if she fails of consistency even to her separated condition it is easy to see toward which persuasion she will wobble. No one, it is also easy to see, is to take offense of Isabel: If she is out of the True Faith it is only the tail end of a historical accident.

Unlike Isabel Archer, and very like Henry James, Gilbert Osmond is a consummate master of Catholic *tone* (but Henry James is a consummate master of *him*). Is Osmond Catholic or isn't he? Is his sister Amy? When he says to her, "Pansy is a little convent-flower," we hear her respond, "Oh, the convents, the convents! . . . Speak to me of the convents. You may learn anything there; I am a convent-flower myself." If Osmond is a Catholic he is a very bad one. Perhaps he is only a Catholic-monger, as suggested by his speech about convents:

> "This bustling, pushing rabble, that calls itself society – one should take her [Pansy] out of it occasionally. Convents are very quiet, very convenient, very salutary. I like to think of her there, in the old garden, under the arcade, among those tranquil, virtuous women. Many of them are gentlewomen born; several of them are noble." . . . And then he went on – "The Catholics are very wise, after all. The convent is a great institution; we can't do without it; it corresponds to an essential need in families, in society. It's a school of good manners; it's a school of repose. Oh, I don't want to detach my daughter from the world," he added; "I don't want to make her fix her thoughts on the other one. This one is very well, after all, and she may think of it as much as she chooses. Only she must think of it in the right way."

Osmond's fatuities may be severally enjoyed by different classes of reader, Protestants relishing one more evidence of the hierarchical corruptibility of Rome, Catholics reveling in self-righteous umbrage over the social-climbing desecration of an exalted spiritual ideal. "And that is my little girl . . . who has just come out of a convent" is how he introduces Pansy to Isabel (Pansy "stood there as if she were about to partake of her first communion"). Osmond envies the Pope, "for the consideration he enjoys." He (Osmond) collects old silver crucifixes. He says his daughter "is a little saint of heaven!"

Catholic reference in *The Portrait of a Lady* is clustered in chapters, not uniformly spread (there are long stretches with no trace of it) – in chapter 22, where Osmond entertains the nuns at his villa and he and Madame Merle bicker about nuns and convents, she approving them less than he;

in chapter 24, where Osmond introduces his little convent-flower to her prospective stepmother and exhibits so much Catholic tone; in chapter 50, where Osmond makes his great speech about convents and Isabel retreats to her old Protestant tradition. Chapter 45 is another very good Catholic chapter. In it we discover how Isabel is the veritable embodiment (personification) of the Jamesian metaphor that I have called the sacred secular, as revealed in her view of marriage, elsewhere given as variously moralistic, pragmatic, and prideful: "[A]lmost anything seemed preferable to repudiating the most serious act – the single sacred act – of her life." Half of Isabel sees marriage as serious (and secular), half as sacred (if not quite a sacrament). She is split right down the middle, but the halves join: There is after all only the one woman. A few pages later, Ralph Touchett tells Isabel, "I am very glad he [Lord Warburton] should not become your step-daughter's husband. It makes such a very queer relation to you!" (as in the fables of Catholic *ménage*, "De Grey: A Romance," *Guy Domville*, *The Golden Bowl*). And then Isabel goes to Pansy "a little as a confessor" – but who is the penitent and who the priest?. Pansy speaks to Isabel "as if she were praying to the Madonna" and in the next sentence text tells us that Isabel *is* the Madonna. What can you do with a passage like that but accept it? It is irreducibly metaphor. But so is language, religious language not least – *Hoc est enim Corpus meum*.

The Princess Casamassima (1886) is so conspicuously political ("the social question," class warfare, capital and labor, affluence and poverty) that some will be surprised to hear that the novel also carries a considerable, if undeniably lesser, burden of intermittent religious discourse, what you might call an interruptive counterpoint in a minor key. At the same time, the text of the novel displays an apparent solicitude on the part of its author that the religious identifications of the personages shall be unusually scrupulous and unambiguous. Moreover, there appears to be an equal solicitude, perhaps under the influence of the nonconformist Princess, to avoid any the least impression of conventional stereotyping. Radicals, liberals, and conservatives consistently fail to line up with any banal equations between politics and religion: The Prince Casamassima may well be the most reactionary personage in the novel, but the Princess, his separated wife, is the most recklessly radical, and both are Roman Catholic.

Hyacinth Robinson seems not to line up at all. Narrative voice, speaking for and by means of Millicent Henning, speaks of his "general secularity," his "godlessness," and his "heretical impatience" displayed at divine worship (Anglican). Paul and Rosy Muniment are at least once found guilty by association with a Wesleyan Chapel. Various personages are anti-clerical but in various ways: Hyacinth superficially, the Poupins programatically, Lady Aurora meekly and modestly, Mr. Vetch decreasingly. Les Poupins are presumptively French Catholic – the others Anglican – and we may remember that anti-clericalism or the furious rejection of "priest-craft" is in its origins and in the main a French Catholic phenomenon. In Paris the ghost of Hyacinth's revolutionary French grandfather shows himself surprisingly tolerant about the visitation of churches. Millicent Henning is by the inflamed imagination of Hyacinth figured as an English version of the French revolutionary Goddess of Reason whereas in fact she is the most religiously oriented of the Protestant personages (Church of England). Yet even Millicent Henning is by textual innuendo given her little Romish leanings: "[S]he seemed to answer, in her proper person, for creeds and communions and sacraments; she was more than devotional, she was almost pontifical." She declines more than a single attendance per day, "once she had lifted her voice in prayer and praise, she changed her *allure*" (a typical Henry James Frenchism).

Paradoxically, this novel of atheist political conspiracy, so largely set in Protestant England (chiefly London), is positively overrun by Roman Catholics, mostly of continental origin. Not one of them is ever observed going to mass; they represent that "social *régime*" of the Catholic church recognized by James in his reading of Balzac. The visit of Pinnie and young Hyacinth to Florentine Vivier his mother dying in prison is benevolently expedited from inside that abominable institution by a solicitous Catholic chaplain. The "sceptical Assunta" (from *Roderick Hudson*) we suppose to be as devout as ever, but we hear no word of her ability to pray for half an hour without letup. Madame Grandoni, "the ironical old woman," also from *Roderick Hudson,* who is German but has lived her long years in Rome, is now Catholic, as we learn from the following bit of dialogue between her and Prince Casamassima – we had an early hint in her droll description of how English families in Rome "squeezed into the great ceremonies of the church":

> "The misery of London is something fearful."
> "*Che vuole?* There is misery everywhere," returned the Prince. "It is the will of God. *Ci vuol' pazienza!* And in this country does no one give alms?"
> "Every one, I believe. But it appears that it is not enough."
> The Prince said nothing for a moment; this statement of Madame Grandoni's seemed to present difficulties. The solution, however, soon suggested itself; it was expressed in the inquiry, "What will you have in a country which has not the true faith?"
> "Ah, the true faith is a great thing; but there is suffering even in countries that have it."
> "*Evidentemente.* But it helps suffering to be borne, and, later, it makes it up; whereas here! . . ."

May I once more point out, perhaps for the last time, that such a passage will be read quite differently by a Catholic reader, a Protestant reader, and (to take a case) a freethinking worshipper of "the State"?

There is naturally in all James (or anywhere else) no Catholic like Christina Light the Princess Casamassima. As in *Roderick Hudson,* she gladly displays a modicum of Catholic learning. She alludes (in English) to the *gran rifiuto* of Dante's *Commedia,* and she foolishly thinks Lady Aurora "as good in her way as St. Francis of Assisi." Although a revolutionist, she is also a *liberal* Catholic who "had cast off prejudices and gave no heed to conventional danger-posts." In quiescent moods, she prefigures Milly Theale, "a creature capable, socially, of immeasurable flights," now sitting "dove-like, with folded wings." She scatters money among the London poor "as simply as the abbess of some beggar-haunted convent, or a lady-bountiful of the superstitious, unscientific ages who should have hoped to be assisted to heaven by her doles." Like Henry James in certain moods, she is almost proud of being superstitious; "I don't know whether I am religious, and whether, if I were, my religion would be superstitious. But my superstitions are certainly religious." Like Miss Barrace of *The Ambassadors* she is freely contradictious. Even Paul Muniment notes the oddity of her feeding revolutionary groups "with money extorted from an old Catholic and princely family." (An uncle of the Prince is a "powerful prelate.") She is just as freely immodest about her graces: "Already, when I was fifteen years old, I wanted to sell all I had and give to the poor." Later she claims to have done so but continues to live rather well. More than anything else, the Princess glories in a high traditional aristocratic Catholic attitude of cultural superiority, especially toward Protestant English upstarts: "[P]eople oughtn't to be both corrupt and dull." Yet like Catholics who claim to be amoral because it makes them so aesthetic and so un-Protestant, "She remarked that she herself was very corrupt," meaning sophisticated. She goes on and on to Lady Aurora, "Do you do your work in connection with any ecclesiasticism, any missions, or priests or sisters? I'm a Catholic, you know – but so little!"

In case we should have missed her Catholic identification, narrative voice occasionally spells it out, plus a little English Catholic history, romantic and vague, perhaps from Thackeray's *Henry Esmond* (1852): "She showed Hyacinth everything: the queer transmogrified corner that had once been a chapel; the secret stairway which had served in the persecutions of the Catholics (the owners of Medley were, like the Princess herself, of the old persuasion)." Sacred seculars abound, some quite sacriligious, as Hyacinth to the Princess, "I was hanging about outside, in the steps of the temple, among the loafers and the gossips, but now I have been in the innermost sanctuary – I have seen the holy of holies," meaning that he is now pledged to political assassination. Then narrative shifts from Judaic to Counter-Reformation ambience, Hyacinth in indirect discourse: "He had taken a vow of blind obedience, as the Jesuit fathers did to the head of their order. It was because they had carried out their vows (having, in the first place, great administrators) that their organisation had been mighty." We may sense that the remarks about Jesuit administrators derive rather more from Henry James (or even Francis Parkman) than from Hyacinth Robinson. But we also sense the reason for his interpolation: Henry James is determined, if only this once, to be clear about his religious points, and if necessary he will break in to establish them.

Perhaps in no other major work by Henry James are the religious aspects of the narrative more coyly hinted at and cunningly left open than in *The Spoils of Poynton* (1897). The text has nothing so determinant as a convent or a conversion, and the words *Protestant* and *Catholic* do not appear. The novel opens quietly at a country house, Waterbath, on a Sunday, when, as so often in a James fiction set in England, the personages are or are not on their way to church. We naturally assume the houseguests and the church to be Anglican, and that assumption seems later confirmed by news that the sister of Fleda Vetch will marry a curate – Anglican parlance. So we read along until chapter 10, when we are knocked across the chops by the following bit of dialogue:

> Fleda stopped in front of her hostess. "I gave him [Owen] my opinion that you're very logical, very obstinate and very proud."
> "Quite right, my dear: I'm a rank bigot – about that sort of thing!" Mrs. Gereth jerked her head at the contents of the house. "I've never denied it. *I'd kidnap – to save them, to convert them – the children of heretics.* When I know I'm right I go to the stake." (emphasis added)

What is so devilish about that passage is the way the reader must simultaneously discount the weight of metaphor while at the same time giving weight to the diction: Mrs. Gereth will not literally kidnap children or go to the stake; on the other hand, who but a Catholic would be likely to use this kind of language – "heretics" – or, in James' view, take such an indecent interest in the necessity of conversion?

Now the wary reader begins to turn pages backward and forward, not altogether surprised to find them loaded with sacred idioms and images, most often applied to secular objects, emotions, and behaviors: "they [the things] were our religion!"; "her [Fleda's] sacred solitude"; "the consecrated Madame de Jaume"; "pledges [to be married] so deep and sacred"; "If you'll take him, I'll give up everything. There, it's a solemn promise, the most sacred of my life"; "you've behaved like such a saint"; "he [Owen] must only trust her [Fleda] and pray for her"; "One would be more at peace in some vulgar little place that should owe its *cachet* to a Universal Provider"; "He clasped his hands before her as he might have clasped them at an altar . . . as if she had been truly something sacred"; "You're not quite a saint in heaven yet"; "I had been an angel of delicacy – I had effaced myself like a saint"; "She equally, she felt, was of the religion, and like any other of the passionately pious she could worship now even in the desert"; "She would go down to Poynton as a pilgrim might go to a shrine," specifically for the Maltese cross, "a small but marvellous crucifix of ivory." These various religious ways of putting largely but not altogether secular things are about equally proffered by Mrs. Gereth and by narrative voice; many of them, as is obvious, refer to Fleda.

At this point the reader is probably ready to suspect the whole kit and caboodle. Reader's next shock comes in chapter 18, when Mrs. Gereth quite unexpectedly (and "out of character," some will now be coming to feel) bursts out to Fleda (about Owen): "Any one but a jackass would have tucked you under his arm and marched you off to the Registrar!" Catholics are not supposed to be that keen on civil marriages – it is one way James surreptitiously suggests the religious affiliations and practices of his personages. Fleda in return says, "To the Registrar?" so that now we do not know if she is mainly upset by Mrs. Gereth's bold talk (she is) or if in her innocence she is unaware of what the Registrar is and does. (This is also possible.) It is almost enough to make us wonder if maybe Fleda is a Catholic and Mrs. Gereth is not. But when Owen actually marries Mona Brigstock, everything reverses again. Fleda, still innocent, asks, "At that place you spoke of in town?" and Mrs. Gereth lets her (and us) have it: "At a Registry-office – like a pair of low atheists." *Is* she or *isn't* she? She sounds like it and then she does not, and then again she does. *The Spoils of Poynton* is like two alternating or intertwined ribbons of different color, one stamped with the word *yes* and one stamped with the word *no*. You can take hold of either or both ribbons, but inattention to both does not, in my book, make for a great reading. Mona and Owen are finally married at Waterbath church, with "two ecclesiastics," rite not specified. After the wedding, Mrs. Gereth fondly supposes that Owen won't live with Mona; divorce is out of the question; "Our only chance," she says, "is the chance she may die." Fleda then indirectly promises not to desert Mrs. Gereth so long as Mrs. Gereth shall live and "her silence committed her as solemnly as the vow of a nun."

Interpretations of *The Spoils of Poynton* will vary according to how Catholic a reader takes Mrs. Gereth as being – *if* she is, then Owen probably is, Mona more than possibly is, and even Fleda may be. *If* any or all of them are, then the Poynton–Waterbath contrast may be a contrast not only between taste and vulgarity but between old Catholic family and a parvenu Catholic setting. Mrs. Gereth is, I should guess, very faintly outlined, your fairly typical Jamesian Catholic in the satiric–heroic mold, eccentric, cynical, tyrannical, amoral, and as Machiavel as Maggie Verver or Balzac. She is also as bold and passionate as Adina Waddington, in that early Italian tale, and magnanimous to a fault ("even in her shrunken state the lady of Ricks was larger than her wrongs"). More than anything else, Mrs. Gereth is outspokenly sexual and sexually manipulative: "Only let yourself go, darling – only let yourself go!" She is quite convinced that Mona got Owen by so doing. "Mrs. Gereth spoke as if she meant it to the fullest extent of her cynicism and saw it in every detail." ("She did what you wouldn't. . . . Before he could turn round he was married.") Earlier, she recalls her own youth: "Lord, what a creature you'd have thought me in my good time!" Earlier still, she asks Fleda if Owen has any romantic-erotic feeling for her:

> "For me?" Fleda stared. "Before he has even married her?"
> Mrs. Gereth gave a sharp laugh at this. "He ought at least to appreciate your wit. Oh my dear, you *are* a treasure! Doesn't he appreciate anything?"

Turn-of-the-century people of the ordinary Protestant sort don't in fictions by Henry James talk with such indecency and worldly wit. Roman Catholics, even when not Latin or continental, sometimes do. It is because Catholics may not divorce that they are so prone to thoughts of adultery. It is because they are not Protestant that they are so sophisticated.

In some of these novels there seems to be on James' part a moderate desire to be reasonably clear about religious affiliation, but in others that desire seems to have been replaced by a desire – reasonable or not, one is hardly in a position to say – to be secretive and even misleading. *The Awkward Age* (1899) falls into the second category, though it is by no means such a hard case as *The Wings of the Dove*. Catholic interest circles around the Duchess (Jane). Her protégée and the cover for her own licentious behavior, her dead husband's niece, is a palpably Italian young lady, called by their English friends Little Aggie, but properly named, in good Catholic Italian, Agnesina (the Lamb, feminized and *diminuendo*), stereotypically too cold before marriage and too hot after. Narrative voice is fond of laying on her Catholic background good and thick, almost Osmondized: "She might have been prepared for her visit by a cluster of doting nuns, cloistered daughters of ancient houses and educators of similar products, whose taste, hereditarily good, had grown, out of the world and most delightfully, so queer as to leave on everything they touched a particular shade of distinction." Mr. Longdon's conversation with her at Mertle elicits for the attentive reader the almost certain knowledge that their Dr. Beltram (hers and Duchess') is an English Catholic priest, James' vexatiousness largely consisting of such distracting terms as *doctor* and *clergyman*. Dr. Beltram is "The most intimate friend of all," "We tell him everything," he "takes away" all their troubles, that is to say, he is their confessor and their spiritual director:

> "Oh I don't mean he's a doctor for medicine. He's a clergyman – and my aunt says he's a saint. I don't think you've many in England," little Aggie continued to explain.
> "Many saints? I'm afraid not. Your aunt's very happy to know one. We should call Dr. Beltram in England a priest."
> "Oh but he's English. And he knows everything we do – and everything we think."

Readers who still find it an open question whether Dr. Beltram might not be (after all) Church of England don't know their Duchess; here she is in full flood to the assembled company in the second chapter of Book Eighth ("Tishy Grendon"):

> "Things have turned out so much as *I* desire them that I should really feel wicked not to have a humble heart. There's a quarter indeed," she added with a noble unction, "to which I don't fear to say for myself that no day and no night pass without my showing it. However, you English, I know, don't like one to speak of one's religion. I'm just as simply thankful for mine – I mean with as little sense of indecency or agony about it – as I am for my health or my carriage."

It is a splendid example of "Catholic tone" à la James – with, of course, Catholic *unction*. Mr. Longdon is a sort of Anglican saint of the old England rural order, even though James shows a certain penchant for pushing him, from time to time, Romeward, or perhaps only so far as Canterbury, as in Vanderbank's feeling that Mr. Longdon "might almost have been a priest if priests . . . were ever such dandies," or as in Mrs. Brook's figure for the impossibility of patronizing him, "As if he were the Primate or the French Ambassador?"

On the other hand, nothing could be more gratefully pellucid – to a reader already sufficiently burdened with other matters of interpretation – than James' handling of religious affairs in *The Ambassadors* (1903). We readily recognize Lambert Strether as a good but slightly disturbed Protestant of the Isabel Archer gentle heretic type. We see him frequent Notre Dame, where he broods, neither a sightseer of the inexcusable (vulgar American) kind nor a prospective convert. We infer that his Woollett associates are also Protestant, variously as to their indifference (passing for tolerance) or their moralistic self-righteousness. We infer that little Bilham is as untouched by his sojourn in a Catholic country as he is consumed with homesickness for the land he left behind him. And there is not even a hint that Chad Newsome is aware of his new French friends' religious faith. They are all, these Americans abroad, Protestants or post-Protestants, including Miss Barrace and Maria Gostrey. Or they are nothing at all – for novelistic purposes, their religious convictions, if any, don't signify. When Maria Gostrey explains Madame de Vionnet to Strether as pluralistically represented by "the many-tongued cluster of confessionals at St. Peter's," we know that the much-traveled Gostrey has been there – but in her capacity as courier, not as a pilgrim. Only reactionary Waymarsh among these Protestant Americans is a fierce anti-Catholic paranoid bigot of the early or middle-nineteenth-century type, fortified in an interlocking set of fiercely connected anti-papist and related prejudices, hatreds and fears centered on the ancient fear of conversion James had made so much of in his early conversion narratives (and even so late as *The Turn of the Screw*). Strether imagines Waymarsh imagining Maria Gostrey as "a Jesuit in petticoats, a representative of the recruiting interests of the Catholic Church. The Catholic Church, for Waymarsh – that was to say the enemy, the monster of bulging eyes and far-reaching quivering groping tentacles – was exactly society, exactly the multiplication of shibboleths, exactly the discrimination of types and tones, exactly the wicked old rows of Chester, rank with feudalism; exactly in short Europe." Exactly Henry James inserting from time to time his little bits of Roman Catholic practice, partly for local color, mainly to represent, perhaps also, a little, to annoy, and, in one famous instance, because he happened to have it to hand, the quite uncalled-for elaboration of Catholic institutions and religious surrounding Gloriani's garden, suggesting to Strether "the sense of a great convent," and then, the text irrelevantly expansive, as in an unbounded epic simile, "a convent of missions, famous for he scarce knew what, a nursery of young priests," flock after flock of Guy Domvilles, "of scattered shade, of straight alleys and chapel-bells." In "Project of Novel" (1 September 1900) James had recalled for his own pleasure and the benefit of a prospective publisher Whistler's garden in Paris, which he had overlooked before it was Whistler's, which reminded him of Chateaubriand and Madame de Récamier, and which abutted "a great convent of which I have forgotten the name, and which I now think was one of the places of training for young missionary priests."[1]

The central Catholic–Protestant passage of *The Ambassadors* features nice tolerant easygoing nondoctrinal Strether vis-à-vis nice tolerant easygoing nondoctrinal Madame de Vionnet, two different kinds of churchgoer, equally yet quite differently civilized. We readers are also variously civilized in our religious differences and thus in our response to texts that represent such differences; some will gladly attribute Strether's outsider status mainly or entirely to his being abroad in a "foreign" culture that

just happens to be French and Catholic (Notre Dame is in fact the arch-
bishopric cathedral of Paris), and others will as gladly attribute his outsider status to his being a separated brother. Text, determined to please
all parties, is noncommittal.

Strether is by now a Notre Dame *habitué*. Notre Dame has a "benefi-
cent action on his nerves." He has made previous visits, with others or
by himself. He has lately tended to come alone and to conceal his visits
from his friends. In several senses, he is increasingly secretive, evasive
(but a desire to become a Catholic does not seem to be among those
senses): "He was aware of having no errand in such a place but the desire
not to be, for the hour, in certain other places," surely a minimalist desire. Notre Dame thus becomes for him a secularized sanctuary. Being
Protestant, "The great church had no altar for his worship, no direct
voice for his soul," the idea of Romanism doubtless interfering with his
direct access to "God," and still it is "soothing even to sanctity," perhaps
because his Protestant secularism renders it, for him, comparatively un-
Poped. The nave and chapels of Notre Dame are mentioned. It is likened
to a museum. The experience is for Strether largely aesthetic.

But not entirely so. Novelistic point of view determines Strether as
subject, other persons as objects. Strether is, as usual, at his people-
watching. He specializes in fellow visitants, especially if they appear devout, that is to say, almost by definition, Catholic (considering where
they, i.e., "we," are), "remarking some note of behavior," and then,
more specifically, "of penitence, of prostration, of the absolved, relieved
state." We perceive Strether making out an individual visitant. She sits
and gazes. She "had placed herself, as he never did, within the focus of
the shrine [and likewise we may never ascertain why a shrine has a "focus" as if it were some sort of ecclesiastic lens], and she had lost herself,
he could easily see, as he would only have liked to do. She was not," like
him, "a wandering alien," as in so many Jamesian texts from "Travelling
Companions" on, "keeping back more than she gave, but one of the
familiar, the intimate, the fortunate, for whom these dealings had a method
and meaning," from which apparently desirable method and meaning
Strether–James is determined to keep a proper distance – the word *dealings* measures the distance and hints the "reasons" for it. Yet Strether, if
not James, is naturally naïve, quite ignorant, in fact: "[H]e wondered if
her attitude were some congruous fruit of absolution, of 'indulgence,' "
and once more we wonder if James has his terms quite straight. "He
[Strether, that is] knew but dimly what indulgence, in such a place, might
mean; yet he had . . . a vision of how it might indeed add to the zest of
active rites," a vision not easily particularized by the skeptical reader,
Catholic or otherwise. Finally Strether recognizes his visitant as Madame
de Vionnet, who obliges him, and us, with some good Catholic talk: "I

love this place, but I'm terrible, in general, for churches." She being "on her own ground," and Strether not, graciousness befalls her: "When people were so completely in possession they could be extraordinarily civil; and our friend had indeed at this hour a kind of revelation of her heritage," at this point rather more Catholic than French. According to Protestant prejudice, Strether promptly misreads her presence in church; she must be innocent because sinners don't go near churches, they take right hold of themselves and amend their lives. But Strether is not so brainwashed as to lose opportunity to invite Madame de Vionnet to *déjeuner* at a favorite restaurant of his, "a place of pilgrimage for the knowing." So the religious set-piece slides from the marginally sacred to the clearly secular, from the suggestively pro-Catholic to the comfortably touristic.

The Wings of the Dove (1902) is perhaps the least clear-cut of all the Jamesian religious performances at novel length. With little help from the author – rather, one may well come to feel, with considerable hindrance – the reader is invited to interpret such presumptively Catholic or pro-Catholic behavior as Merton Densher on Christmas morning dashing into the (very, very Catholic) Brompton Oratory at the behest of Aunt Maud (and also at the extrasensory behest of Milly Theale from beyond the grave?). Is he suddenly turning Catholic? Or is it no more than a momentary and seasonal enthusiasm? There is no further indication (than what I have just given) that Densher is religious at all, but a provocative idea has been powerfully obtruded; and of course there is no further indication that he is *not* turning Catholic. All along we had thought him safely Protestant – if we had thought about the matter at all, basing our inference on his talks with Kate Croy about a civil marriage, ever an indicator in a James fiction. But now he has come out of Kate Croy's sphere of influence and entered that of Milly Theale.

And what of her? And if we think that she is, will we read the novel differently? Two passages subtly – I also say defiantly–insinuate that she might very well be Catholic. The first of these is her speech to Kate Croy after seeing Sir Luke Strett: "Of course I like it [her relieved condition]. I feel – I can't otherwise describe it – as if I had been on my knees to the priest. I've confessed and I've been absolved. It has been lifted off." (For once James has the word *absolved* correct.) Readers still determined to secularize the Jamesian text will naturally conclude that the "as if" phrase renders the whole statement figurative, hence without religious substance, hence to be ignored, while they return Milly Theale to, or continue her in, her purely American abroad post-Protestant status, plus religious "symbols." In fact, what the text *says* she says (she is after all only a fictive personage, a linguistic function of textual asserveration) is that she has a feeling which can be expressed only by comparison-conflation with one other feeling – and then she so expresses it. But in order to "have" the feeling, she must first have "done" what is the only possible source of that feeling, that is, she must have been on her knees to a priest. She doesn't even say "a priest"; she says "the priest." Unless of course she has been reading William James, *Varieties of Religious Experience,* just published, where she would have found such illumination as "The Catholic practice of confession and absolution is in one of its aspects little more than a systematic method of keeping healthy-mindedness on top. . . . Any Catholic will tell us how clean and fresh and free he feels after the purging operation" ("Lectures VI and VII: The Sick Soul").

Henry James' Milly Theale does *not* say "as if I had been on my knees to a priest, as naturally you will assume I never have been, although I can so easily imagine it!" It seems almost certain that Henry James had never been on his knees to a priest either but could quite easily imagine it, and there our perception of his own religious experience must once again stop. But with a fictive personage it is different. Unless there is a clear reason to doubt, you have to honor what she says; you can't go behind it. Either Milly Theale is or has been a Catholic, or Henry James is a novelistic bungler. That he is not a bungler but conceivably too subtle, or too sporadic, for his own good may appear from a subsequent passage in *The Wings of the Dove* about Milly Theale in Venice: She "had expressed as yet – he [Densher] could feel it as felt among them all – no such clear wish to go anywhere, not even to make an effort for a parish feast." *A parish feast?* Why in the world should a sick and dying American woman, terminally resident in Venice, make an effort to assist at a parish feast? Why should that be her chief reason for wanting to leave the house? Who would ever think of it in the first place but a devout Catholic abroad presupposing the universality of her church together with her right and even her obligation to participate in its liturgical and social life regardless of her whereabouts? And who else would ever think of helping out with the local religious rites? Maggie Verver would.

Let me now indulge in a few summary remarks about how to read, and a fortiori how *not* to read Henry James on his religious, which is pretty much to say his Catholic, side, *The Wings of the Dove* furnishing the test case. First, a closer look at Merton Densher and the Brompton Oratory. Densher's precipitate dash in the Romish direction is vaguely prefigured by an earlier scene in which Aunt Maud reveals that she has lied for him ("So Milly was successfully deceived"). Apparently as a consequence of her revelation, "He walked up the Bayswater Road, but he stopped short, under the murky stars, before the modern church." Does the reader remember the outdoor light conditions in "The Altar of the Dead"? Is the reader aware that "modern" churches in Henry James texts are almost never Anglican? (Why should they be?) In the much later incident of the Brompton Oratory, has the reader noticed that Densher leaves his apartment that Christmas morning "dressed with more state than usual and quite as if for church," Church of England church, we should suppose, his father having been a British overseas government chaplain? Has the reader looked long and hard, and cogitated the same, at the actual text describing Densher's bizarre "Catholic" (to give it a name) behavior? If not, here is the passage, for contemplation and bewilderment:

> To what church was he going, to what church, in such a state of his nerves, *could* he go? . . . He was just then however by a happy chance in the Brompton Road, and he bethought himself with a sudden light that the Oratory was at hand. He had but to turn the other way and he should find himself soon before it. At the door then, in a few minutes, his idea was really – as it struck him – consecrated: he was, pushing in, on the edge of a splendid service – the flocking crowd told of it – which glittered and resounded, from distant depths, in the blaze of altar-lights and the swell of organ and choir. It didn't match his own day, but it was much less of a discord than some other things actual and possible. The Oratory, in short, to make him right, would do.

The questions opening this passage are loaded, and the concluding remarks maddeningly undecideable. Are we to think that any old church would have done? or that a Catholic church would do better than some others? or than any others? that only a Catholic church would do? why?

It is incomparably easier to ask such questions than it is to answer them – which is at times the pleasure of reading Henry James. And so we arrive at the very end of our argument, which is mainly speculation (plus evidence). We arrive at the total, the absolute, the eternal impossibility of interpretation in certain cases and with respect to the religious implications of the text. Faced with such problematic puzzles as Milly Theale and confession, Milly Theale and her parish feast, Merton Densher and his Roman Catholic mass, we will naturally want to read "in context." The final turn of the screw is to find that the context is more problematic than the problem we hoped it would solve. Take, for example, Milly Theale's "confession" of confession. There are in *The Wings of the Dove* at least a dozen verbal allusions to the idea of confession, but not one of these references is in any degree Catholic, sacramental, or religious, whereas in the one instance where Catholic confession is so strongly implied the word *confession* does not appear – they are all extreme cases of what I have called sacred seculars, each of these dozen allusions strongly inclining to the secular rather than to the sacred aspects of human experience. They are what are generally referred to as dead metaphors, part of the weave, contributive to the tone, but you bring them to full life at your peril. Possibilities of misinterpretation abound, not only for Milly's confession but for references to providence, to things sacred (*joy, essence, proof, script, corner, hush* – these seem to be some of the nouns at which the adjective is directed), to catechesis, to following Jesus (Milly, in fact), to crucifixion (Densher, obviously), to the court of heaven, to Milly's "almost monastic" black dresses, to advent (none other than Kate Croy, who is also said to "consecrate"), and, at last, to Milly Theale (Minny Temple) as Christ, who, in the insufferable language of Kate Croy, "died for you then that you might understand her."

Back in Book Third, James was slightly more accommodating, chiefly in the conflicted Catholic–Protestant differentiations there hinted, if never quite clarified, between Milly Theale and Susan Shepherd Stringham. In Susie's string of Milly's attributes we easily sail over *alone* and *stricken* and *rich* but then we touch keel to bottom with the word *strange* – in what sense(s)? To the perfervid Protestant literary imagination, Milly is "the real thing, the romantic life itself." The two women, we further note, "had met thus as opposed curiosities," a suggested antithesis oddly reminiscent of the Catholic–Protestant face-offs in James' early book reviews. Has Milly Theale's (imputed – we still do not "know") Catholicity anything to do with her being "the potential heiress of all the ages"? Does that phrase mean that she is a stunning witness to American democracy in all its wonders (see *The American Scene* for the deflation of any such wonders) or because she has all the money in New York or because she inherits two thousand years of Catholic Christendom? What are we to make of Milly's already having been to Italy (Catholic) and Susie to (Protestant) Switzerland–Germany (which she thinks makes her "a woman of the world")? Certainly we should be sorry to miss the comic grandeur of Protestant Stringham's proposing something or other to "Catholic" Theale as "fun," with the response, "the indescribable look dropped on her, at that, by her companion . . . the look was long to figure for her as an inscrutable comment on *her* notion of freedom." What most readings of *The Wings of the Dove* most fall short of is wit, for example recognition of the wit displayed by Milly Theale, when, after Kate Croy has first called her a "dove," she begins to play, in the recesses of her soul, with the tonal complications of that metaphor: "*That* was what was the matter with her. She was a dove. Oh, *wasn't* she?" Frustrated of final answers to our (as *we* think!) most demanding questions, we may still hear with the greatest of pleasure the tones of voice through which a text by Henry James gets itself constituted. Knowing a thing or two about Henry James enables us to tune our ears to what it is we might listen for.

Notes

Part One

1 "The average Protestant American of the 1850's had been trained from birth to hate Catholicism; his juvenile literature and school books had breathed a spirit of intolerance; his illicit dips as a youth into the parentally condemned but widely read Ned Buntline tales had kept his prejudice alive; his religious and even his secular newspapers had warned him of the dangers of Popery; and he had read novels, poems, gift books, histories, travel accounts, and theological arguments which confirmed these beliefs. Only the unusually critical reader could distinguish between truth and fiction in this mass of calumny; more were swept away to a hatred of Catholicism which endured through their lives." Ray Allen Billington, "The Literature of Anti-Catholicism," *The Protestant Crusade, 1800–1860* (New York: Macmillan, 1938), 345.

2 Decidedly no influence on the literary Catholicizing of Henry James.

3 "We can measure the great advance made on the corruptions of the Romish Church by the early reformers, by Wicliffe and Erasmus and Luther. We can estimate the progress made by our fathers, the Puritans, on the English re-formed Church. And now, our hearts and our understandings can approve the simplicity and beauty of that purified Christianity, which a better under-standing of the scriptures and of the character of God have taught us, over some of the dark superstitions which our fathers received." *The Complete Sermons of Ralph Waldo Emerson,* ed. Albert J. von Frank, et al. (Columbia: University of Missouri Press, 1989–   ), 1:152, Sermon XIV.

4 The full title reads: *Awful Disclosures of Maria Monk, As Exhibited in a Narrative of Her Sufferings During a Residence of Five Years as a Novice, and Two Years as a Black Nun, in the Hotel Dieu Nunnery at Montreal.* The title page further flaunts a quotation from Revelation 17.4, viz., "Come out of her, my people, that ye be not partakers of her sins, and that ye receive not of her plagues," where "her" is arguably the Roman Catholic Church in general as well as a particular nunnery and "my people" are the Americans and "her sins" are

idolatry and superstition and popery and "her plagues" are syphilis – see my comments on Henry James, "De Grey: A Romance."

Part Two

1 The very idea of Methodism was apparently enough to send James off in a Catholic direction. About a decade later (the *Nation*, 8 July 1875), excoriating Gilbert Haven's *Our Next-Door Neighbor*, he indulges in such rarely abusive language as "Mr. Haven's tone is inordinately ignorant, bigoted, flippant, conceited, and ill-conditioned generally . . . the most offensive literary performance it has lately been our fortune to encounter." Haven's text is furthermore "singularly diffuse, ill-written, and vulgar." Specifically, "He went to Mexico, as an agent of the Methodist Episcopal Church, to arrange for the establishment of a mission in the capital, and he informs us that he was successful, in so far as that a building suitable for a meeting-house was purchased and opened, in spite of much perfidious counter-plotting on the part of the Catholic authorities. This establishment is now in operation, and with 'its dear, delightful prayer-meetings,' as the author has it, is hastening on that immediate millennium which he promises the depraved Mexicans at the end of each chapter."

2 These assignments he solicited (9 August 1864 to Charles Eliot Norton).

3 E. F. Benson, ed., *Henry James: Letters to A. C. Benson and Auguste Monod* (London: Elkin Mathews & Marrot, 1930), 3.

4 See C. S. Lewis, *Studies in Words* (Cambridge: Cambridge University Press, 1960), pp. 126–32 (" 'Liberal' as a Cultural Term"); Robert C. Broderick, *The Catholic Encyclopedia* (Nashville: Nelson, 1976), especially p. 347, "Liberals, Catholic"; Thomas Bokenkotter, *A Concise History of the Catholic Church*, rev. ed. (New York: Doubleday, 1979), chapters titled "Pius IX Says 'No' to the Liberal Catholics" and "The *Syllabus of Errors* Squelches the Liberal Catholics"; Edward Norman, *The English Catholic Church in the Nineteenth Century* (Oxford: Clarendon, 1984), passim.

5 Behold a distinguished church historian attempting to disentangle religion and *realpolitik* from the ideologies and innuendoes: "Lamennais preached a free press and freedom of thought and religion; he sought an independence of Church from the State. That, too, was the burden of Montalembert's famous address at the Malines Congress in 1863: a free Church in a free state – the slogan of the Italian Risorgimento. Hence the attack on Montalembert by Ward, precisely because the union of Church and State had always been Catholic teaching, and because its disruption lay at the heart of the Italian liberals' assault upon the States of the Church in Italy. But those principles were just the ones that the Irish Catholic hierarchy were opposing, in their campaign for the disestablishment of the Protestant Church in Ireland, and which, during the Catholic Emancipation movement in England, the Vicars Apostolic had absorbed from the surrounding pool of English liberalism and radicalism." Norman, *English Catholic Church in the Nineteenth Century*, 302. In comparison, Henry James seems almost simple.

6 *A Small Boy and Others* (London: Macmillan, 1913), 244–6.

7 Percy Lubbock, ed., *The Letters of Henry James*. 2 vols. (New York: Scribners, 1920), 1:321.

8 Howard R. Greenstein, *Judaism, An Eternal Covenant* (Philadelphia: Fortress Press, 1983), p. xii. More or less the same point is made in Nicholas de Lange, *Judaism* (New York: Oxford University Press, 1986), 4–5.

9 In the 1905 essay on Balzac we find: "His system of cellular confinement, in the interest of the miracle, was positively that of a Benedictine monk leading his life within the four walls of his convent and bent, the year round, over the smooth parchment on which, with wondrous illumination of gold and crimson and blue, he inscribes the glories of the faith and the legends of the saints. . . . Only, as happened, his subject of illumination was the legends not merely of the saints, but of the much more numerous uncanonized strugglers and sinners."

10 Leon Edel, ed., *The American Scene* (Bloomington: Indiana University Press, 1968), 381, 93. "Art protects her children in the long run – she only asks them to trust her. She is like the Catholic Church – she guarantees paradise to the faithful" ("'Collaboration,'" 1892).

11 Marcia Jacobson, *Henry James and the Mass Market* (Tuscaloosa: University of Alabama Press, 1983); Anne T. Margolis, *Henry James and the Problem of Audience: An International Act* (Ann Arbor: UMI Research Press, 1985); Michael Anesko, *"Friction Within the Market": Henry James and the Profession of Authorship* (New York: Oxford University Press, 1986).

12 *A Karamazov Companion: Commentary on the Genesis, Language, and Style of Dostoevsky's Novel* (Madison: University of Wisconsin Press, 1981), 96–7, 99–100.

13 Edward Norman, *Roman Catholicism in England from the Elizabethan Settlement to the Second Vatican Council* (New York: Oxford University Press, 1986), 30, 71, 108.

14 Bokenkotter, 383.

15 A very considerable body of recent criticism, not only of Henry James, handles religious terms as if they were "null terms," as defined by Peter Schneider in "Is There a Europe?" *Harper's* 277 (1988), 57. "Null terms are words whose meanings inexorably tend toward zero as a result of constant, inflationary misuse. . . . The passenger who chose to open a conversation with his West Berlin cabbie by introducing himself as an anti-communist was stopped cold with the statement, 'I don't care what kind of communist you are.' "

16 Her speech is retained and revised in dramatic form. Leon Edel, ed., *The Complete Plays of Henry James* (Philadelphia: Lippincott, 1949), 538.

17 Benson, 33.

18 Lubbock, 2:159.

19 Lubbock, 2:394.

20 Lubbock, 2:165.

21 Lubbock, 2:279.

22 Lubbock, 2:476.

23 Lubbock, 2:476.

24 Lubbock, 1:238.

25 Leon Edel and Lyall H. Powers, eds., *The Complete Notebooks of Henry James*

(New York: Oxford University Press, 1987), 161, 109, 31, 56, 73, 77, 92, 97, 127, 145, 167, 173, 187, 237, 243, 259, 318, 406, 195.

26 *Notebooks,* 260–1.

27 Lubbock, 2:70.

28 See also the 9 September 1910 letter to Edith Wharton; Lubbock, 2:169.

29 Lubbock, 2:330.

30 Leon Edel, *The Middle Years* (Philadelphia: Lippincott, 1962), 166. Again, "[H]is letters of condolence are muted and exquisite prose elegies." *Henry James Letters,* 3:194.

31 Lubbock, 1:371–2.

32 "Is There a Life After Death?" was first published in a symposium, *In After Days* (New York: Harpers, 1910). Rpt. in F. O. Matthiessen, *The James Family* (New York: Knopf, 1948), 602–14, from which I quote.

Part Three

1 As Mrs. Light remarks, "The man first – the money afterwards: that was always my motto, and always will be."

2 In a 21 November 1869 letter to his mother from Rome: "I don't at all agree with the people who assume that Rome is the place to discuss [disgust?] and disenchant you with the Church. On the contrary, a faint impulse once received (an essential premise) Rome makes the rest of the journey all downhill work. The sense you get here of the great collective Church must be far more potent than elsewhere to swallow up and efface all the vile and flagrant minor offenses to the soul and the senses. Once *in* the Church you can be perfectly indifferent to the debased and stultified priests and the grovelling peasantry: out of it you certainly can't. But enough on this chapter. There is a better Rome than all this. . . ." The flagrant differences of tone between James' published writings and his letters home often raise, in my mind at least, the question of whether he is writing his family what he really thinks or what he thinks they want to hear (or perhaps a combination of the two). Certainly he appears to assume that his family will dote on an amount and extent of anti-Catholic abuse that the general public can hardly be expected to relish or even put up with. It is the same difference in tone as that between the Italian sketches and the Italian tales. Late in life, James spoke quite sentimentally of "the old vanished Pio Nono Rome, *my 1st* old Rome of 1869." Rayburn S. Moore, ed., *Selected Letters of Henry James to Edmund Gosse* (Baton Rouge: Louisiana State University Press, 1988), 229; letter of 14 October 1907.

3 Leon Edel, *The Conquest of London* (Philadelphia: Lippincott, 1962), 112–13.

4 That Henry James knew of the Kingsley–Newman controversy is no mere conjecture, for he wrote about Kingsley three times, twice prior to *The American* and once while it was running in the *Atlantic:* in 1866 (25 January in the *Nation*), "We have never been partial to Mr. Kingsley's arrogance, his shallowness, his sanctified prejudices; but we have never doubted that he is a man of genius," as a novelist, that is; in 1875 (28 January in the *Nation*), James identifies Kingsley "as the exponent of 'muscular Christianity' "; and in an

1877 review of his wife's biography (25 January in the *Nation*) he refers to Kingsley's "hatred of 'Popery,' " his "theological controversy with Dr. Newman," and again his "fit of ill-starred controversy with Dr. Newman."

5 Generally signaling a kind of vague Protestant tonality, *here below* is variously encountered in Jamesian texts, as his 1875 review of the *Correspondence* of William Ellery Channing, a 28 February 1877 letter to William James, a 3 March 1885 letter to Edwin L. Godkin (denominating just where his father's literary reputation happened not to be), in such tales as "A Passionate Pilgrim" and "Master Eustace" (both in 1871) and doubtless in many another place where I have missed it for want of appropriate zeal.

6 Robert C. Broderick, "Communion of Saints," *The Catholic Encyclopedia* (Nashville: Nelson, 1976), 126–7.

7 To be sure, James is fond of the phrase and will sometimes use it in the most uninteresting ways, for example, in a personal letter, "I have indeed kept watch & ward over Saturday week 6*th*" (*Letters to Gosse*, 39; 28 January 1886), or in the *Notebooks,* "She waited and watched in short" (Leon Edel and Lyall H. Powers, *The Complete Notebooks of Henry James* [New York: Oxford University Press, 1987, 201, entry of 26 December 1908). Still there are good textual reasons for suspecting that ancient title of latent and lingering Roman Catholic ambience, for here it is again full tilt in *The Golden Bowl,* "watch and wait," "he too watched and waited," "to wonder and watch," too much of a good thing for sheer accident. *The Golden Bowl* also contains a fantastic little scene ("The Princess"; Book Fourth; end and climax of chapter fifth), in which Prince Amerigo ("he bareheaded") and Charlotte Stant are by Maggie Verger recuperated as Peter Quint and Miss Jessel. Maggie "sees" them as perched "to watch for the return of the absent, to be there to take them over again," including the Principino. "The group on the pavement," she, her father, the child, the nurse, "stared up as at the peopled battlements of a castle. . . . Maggie's individual gape was inevitably again for the thought of how the pair would be at work." Life Among the Catholics.

Part Four

1 "There is notoriously no glamour over the suburbs," Henry James on Henrik Ibsen in the *New Review,* June 1891; Allan Wade, ed., *The Scenic Art* (New Brunswick, N.J.: Rutgers University Press, 1948), 250. In *The Wings of the Dove* (Book Fourth, chapter second), Milly Theale and Kate Croy "attack" London, "shops and streets and suburbs oddly interesting to Milly." In Book Tenth, chapter first, Aunt Maud is "engaged with an old servant, retired and pensioned, who had been paying her a visit and who was within the hour to depart again for the suburbs," evidently far from Lancaster Gate.

2 *The Notebooks of Henry James* (New York: Oxford University Press, 1947), 165–6.

3 "If such resources were open to us poor heretics, I should suppose she meant to go into a convent" ("The Impressions of a Cousin," 1883). In the suspicion that the reader may already have taken a surfeit of James' conventual references, I omit all further examples but one or two, for instance a letter from

Hotel de Rome, Roma, 8 January 1873, to his father: "A hotel gives one a disagreeable *tourist* feeling, but this one is so large and grave and tranquil, that I feel as if I were a pensioner by the year in some soundless old convent." In "The Death of the Lion" (1894), James speaks of "The monastic life, the pious illumination of the missal in the convent cell." As the desk was an altar, the room in which you wrote at it was a cell, and the text there created was a missal.

Part Five

1 So Sallie Sears speaks of *The Golden Bowl:* "It is a *ménage à quatre,* or *à cinq* if one includes Fanny Assingham. . . . And that such a situation, ripe by its very nature for the strongest yet most ambiguous loves, involvements, rivalries, occurs in a near social vacuum contributes to the intensity." *The Negative Imagination: Form and Perspective in the Novels of Henry James* (Ithaca, N.Y.: Cornell University Press, 1968), 165. In his 1909 preface, James speaks of "a group of agents who may be counted on the fingers of one hand."
2 *Henry James: A Reader's Guide* (Ithaca, N.Y.: Cornell University Press, 1966), 34.
3 *Experiment in Autobiography* (London, 1934), rpt. in Leon Edel and Gordon N. Ray, *Henry James and H. G. Wells* (Urbana: University of Illinois Press, 1958), 45.
4 Matthiessen–Murdock *Notebooks* (New York: Oxford University Press, 1947), 174. Edel, ed., *The Complete Plays of Henry James* (Philadelphia: Lippincott, 1949), 61; Edel, *The Treacherous Years* (Philadelphia: Lippincott, 1969), 88; *The Master* (Philadelphia: Lippincott, 1972), 210.
5 In Allan Wade, ed., *The Scenic Art* (New Brunswick, N.J.: Rutgers University Press, 1948), 133–4.

Part Six

1 Leon Edel and Lyall H. Powers, *The Complete Notebooks of Henry James* (New York: Oxford University Press, 1987), 542 and 542 *n* 2.

Index

Continued from the front of the book